LOCOMOTIVE HEADBOARDS

THE
COMPLETE
STORY

DAVE PEEL

ACKNOWLEDGEMENTS

The author gratefully acknowledges the support and cooperation of the following in the preparation of this book: National Railway Museum (especially Martin Bashforth and David Wright), Science & Society Picture Library, Tim Bryan ('Steam' Museum, Swindon), Topham Picturepoint, Getty Images, Millbrook House, Milepost 92½, University of Hull (Brynmor Jones Library), Ipswich Transport Museum, Bob Clow (Harwich Railway & Shipping Museum), Ian Wright (Sheffield Railwayana Auctions), Sheffield Star Newspapers, Public Record Office, Mitchell Library (Glasgow), Southampton City Library, Swanage Railway Library, Ken Hoole Study Centre, Bradford Industrial Museum; also Frank Burridge, Bob Withers, Graham Kelsey, Adrian Crafer, Barry Fletcher, Chris Halsall, Nelson Twells, Hamish Stevenson, Bill Lynn, John Mander, and in particular John Fleetwood, Peter Townend and William Cattermole for their personal insights into headboard production and embellishments.

Plus, of course, all those who generously supplied the very many individually credited illustrations. While every effort has been made to ensure that the attributions are accurate, if this is not the case, the author would welcome contact from the true copyright holder.

Thanks are also due to Eric Youlden and Frank Burridge for their proofreading, and especially to Sheila Ashworth who did my typing.

First published in 2006
This edition published in 2010

The History Press
The Mill, Brimscombe Port
Stroud, Gloucestershire, GL5 2QG
www.thehistorypress.co.uk

British Library Cataloguing in Publication Data.
A catalogue record for this book is available from the British Library.

ISBN 978 0 7524 5599 0

Typesetting and origination by The History Press
Printed in Great Britain

CONTENTS

The northbound FLYING SCOTSMAN leaving York in 1950 past the site of the current National Railway Museum, then York's motive power depot (50A). A smart rake of fully roofboarded postwar LNER stock, mostly in 'varnished teak' finish, trails the blue-liveried A4 *Gannet*, and an LNER-style painted steel headboard proclaims the service. *(Millbrook House Collection)*

HISTORICAL INTRODUCTION: DEVELOPMENT AND DECLINE

The practice of naming trains has a long history. The IRISH MAIL was known thus, unofficially, from about 1848, and the FLYING SCOTSMAN – as the 10 a.m. Scottish express – from 1862, to name but two. Official recognition of either of these did not come until many years later, however, with the IRISH MAIL being named in the London & North Western Railway timetable for 1921 and the FLYING SCOTSMAN first seeing its name in print in the London & North Eastern Railway timetable for 1927. Moreover, it must not be thought that officially conferring a title on an express did, either instantaneously or even automatically, bring with it a loco headboard advertising the fact, though in many cases this was indeed so. The IRISH MAIL, for instance, had to wait a further thirty years (well into British Railways days) before first bearing a headboard, while the FLYING SCOTSMAN gained one merely a year after its official naming in the timetable.

The train names themselves were usually selected by the various Public Relations & Publicity offices, though not always. The title CORNISH RIVIERA LIMITED, for example, conferred by the Great Western Railway in 1906 on the through Paddington–Penzance service introduced two years earlier, was the result of *The Railway Magazine* asking its readers to submit a suitable name, though in the event the winning entry itself was not used. Even when a title was published in the timetable and a headboard provided, the two did not always correspond. During the 1930s the CHELTENHAM SPA EXPRESS (in the timetable) translated to CHELTENHAM FLYER on the engine headboard, and this was the GWR's only venture into the provision of headboards. Of the other three major pre-nationalisation companies, the London, Midland & Scottish Railway was equally reluctant to make the move into headboards[1] and the Southern Railway delayed their use on timetabled expresses until the last two years of its independent existence, 1946–7.

It was therefore on the LNER that the habit of providing headboards originally flourished. The LNER did, however, inherit the precedent for this from the railway that began the practice in the first place – the North British. Here it was company policy to place destination boards on the front of the engine, high up, just below the chimney. A single word only, on a curved metal plate. When in June 1912 the NBR began running its LOTHIAN COAST EXPRESS, these three words, on two lines, again on a curved metal plate, were placed in the same position as the destination board. Thus was born the first titled train headboard, concurrent in this case with the naming of the train in the timetable. This was quickly followed a month later by the FIFE COAST EXPRESS and these services transferred, with headboards, to the LNER in 1923. For the next five years these two were the only headboarded trains, until the FLYING SCOTSMAN was added in 1928. Even then, four more years were to elapse before widespread use on the LNER was sanctioned in 1932, with usage growing to fourteen services in 1939.

During the Second World War the naming of trains ceased almost entirely[2] and the carrying of headboards was completely discontinued. Only in 1946 did the LNER resume both practices and, as noted above, the Southern entered the field also. The period 1946–64 saw the introduction of just about all the remaining headboards ever used. Indeed, in the vast majority of cases they were both introduced and withdrawn during these years.

1948 saw the first use, by the Eastern Region of BR, of cast aluminium headboards. These not only replaced the painted steel plates previously displayed on their own services, but the use of this metal then became standard for the headboards of all other regions as well. There were a few exceptions to this, and in the early 1960s fibreglass was also tried, but the overwhelming number of headboards in the BR period were aluminium. Festival of Britain year, 1951, saw the greatest increase in headboarded trains in any one year, and the next ten years after that witnessed the maximum number and diversity of headboards.

As the steam age came to an end and diesels (in the main) began to take over the powering of the named expresses, so the carrying of headboards declined. This decline was not uniform across BR, but few headboards remained in regular service anywhere after 1966, when electric services between Euston, Manchester and Liverpool commenced, accompanied by a mass withdrawal of train titles.

After this, although a handful of the existing headboards saw fitful use for a while longer, the period of regular headboard-carrying on a widespread basis could be said to have finished. True, isolated instances of new headboards being introduced have occurred since then, notably for THE SILVER JUBILEE in 1977, and in the privatised era Virgin Trains did attempt a brief resurrection of a ROYAL SCOT headboard. Even now, the timetable contains a number of titled services, but the special, identifiably different nature of these has long since disappeared.

NOTES

1. The only exception to this was THE ROYAL SCOT headboard permanently fixed to the smokebox of the loco that toured the USA and Canada in 1933 with the ROYAL SCOT train set. This was not removed until the engine's rebuilding in 1950.
2. On the LNER, the FLYING SCOTSMAN, ABERDONIAN and NIGHT SCOTSMAN continued to be named in the timetable throughout the war, though even these were not present in the Emergency Timetable October–December 1939. The IRISH MAIL was initially retained in LMS timetables, but became anonymous from December 1942.

GENERAL COMMENTS

The text of this book is heavily based on the photographic evidence. Few records survive from official sources as to exactly how many headboards there were, or when and where they were manufactured. A dozen or so drawings from Doncaster and Eastleigh drawing offices have survived (in the National Railway Museum) and some of these are included in the illustrations. However, there is no 'master list' to work from, and it may still be the case that, despite the author's best efforts, some headboards have escaped detection. Photographically this is certainly the case, and these few omissions are pointed out where applicable.

Since most illustrations are in black and white, the often emotive question of colour – particularly shades thereof – is largely bypassed. Generally, where a colour is quoted, it is that which it was intended to be, since that which prevailed usually differed by virtue of grime, weathering, repainting, cleaning with oily rags, etc. Those illustrations that are in colour are, however, thought to represent the original intentions fairly accurately.

For the most part, titles were bestowed on existing trains – some of very long standing – only a few, relatively, being brand-new services. For those seeking greater detail of all the titled services themselves, a source other than this book will be required. Here, only the briefest of facts relating to the routes, timings, loadings and changes to these over the years are included. Where service duration dates are given, these are taken from the public timetables then current (see Guidance Notes). Because a service was titled in the timetable, this does not necessarily imply that the locomotive bore a headboard, the THAMES-FORTH EXPRESS (LMS/LNER, pre-war) being a case in point. Nor was it true that all headboarded services appeared in the public timetables. Boat trains were the prime examples of these, as were regularly-run holiday trains where local posters and handbills were a more appropriate means of promotion. The handful of freight services that carried headboards is also in this category and is included for completeness. Clearly, for most boat trains, holiday trains and freight trains, finding their respective starting and finishing dates presents a problem, and in these cases the dates quoted are either approximate or absent.

Of the numerous titled trains appearing in this book, a small number were also provided with 'tailboards' to bring up the rear. These closed off the corridor connection of the last carriage and provided a second opportunity to identify the service. The Pullman Car Company sometimes, but not always, supplied their own version, but largely the various Carriage & Wagon workshops were responsible for these. The first instance of their use would appear to have been in the summer of 1932 when the FLYING SCOTSMAN was so equipped, but the last usage is unknown, as is the precise figure for the number of services carrying these devices. Generally they were not carried for any great length of time, and were rarely photographed. Although illustrations are provided for those that have been found, this is an area where the author would welcome input from those with photographic evidence of additional examples.

Another aspect of titled train 'advertising' that is merely touched upon in this book (largely in the London Midland section) is that of carriage roofboards. Very many untitled trains carried roofboards announcing the various destinations. Titled trains displayed both these and additional roofboards showing the train name, sometimes embellished with extra devices, the better to distinguish the service. This entire field is however only glimpsed here, leaving the interested reader to pursue the matter further if he or she so wishes.

GUIDANCE NOTES

Routes

Generally only the end points of the services are given, and where one of these is London, this is quoted first. It is of course recognised that in many instances the principal reason for the train's existence was to take passengers to and from London, i.e. the capital was the destination, rather than the starting place. However, in stating the basic route, rather than describing the service, putting London first is judged to be more appropriate here. Where an express served multiple end points by having several portions, the various end points are usually quoted. If some of these changed over the years then generally only the longest-served are listed.

THE ROYAL HIGHLANDER leaves Aviemore on a misty morning in September 1957 on the last stage of its overnight run from Euston. The thirteen-coach formation heads north on single track towards Slochd summit (1,315ft above sea level) and finally Inverness. This was the only headboarded service to operate over the Highland main line. *(W.J.V. Anderson/Rail Archive Stephenson)*

Opposite: Swindon Works yard is the location for visual inspection of the fibreglass headboard that was being proposed for use on the more powerful 2700hp 'Western' class diesel-hydraulic locos diagrammed to take over the South Wales expresses. A second of similar appearance was made for the CAPITALS UNITED EXPRESS. These two were the work of Mr Milner Gray, a consultant with the Design Research Unit, who was responsible for (among other things) the design for the D800 class 'Warship' nameplates. As seen here in 1961, the dragon's background was dark; however, as preserved in Swindon's Steam Museum, the dragon is now chocolate brown on an off-white background. When and where these changes took place is unknown. *(NRM/SSPL)*

Dates

It is important to note that, overwhelmingly, the date quoted in the text for the 'inaugural titled run' corresponds to the train's first appearance, as titled, in the relevant public timetable (exceptions to this are noted in the text). These dates are therefore thought to be accurately established. Note, however, that the commencement of a timetable's validity does not necessarily coincide with the inauguration date, as the service may only have operated on certain days of the week (e.g. THE HARROGATE SUNDAY PULLMAN) and/or have

a restricted period of running (e.g. a train might not run for the full extent of the summer timetable). These comments apply equally to both pre- and postwar introductions.

Exactly when certain titles ceased to be carried at the outbreak of the Second World War is more difficult to determine. It seems that the companies continued to operate their summer timetables for one week after 3 September 1939 and that thereafter (with the exceptions noted earlier) all titles disappeared until 1946. However, some services were withdrawn before the outbreak of hostilities, all the LNER/LMS streamline trains for example. Additionally, some ports were closed to civilian traffic before 3 September and boat trains running in conjunction with ferry sailings were therefore early withdrawals, such as the NIGHT FERRY from Dover.

Dates for the 'last titled run' are similarly taken from the public timetables. Sometimes the title and the service disappeared at the same time; sometimes the service continued for some considerable time after the title had been dropped; sometimes the title reappeared after a lapse of several months or even years. In the latter circumstance, if no headboard was carried during the service's reincarnation, no dates are given at all for this second coming.

Regarding headboard introduction and withdrawal dates, these are much less secure. Although introduction dates can often be quoted accurately or with little error, most last-run-with-a-headboard dates can only be guessed at as headboard usage became less and less frequent although the service itself continued to run. In many instances, therefore, only an approximate period can be stated, if any is stated at all.

AUTHOR'S NOTES

This is the first book in which a comprehensive treatment of this topic has been attempted. As such, the author is aware that it has its shortcomings, but nevertheless trusts that the majority of readers will find it to be a satisfactory account. Where gaps in knowledge exist these have been brought to the reader's attention, and anyone with specific information that would enhance the record is invited to contact the author (via the publisher), who would welcome both corrections and additions.

An index of all the titles described in this book is provided at the end. While this list is displayed alphabetically, within the five book sections this is not the case. The Western Section expresses are ordered more or less chronologically (postwar), while the Southern Section proceeds on a destination basis moving west to east. The three remaining sections are different again, each grouping together services using specific London termini. Internal Scottish titles are contained within the London Midland or Eastern Sections. All five sections also include some Additional Titles covering subjects that are, in some way, not mainstream. Largely these are titles not contained in the public timetables: boat trains, holiday trains or freight services, for example. Others may be special events, non-public trains, those having tailboards only, or short-lived HST services with 'sticker' headboards.

Opposite: The approach to Reading General from the west in the early summer of 1953 finds No. 70025 *Western Star* whistling its way onto the Berks & Hants junction with the up RED DRAGON from Swansea and Carmarthen. Not only has the headboard gained a red background, but the additional decoration displayed above (but attached to) the headboard is there in recognition of the Queen's Coronation, and was only carried during the period 22 May to 14 June. Four of the region's expresses had the distinction of carrying this device: CORNISH RIVIERA, THE BRISTOLIAN, THE INTER-CITY and of course THE RED DRAGON. *(NRM/SSPL)*

TITLED EXPRESSES OF THE GWR AND BR (WR)

INTRODUCTION TO 'WESTERN' HEADBOARDS 1932–67

The following pages give details of the loco headboards carried by titled trains running on the Western Region of BR during the 1950s and 1960s. Each is illustrated in some manner, and every headboard regularly carried is portrayed. The only pre-war headboards used are included for completeness, as are two experimental types designed solely for diesel traction, and one anniversary headboard produced for publicity purposes and used on one day only.

This latter headboard did, however, influence the introduction and design of Swindon's own individualised headboards a couple of years later. It had been duly noted that the yellow background of this headboard, and its large size, had shown up at a distance much better than those then in use. The additional provision of some civic heraldry also found favour, and this feature was included in most of the later headboards, though this idea may well have been borrowed from existing Eastern Region practice. The types of headboard manufactured for general use fall into three broad categories: the variety illustrated by the first style of the CORNISH RIVIERA or CHELTENHAM SPA EXPRESS headboards; the variety common throughout BR, illustrated typically by the first-style headboards for THE INTER-CITY or the CAMBRIAN COAST EXPRESS; and the individualised variety in the house colours of brown letters on a cream background embellished with crests and/or shields, latterly carried by most of the WR named expresses then running. The only titles not to receive this individualised variety were THE WILLIAM SHAKESPEARE (which ran only in the summer of 1951), THE SOUTH WALES PULLMAN (which was taken over by diesel 'Blue Pullmans' in 1961) and THE DEVONIAN (which was inter-regional). The last WR design

to be introduced, the CATHEDRALS EXPRESS, whose colours were blue, red and gold, broke the mould again by having Gothic-style lettering in both small case and capitals. The first two varieties both used Gill Sans Medium letter face, whereas the final variety used Clarendon Regular. With the one exception noted above, all headboards used capital letters only.

The non-Swindon BR headboards were all aluminium castings with polished beaded edges and raised, polished letters. The background was generally painted black, though exceptions to this are noted in the individual descriptions for each titled train. The headboards were of three basic sizes as shown in the following table (the 'Type' designation is for convenience only; it is not a BR description).

Dimensions are in inches	Type 1	Type 3	Type 7	
Length of top arc	40	24	35	
Distance between lowest points	31	31	31	Letter size 3¾ for each Type
Distance between top/bottom edges	9⅞	9⅞	14⅜	

(For a full listing of all the various BR headboard sizes, see the Eastern Section.)

These sizes were carried on the Western Region expresses as follows:

Type 1
CORNISH RIVIERA★
TORBAY EXPRESS★
CHELTENHAM SPA EXPRESS

★ Headboards 7in narrower than standard, i.e. length of top arc is 33in.

Type 3
THE DEVONIAN
THE RED DRAGON
THE INTER-CITY
THE BRISTOLIAN
THE CORNISHMAN
THE MAYFLOWER

Type 7
THE MERCHANT VENTURER
THE WILLIAM SHAKESPEARE
CAMBRIAN COAST EXPRESS
PEMBROKE COAST EXPRESS
THE SOUTH WALES PULLMAN
CAPITALS UNITED EXPRESS

For most of the Swindon-cast headboards, some dimensions are also given on the particular page relating to that title. This provision of non-standard headboards arose from the extra autonomy granted by BR to its various regions in 1956 in respect of introducing some colour variations to their rolling stock, locos as well as coaches. This latitude allowed the WR to reinstate the old GWR colours of chocolate and cream for its main expresses' coaches. This was the impetus needed to design new headboards to advertise each title, and as complete rakes of new (or newly repainted) chocolate and cream stock became available, a new headboard was supplied. On 11 June 1956 three expresses became thus equipped:

CORNISH RIVIERA LIMITED, TORBAY EXPRESS and THE BRISTOLIAN. Others followed suit on a one-by-one basis, and the WR was the only region on which the equation 'repainted coaches = new headboard' was valid. (The Southern Region opted to go back to green coaches, whereas the LMR, ER and ScR were content with BR's new 'national' coach colour of maroon. The LMR did, however, introduce some new carriage roofboards for four of its main expresses at this time.)

All WR headboards differed from those of all other regions in one major respect – the fixing bracket. Headboards were attached to the loco by slotting the bracket (on the rear) onto the lamp irons, usually the one just below the chimney. On the WR (following GWR practice) the vertical strut of the lamp iron, onto which the headboard was seated, was edge-on to the direction of travel. Throughout the rest of BR the strut was face-on, i.e. at 90 degrees to the WR style. On the WR this resulted in both in the point of attachment of the headboard being offset from the centre, and any inter-regional working requiring a different headboard when non-WR-allocated engines replaced WR locos.

As will be seen from the dates provided some trains operated for considerably longer periods than others. The dates during which headboards were carried are, however, less well-defined. While most introduction dates coincided, more or less, with the inaugural titled run, few headboards had definite withdrawal dates, but the last to be carried was the CAMBRIAN COAST EXPRESS on 4 March 1967 – by steam.

THE MANUFACTURING PROCESS

Of the three categories mentioned above, only those headboards receiving the house colours were actually manufactured at Swindon, being cast in the Brass Foundry No. 10 Shop, and made of LM6 aluminium. Before casting could take place, wooden patterns of the design were made using beech for the crests and lettering, and yellow pine for the base.

At the foundry the headboard pattern was placed, face upwards, onto a large horizontal 'ram-up' board and the lower section of the iron moulding box placed over it. This box was then packed with green sand and rammed tightly over the pattern to create a mould of the pattern's overall shape, together with the lettering and crests. This entire lower section was then turned over so that the flat back of the headboard pattern was now uppermost, and the pattern for the loco attachment bracket was then fixed to the back of the headboard pattern. The separate empty upper section of the moulding box was then located accurately on top of the (upside-down) lower section. This upper section was then filled with green sand deep enough to cover the bracket section by 2–4in and the sand was rammed hard in order to create the mould for the bracket. When this was done, the upper section was lifted from the lower section, the headboard and bracket patterns removed, and the upper section replaced and secured firmly on top of the lower section, thus sandwiching the two halves of the mould together. Aluminium at about 750 degrees Celsius was then poured through the rammed sand using a vertical tube (or 'runner stick') and was led evenly into the mould via several small, horizontal channels (or 'runners') cut into the hard sand for this purpose, Another small channel, cut vertically, allowed expelled air to escape. Cooling took 30–40 minutes before the two sections could be separated and the casting removed for inspection. Generally, two castings were made for each pattern, though replacements because of breakages and so on often increased this number at later dates. If perfect, the headboards were then taken to the paint shop for painting and varnishing before being released for use.

All the 'Swindon' headboards were cast in this way during the period 1956–9, and the piecework rate at that time was 23s per headboard for the three-quarters of a day's work by the foundry foreman John Fleetwood, assisted by three workmates only when lifting and turning the heavy moulds. The patterns were prepared by the late 'Viv' Rogers and both patterns and castings were unsurpassed examples of the craftsmanship involved.

TRAIN REPORTING NUMBERS

While the main object of this book is to describe and illustrate the loco headboard, another even more prominent feature is seen in many of the following photographs. This is of course the three-digit train reporting number.

This facet of operation was introduced by the GWR in 1934. Initially this was so that the large number of relief trains to and from the West of England on summer Saturdays could be more readily distinguished by signalmen. The timetabled services were allocated three-digit numbers ending in either 0 or 5, while their various relief trains would have the same two first digits, but end in either 1–4 or 6–9 so that, for instance, 130 might relate to the westbound CORNISH RIVIERA while 132 would identify the second relief train to this.

Postwar, and especially post-nationalisation, the system was expanded and applied to the majority of express services, including inter-regional trains. It should be emphasised, however, that although these numbers appeared in the Working Timetable they did not appear in the Public Timetable. Even the trains themselves sometimes did, and sometimes did not, display the reporting number. The numbers allocated were changed slightly from year to year, with additions and deletions as necessary, and the sequence illustrated was itself overhauled totally in 1958.

In 1960 the WR began using new four-character headcodes, in which the second character was a letter, the others numerals. In this system the first numeral referred to the class of train (e.g. 1 = express passenger), the letter referred to the destination area (e.g. F = South Wales district), and the second and third numerals referred to the individual train itself.

WESTERN REGION TRAIN REPORTING NUMBERS—SUMMER, 1955

BY courtesy of the Western Region we are able to publish below the reporting numbers carried by W.R. passenger trains in the current summer timetable, in answer to many requests. The number allotted to each train is displayed in a metal frame carried on the smokebox of the engine, but is not necessarily carried every day or for the whole of the train's journey. The numbers shown in this list refer to ordinary trains only ; those carried by relief or duplicate trains are shown only in the Western Region's official working notices, as required, and do not appear in this list.

§ Every weekday. * Sats. exc. † Sats. only. ‡ Fris. only. • Sats. & Suns. ‖ Tues. to Sats. or Suns. incl. ** Weekdays and Suns. †† Mons. only. ‡‡ Suns. only

Train No.	Time	From	To	Train No.	Time	From	To	Train No.	Time	From	To
010	9.50 p.m.‡	Paddington	Penzance	138	11. 0 a.m.†	Paddington	Penzance	181	9. 0 a.m.*	Paddington	Wolverhampton
011	10.12 p.m.‡	,,	,,	140	11. 5 a.m.*	,,	,,	..	9. 0 a.m.*	,,	Pwllheli
012	10.35 p.m.‡	,,	,,	142	11.15 a.m.§	,,	Weston-s.-Mare	183	10.10 a.m.*	,,	Aberystwyth
013	10.50 p.m.‡	,,	Newquay	144	11.30 a.m.*	,,	Penzance	185	11.45 a.m.§	,,	Hereford
015	11.35 p.m.‡	,,	Penzance	..	11.30 a.m.‡	,,	Minehead	186	1.45 p.m.§	,,	,,
016	11.50 p.m.‡	,,	,,	146	12. 0 n.n. ‡	,,	Kingswear	187	4.10 p.m.§	,,	Birkenhead
018	12.30 a.m.†	,,	,,	147	12. 5 p.m.†	,,	Plymouth	189	4.45 p.m.‡	,,	Hereford
	(News)			149	1.25 p.m.‡	,,	Kingswear	192	5.10 p.m.*	,,	Wolverhampton
019	12.35 a.m.†			150	1.35 p.m.†	,,	Penzance	195	6.10 p.m.§	,,	Birkenhead
038	10.50 a.m.‡‡	Manchester (L.R.)	Cardiff	152	3.20 p.m.*	,,	Kingswear	198	6.45 p.m.§	,,	Hereford
100	5.30 a.m.*	Paddington	Penzance	153	3.30 p.m.§	,,	Penzance	201	10.22 p.m.‡	York	Swindon
..	5.30 a.m.†	,,	Minehead	154	4.15 p.m.§	,,	Plymouth	202	11.35 p.m.§	Liverpool	Penzance
102	6.55 a.m.†	,,	Penzance	155	5. 5 p.m.*	,,	Weston-s.-Mare	204	8.10 a.m.†	Manchester(L.R.)	Penzance
103	7. 0 a.m.†	,,	Kingswear	156	11. 4 a.m.†	Bournemouth	Sheffield	..	11.16 a.m.†	Bournemouth	Newcastle
105	7. 5 a.m.†	,,	Penzance	157	5.30 p.m.‡	Paddington	Plymouth	205	12. 0 n.n. ‡	Penzance	Crewe
..	7.25 a.m.†	Ealing Bdy.	,,	158	6.15 p.m.‡	,,	Bristol	206	8. 5 a.m.§	Bournemouth	Newcastle
107	7.30 a.m.†	Paddington	Paignton	159	6.30 p.m.‡	,,	Weston-s.-Mare	208	9.10 a.m.‡	Liverpool	Plymouth
108	7.40 a.m.†	,,	Paignton	161	7.55 a.m.‡	,,	Carmarthen	..	9.15 a.m.†		
110	8.10 a.m.†			162	8.50 a.m.†	,,	Pembroke Dock	..	10.40 a.m.‡‡		
113	8.20 a.m.†	,,	Weymouth	..	8.40 a.m.†	,,	,,	..	9.40 p.m.†	Swindon	York
114	8.25 a.m.*	,,	Penzance	163	8.55 a.m.§	,,	,,	210	9.25 a.m.‡	Manchester (L.R.)	Swansea
115	8.20 a.m.*	,,	Weymouth	164	9.55 a.m.*	,,	Swansea	212	9.10 a.m.†	,,	Plymouth
..	8.30 a.m.†			..	9.55 a.m.†	,,	Neyland	..	9.10 a.m.†	,,	Paignton
116	8.45 a.m.†	,,	Bristol	165	10.55 a.m.§	,,	Pembroke Dock	214	5.30 p.m.‡	Glasgow	Plymouth
117	8.50 a.m.†	,,	Paignton	166	11.35 a.m.‡	,,	Neyland	215	12. 5 a.m.†	Cardiff	Liverpool
119	9. 5 a.m.‡	,,	Bristol	167	11.55 a.m.§	,,	Pembroke Dock	216	9. 5 a.m.†	Birkenhead	Plymouth
120	9.15 a.m.†	,,	Durston	168	1.50 p.m.†	,,	Carmarthen	217	12.10 a.m.††	Bristol	Manchester (L.R.)
122	9.30 a.m.†	,,	Falmouth	169	1.55 p.m.§	,,	Pembroke Dock	..	4.45 p.m.‡	Penzance	,,
..	9.30 a.m.†	,,	Newquay	170	3.45 p.m.‡	,,	Fishguard Harbour	221	7. 5 p.m.§	,,	(V.)
123	9.35 a.m.†	,,	Minehead	171	3.55 p.m.§	,,	Neyland	223	10. 4 a.m.†	Exeter	(L.R.)
125	9.40 a.m.†	,,	Paignton	172	4.55 p.m.§	,,	Cheltenham	227	8.20 a.m.*	Cardiff	(May.)
128	10.20 a.m.†	,,	Kingswear	173	5.55 p.m.§	,,	Carmarthen	228	11.55 a.m.§	Manchester (L.R.)	Plymouth
130	10.30 a.m.‡	,,	Penzance	174	5.50 p.m.§	,,	Swansea	230	12.15 a.m.†	,,	Paignton
131	10.35 a.m.*			176	6.55 p.m.§	,,	Cheltenham	232	12.40 a.m.†	Cardiff	Manchester (Ex.)
133	10.35 a.m.†			178	6.55 p.m.‡	,,	Fishguard Harbour	234	3. 0 p.m.†	Liverpool	Cardiff
135	10.40 a.m.*	,,	Paignton	179	7.15 p.m.‡	,,	,,	..	3. 5 p.m.†‡		
136	11. 5 a.m.†	Swindon	Sheffield	180	9.10 a.m.§	,,	Birkenhead	239	10.15 a.m.†	Bradford (Ex.)	Poole

318 TRAINS ILLUSTRATED August 1955

(Reproduced from Trains Illustrated, *courtesy Ian Allan Publishing Ltd)*

On steam engines the metal frame only had three spaces, so these were used to display the last three characters. The class of train remained identified, as it always had been, by the lamp positioning, an express passenger train being denoted by two lamps on the buffer beam, one above each of the buffers. Of the early diesel hydraulic units, numbers D800–D812 were delivered with three-character panels, with later deliveries incorporating the full four-character panels from new.

THE TITLED EXPRESSES

CHELTENHAM FLYER
CORNISH RIVIERA★ / LIMITED / EXPRESS
THE DEVONIAN
TORBAY EXPRESS
THE RED DRAGON★
THE INTER-CITY★
THE WILLIAM SHAKESPEARE
THE MERCHANT VENTURER
THE BRISTOLIAN★

CAMBRIAN COAST EXPRESS
THE CORNISHMAN
PEMBROKE COAST EXPRESS
THE SOUTH WALES PULLMAN
CAPITALS UNITED EXPRESS
CHELTENHAM SPA EXPRESS
THE MAYFLOWER
THE ROYAL DUCHY
CATHEDRAL EXPRESS

★ These services also carried a 1953 Coronation commemorative headboard.

ADDITIONAL TITLES

GOLDEN HIND
NORTH WALES RADIO LAND CRUISE

Old Oak Common motive power depot – coded 81A by British Railways in 1950 – supplied London's Paddington station with its engines and all their paraphernalia, such as oil lamps, train reporting numbers, and of course headboards where appropriate. In this internal view, five of the Western Region's own in-house designs are on show – all cast at Swindon Works – while the sixth was of the earlier type, possibly cast at Doncaster, and familiar throughout all regions except the Southern. Those only partially visible are THE ROYAL DUCHY (left) and THE MERCHANT VENTURER (right). *(NRM/SSPL)*

CHELTENHAM FLYER (GWR)

Paddington–Cheltenham Spa (St James)

Inaugural titled run	9 July 1928
Last titled run	9 September 1939
(a) 1st style headboard	**Introduced 14 September 1931** Rectangular wooden board incorporating the legend WORLD'S FASTEST TRAIN, with the train's title split by the GWR roundel. Board 42in wide, 24in high, roundel 9in diameter. Superseded by srtyle (b). (See also Colour Section)
(b) 2nd style headboard	**Introduced 20 May 1936** 'Curved rectangle' with brown lettering on cream background (see Colour Section).

- The train's title in the public timetable was CHELTENHAM SPA EXPRESS.
- The headboard's claim to be the world's fastest train referred to its scheduled 67 min sprint start-to-stop from Swindon to Paddington. The fastest achieved was on 6 June 1932 when the actual time was 56 min 47 sec – an average speed of 81.6mph. The timing was tightened again on and from 12 September 1932, when only 65 min was allowed for the 77.3 miles. This schedule remained in force until the outbreak of the Second World War.
- The progressive accelerations of the Swindon–Paddington timings were:

9 July 1928 75 min (summer only)	14 September 1931	67 min
8 July 1929 70 min (daily Monday–Saturday)	12 September 1932	65 min

The first train to run to the 67 minute timing speeds through Tilehurst on 14 September 1931. The loco is No. 5000 *Launceston Castle* and the youthful throng (quite probably put up to it by the photographer) are giving the crew and passengers a cheery wave. Note the flowerbeds, gas lamps and the tail end of a Down service on the right. *(NRM/SSPL)*

CORNISH RIVIERA / LIMITED / EXPRESS

Paddington–Penzance

Inaugural titled run	21 July 1906
Title withdrawn	1 January 1917 to 6 July 1919; 9 September 1939
Reintroduced	6 May 1946
Last titled run	Still running

(a) 1st style headboard	Introduced 11 June 1951 and usage overlapped styles (c) and (d) CORNISH RIVIERA BR Type 1 but less wide than standard. Fitted with extra Coronation crown and cypher in 1953 for a few weeks.
(b) 50th anniversary	CORNISH RIVIERA EXPRESS Wooden, 52in wide. Yellow background with dark brown lettering. Two inward-facing 'lion and wheel' BR emblem at sides, with the coat of arms of the Great Western Railway Company mounted centrally. One of two, carried by the Up and Down trains on 1 July 1954, though only between Paddington and Plymouth.
(c) 2nd style headboard	Introduced 11 June 1956. Used until Summer 1958 only, superseded by style (d) CORNISH RIVIERA LIMITED brown letters on cream background surmounted by the arms of the Duchy of Cornwall and motto 'one and all'. 52in wide. First boards wooden with painted lettering. Later boards cast, with both painted and cast lettering.
(d) 3rd style headboard	Introduced April 1958, but rarely used after 1961/2 CORNISH RIVIERA EXPRESS as (c) with LIMITED replaced by EXPRESS. Again, some had painted lettering, some had the lettering cast integral with the headboard.

- Unique among headboards in having three different wordings.
- When introduced in 1904, the Paddington–Plymouth leg of the journey was the longest non-stop run yet performed in regular service. The GWR wished the express to bear a title and asked readers of *The Railway Magazine* to suggest a suitable name. The competition was to be judged by Mr J.C. Inglis (General Manager, GWR) and the prize was 3 guineas; it was announced in the July 1904 issue, with the winners published in the September edition. The winning entry was judged to be the RIVIERA EXPRESS and the prize money was shared equally between two entrants. However, as the title officially bestowed on the train (nearly two years later) turned out to be CORNISH RIVIERA LIMITED, the four people who suggested precisely this title had cause to be aggrieved.
- It will be observed that the anniversary headboard celebrated neither of the titles above, nor the correct year. At least the 1956 version reverted to the original 1906 name.

The 1st style headboard had already been in use for two years when this Plymouth-based 'King' stood in Old Oak Common's yard before working the Down service. The date must be within a fortnight or so either way of the Queen's Coronation on 2 June 1953, as the Western Region's commemorative design for this event was only fixed to the headboard during this period. The train reporting numerals are also, identifiably, a full set of Old Oak's own. *(NRM/SSPL)*

One of Old Oak Common's own 'Kings', No. 6018 *King Henry VI* at Paddington on a damp Thursday 1 July 1954. The train is the time-honoured 10.30 a.m. departure, but for this day only the Golden Jubilee headboard is displayed. It is at least arguable that the WR jumped the gun by two years here. While the service itself, namely a through train from London to Penzance, did indeed begin on 1 July 1904, the title CORNISH RIVIERA LIMITED was not conferred in the timetable until 21 July 1906, when the train began using the new Westbury cutoff and was accelerated by 20 minutes. Only then did the express begin its non-stop run to Plymouth at 10.30 a.m., rather than its original time of 10.10 a.m. The Jubilee headboard was only carried as far as Plymouth and the word EXPRESS was not to reappear on the engine headboard until 1958. *(NRM/SSPL)*

On the first day of the summer timetable, the brand-new wooden board (with painted lettering) is given a shine for the press by driver Lewis Parker. The thickness of this board will be noted. Paddington, 11 June 1956. *(Getty Images)*

Cast headboard, painted lettering. Note the absence of an upturned tail to the letter R in comparison to the cast lettering seen below. *(Courtesy Sheffield Railwayana Auctions)*

With the introduction in 1958 of diesel-hydraulic locos the service was retitled EXPRESS, a style it then kept until the end of its headboard-carrying days. Brand-new D800 *Sir Brian Robertson* (then Chairman of the British Transport Commission) stands in Swindon Works yard for an official photo in April 1958. The way that the point of attachment to the lamp iron is offset from the centre of the headboard is clearly seen. *(NRM/SSPL)*

THE DEVONIAN

Bradford (Forster Square)–Paignton
Bradford (Exchange)–Paignton (from 1 May 1967)
Leeds City–Paignton (from 3 May 1971)

Inaugural titled run	26 September 1927
Title withdrawn	9 September 1939
Reintroduced	23 May 1949
Last titled run	3 May 1975

(a) 1st style headboard	Introduced Summer 1951. Usage of LMR versions overlapped style (b) BR Type 3 with black background (WR) or red background (LMR).
(b) 2nd style headboard	Introduced *c.* 1960/1 BR Type 6 with a red background. (See Colour Section). LMR only.

- This long-lived inter-regional service ran during summer only 1949–52 inclusive, but daily (Monday–Saturday) from the summer timetable of 1953.
- 1st style headboard: those with a black background were for use with WR-allocated locos only, as the lamp bracket onto which the headboard was fixed differed from the LMR equivalent, requiring two versions of the securing bracket on the back of the headboard. Hence the same headboard could not be used throughout the journey and was swapped at Bristol when engines were changed.

Rather surprisingly, this famous and popular service was only ever provided, while running on WR metals, with one style of headboard. Just why an 'individualised' headboard was not provided post-1956 remains a mystery, since the WR headboard – of whatever style – was not carried north of Bristol in any case. Here, Newton Abbot's *Powderham Castle* runs along the sea wall at Teignmouth with the northbound service in July 1953. Note the ex-LMS coaches in carmine and cream, complete with roofboards. *(B.K.B. Green Collection/ Initial Photographics)*

TORBAY EXPRESS

Paddington–Kingswear

A wooden pattern from which castings were made for the 'Devon' shield. *(Courtesy Adrian Crafer)*

Inaugural titled run	9 July 1923
Title withdrawn	9 September 1939
Reintroduced	6 May 1946
Last titled run	13 September 1968

(a) 1st style headboard	Introduced Summer 1951 and usage overlapped styles (b) and (c)
	BR Type 1 but less wide than standard.
(b) 2nd style headboard	Introduced 11 June 1956 and usage overlapped style (c)
	Painted brown letters on cream background incorporating the arms and motto of Devon County Council *Auxilio Divino* ('by Divine Aid').
	Two versions, one with circular letter O, one elliptical.
(c) 3rd style headboard	Introduced Summer 1958 but rarely carried after 1963
	Similar to (b) but with different lower edge; cast lettering.

- The shield contains a lion rampant (of the Earls of Cornwall), above which is an ancient ship. This is perhaps a depiction of the *Golden Hind*, since the motto is that of Sir Francis Drake.
- Before the Second World War the service was variously titled (in the timetable) as TORBAY EXPRESS/LIMITED EXPRESS/TORQUAY PULLMAN LIMITED, existing in the latter form from 8 July 1929 to 20 September 1930.
- At the end of the summer season in 1964 this train ceased to run daily (Monday–Saturday) and thereafter ran in the summer months only during 1965–8.

First-generation headboard on second-generation motive power. D813 *Diadem* heads the Down service at Taunton on 14 April 1962. Train description has now grown to four characters, and no fewer than ten small panels warning of overhead electrification have been attached, five of which are visible. *(John Hodge)*

A double-chimneyed 'Castle' sets out from Kingswear at the start of its eastbound journey in 1959. Although deep in the centre, the extremities of this headboard were found to be insufficiently robust to survive for very long in the rough handling conditions encountered at steam running sheds, a fault rectified by the introduction of the 3rd style. Note the elliptical O. *(NRM/SSPL)*

The second version of the above headboard, with the circular letter O, seen in the company of a ROYAL DUCHY headboard in the depths of Old Oak Common. The cast lettering of the DUCHY headboard is evident, and the upward-pointing tail to the cast letter R contrasts with the almost horizontal tail of the painted R, a distinguishing feature. *(NRM/SSPL)*

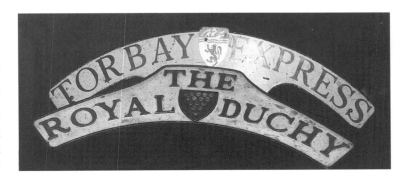

The final form of the Swindon casting. See also the wooden pattern for the central shield.
(Author, with permission of the NRM)

THE RED DRAGON

Paddington–Swansea/Carmarthen

Inaugural titled run	5 June 1950
Last titled run	12 June 1965

(a) 1st style headboard — Introduced Summer 1951 but superseded by style (c)
BR Type 3 with black or red background. Fitted with extra Coronation adornment in 1953.

(b) 2nd style headboard — Introduced 1956 and used only until style (c) became available
As (a) but with colours reversed, i.e. dark letters on light-coloured background.

(c) 3rd style headboard — Introduced 1956, last carried in 1962
'Curved rectangle' containing one line of brown letters on a cream background surmounted by a central disc containing a representation of a red dragon against a slate-grey or cream background. 53½in wide overall. Disc width 15in.

(d) 4th style headboard — Introduced 22 November 1961, for inspection purposes
Experimental only, not used in traffic. Made in fibreglass and designed for diesel traction, but policy changes prevented its introduction. Rectangular, 55in × 12in with 14in-high central plaque, containing a red dragon, as in (c). Not flat, with a 2½in bow, front to back. Illustrated on p. ix.

- Although running titled from the commencement of the summer timetable, the winter 1950/1 timetable is the first to mention the name of the first titled train to serve South Wales.

No. 5099 *Compton Castle* powers the London-bound service through Moreton Cutting, east of Didcot. The thirteen coaches appear to be entirely of ex-GWR design in the early BR colours of carmine and cream, and the first version of the BR crest is carried on the tender of the immaculate Cardiff (Canton) 'Castle'. There is a black background on the nearly new headboard. *(NRM/SSPL)*

Immediately before the introduction of the new-style headboards in 1956 the WR apparently tried out the new colours of dark brown lettering on a light background on three of its current services' headboards, namely THE RED DRAGON, THE MERCHANT VENTURER and CAPITALS UNITED EXPRESS. Here one of the Cardiff-based 'Britannia' class locos waits on the through lines at Cardiff General (as it then was) to take over the Paddington leg of the journey and displays the short-lived colour variant of the standard BR-pattern cast-aluminium headboard. *(Norman Preedy)*

About five years later, 9 May 1961, the Up service is again about to depart from Cardiff but certain things have changed. The stock (still thirteen coaches) is now of the BR Mk 1 design, but in the WR house colours of chocolate and cream, some displaying carriage roofboards, some the BR coaching stock roundel, some both. The engine now carries the later version of the BR crest, hand-holds have been cut into the smoke deflector, an alpha-numeric train reporting number is in use, and of course the individualised headboard has arrived. Here the dragon disc has a dark, slate grey background, whereas on others this was cream coloured. (See also Colour Section) *(John Hodge)*

THE INTER-CITY

Paddington–Wolverhampton (Low Level)

Inaugural titled run	25 September 1950
Last titled run	11 June 1965

(a) 1st style headboard	Introduced Summer 1951 and usage overlapped style (b) BR Type 3 with black background. Fitted with extra Coronation adornment in 1953.
(b) 2nd style headboard	Introduced Summer 1957, last carried in 1962 Similar in overall shape to (a) but with brown letters on cream background together with three shields attached radially, with arms, crests and mottos of Birmingham (left), London and Wolverhampton (right).

- One of only eight cast-aluminium headboards to include a hyphen.
- Mottos: Birmingham: Forward
  London: *Domine dirige nos* ('Lord direct us')
  Wolverhampton: *Out of darkness cometh light*
- Chocolate and cream stock was received in December 1956, but it is thought that the new headboard was not supplied until some months later.

Above: The method by which the Coronation embellishment was attached is clearly seen, being secured by three countersunk screws. *(Courtesy Sheffield Railwayana Auctions)*

Left: Allocated to Wolverhampton Stafford Road, coded 84A, 'Castle' class No. 5022 *Wigmore Castle* calls at Birmingham's Snow Hill station on 19 September 1957 with the Up train. (See Colour Section) *(Michael Mensing)*

THE WILLIAM SHAKESPEARE

Paddington–Wolverhampton / Stratford-upon-Avon

Inaugural titled run	3 May 1951
Last titled run	8 September 1951
Only headboard	Introduced 3 May 1951, last used four months later
	BR Type 7 with black background.

- This was one of two WR expresses named specifically for the Festival of Britain, and was equipped with brand-new coaching stock in the BR colours of carmine and cream (see also THE MERCHANT VENTURER). The service was not a commercial success and ceased after one summer of operation only. However, as the service did not appear in the public timetable for the first two months of its life, this is hardly surprising. The third of May was the opening date for the Festival, but not the start of the summer timetable. This had been scheduled to commence on 18 June but was put back a fortnight to 2 July, as an economy measure.
- The title was bestowed on the 10.10 a.m. ex-Paddington and the 7.23 p.m. return working from Stratford, which had previously run only in the summer timetable.

The first (but not the last) picture of a titled train commencing its journey hauled by a tank engine. This is the Stratford-upon-Avon portion of the through London express, to which it will be attached at Leamington Spa, and the headboard transferred to the main line locomotive. At this stage the engine does not carry lamps in the 'express passenger' position but a single lamp indicating 'light engine'. Hence, either the loco has only just backed on, or the crew have omitted to make the change. The 2–6–2 still displays the insignia of its former owner on the sides of its water tanks, more than three years after nationalisation. *(NRM/SSPL)*

THE MERCHANT VENTURER

Paddington–Bristol/Weston-super-Mare

Inaugural titled run	3 May 1951
Last titled run	9 September 1961

(a) 1st style headboard	Introduced 3 May 1951 and usage overlapped style (b)
	BR Type 7 with black background.
(b) 2nd style headboard	Introduced 1956 and used only until style (c) became available
	As (a) but with colours reversed, i.e. dark letters on a light-coloured background.
(c) 3rd style headboard	Introduced Summer 1957, and usage continued until at least 1960
	Brown letters on cream background surmounted by the arms and crest of The Society of Merchant Venturers with the motto *Indocilis Pauperium Pati* ('Will not learn to endure poverty') below the arms. (See also Colour Section)

- This was one of two WR expresses named specifically for the Festival of Britain (which opened on Thursday 3 May 1951) and was equipped with brand-new coaching stock in the BR colours of carmine and cream (see also THE WILLIAM SHAKESPEARE).
- The Society of Merchant Venturers was granted its first charter by King Edward VI in 1552. Two Masters of the Society have travelled on the footplate of the engine from Bristol to Paddington, one in 1956, the other in 1958 (see also THE MASTER CUTLER, LMR and ER Sections).
- The title was bestowed on the then 11.15 a.m. ex-Paddington and 4.35 p.m. return working from Weston.
- Initially a three-coach Taunton portion was attached/detached at Bristol, but this was soon discontinued.

D829 *Magpie* passes milepost 106½ on the outskirts of Bath with the Down train *c.* 1960. This, the tallest of all the customised headboards, obstructs slightly the clear view ahead afforded by diesel traction, but not for much longer as the title was abandoned with the commencement of the 1961 winter timetable. *(John Ashman, courtesy Mike Esau)*

Along with THE RED DRAGON (already noted) and CAPITALS UNITED EXPRESS (see later), this service was also chosen to trial the colour-reversal scheme on existing headboards. Consequently, this light-background-with-dark-lettering version of the standard three-line large headboard appeared in 1956. *(Courtesy Sheffield Railwayana Auctions)*

Before deciding to order diesel-hydraulic units, the Western Region did give serious consideration to opting for gas turbine locomotives. Two were ordered and the second, more powerful, unit No. 18100 stands at Bristol (Temple Meads) station immediately after arrival from London. Delivered in 1952 from Metropolitan Vickers Electrical Co. Ltd, this two-bogie, six-axle machine had an output of 3000hp and a top speed of 90mph. Officially withdrawn on 1 January 1958, it was converted into an ac electric locomotive and used for driver training on the first stages of the Manchester–Crewe electrification. Renumbered E1000, and then E2001, it was finally withdrawn in 1968 and sold for scrap in 1972. *(NRM/SSPL)*

THE BRISTOLIAN

Paddington–Bristol (Temple Meads)

Inaugural titled run	9 September 1935
Title withdrawn	9 September 1939
Reintroduced	2 July 1951
Last titled run	12 June 1965

A complete pattern with the London and Bristol shields *in situ*. *(Author, courtesy Adrian Crafer)*

(a) 1st style headboard	Introduced Summer 1953 and usage overlapped style (b) BR Type 3 with black ground. Fitted with extra Coronation adornment in 1953.
(b) 2nd style headboard	Introduced 11 June 1956 but rarely carried after 1962 Brown letters on cream background with the arms of London (left) and Bristol, both with crests above and mottos below. Initially a painted wooden board (not illustrated), soon replaced by a cast version of the same design.

• As the coat of arms of the Great Western Railway Co. is a blending of the arms of the cities of London and Bristol (the original limits of the GWR as contemplated by the Bill of 1835), it is perhaps worthwhile to record these in greater detail.
City of London: Red cross on white background with sword of St Paul in the first quarter, with crest above showing a dragon's wing with red cross. Motto below is *Domine dirige nos* ('Lord direct us').
City of Bristol: A silver castle with two domed towers each flying the cross of St George. The castle stands on a cliff and a golden ship sails from a port in the left tower. Above this the crest consists of two bent arms with forearms crossed holding a snake and a pair of scales. Motto below is *Virtute et industria* ('By virtue and industry').
• 1935 was the centenary of the Royal Assent being given to the Great Western Bill of 31 August 1835. The first stretch of line (Paddington–Maidenhead) did not open until 31 May 1838.

A 'King' passes, a Queen is crowned. A perfect sight on a perfect morning *and* sweet rationing had just ended. No. 6009 *King Charles II* heads west with eleven coaches, carrying the extra Coronation embellishments and a spare headboard (reversed) located on the running board in front of the steam pipe. *(NRM/SSPL)*

In May 1958 the WR conducted two tests to ascertain the viability of a 100-minute schedule for the winter 1958/9 timetable, an acceleration of five minutes. To this end No. 7018 *Drysllwyn Castle* was employed on 6 May and is seen here whisking its seven-coach load through Box on the way to Bristol, with Middle Hill Tunnel in the background. Built by BR in 1949, No. 7018 received a name that had already been borne by Nos 5051 and 5076, and by 1958 had been modified by the addition of a double chimney, a four-row superheater and a mechanical lubricator. For the purposes of the test run, it was also paired with a self-weighing tender. *(Ivo Peters, courtesy Julian Peters)*

No. 18100 receives the fitters' attention inside Old Oak Common depot. The WR virtually always carried headboards on the top lamp iron, and to see one fixed on the buffer beam was rare indeed, even if it was the only feasible place on a gas turbine. *(S.V. Blencowe Collection)*

The replacement headboard strongly resembled the shape of the original, but with 'colour reversal' and the addition of two shields overlapping the profile. The lettering style has also changed from the BR version of Gill Sans to a serif style most closely matched by Clarendon Regular. In this 1959 view, No. 5085 *Evesham Abbey* prepares to leave Temple Meads with the Up service. As usual, the train reporting number catches the eye, despite the increased prominence of the individualised headboard. *(Norman Simmons, courtesy Photos of the Fifties)*

CAMBRIAN COAST EXPRESS

Paddington–Aberystwyth/Pwllheli

Inaugural titled run	15 July 1927
Title withdrawn	9 September 1939
Reintroduced	7 July 1951
Last titled run	4 March 1967

(a) 1st style headboard	Introduced 30 March 1953 but superseded by style (b)
	BR Type 7 with black background.
(b) 2nd style headboard	Introduced Summer 1958. Carried by steam traction throughout its life including the final day of service
	Brown letters on cream background, surmounted by the arms of the Cambrian Railway comprising a conjoined half wyvern (left) and half Tudor rose.

- Has the distinction of being the last WR headboard used in service.
- The wyvern/rose badge used here was the third version of the arms of the Cambrian Railway and was used between 1891 and 1909 on the sides of carriages.
- Postwar, this train began running on summer Saturdays only, this being the case in 1951–3. For the summer of 1954 the train operated daily (Monday–Saturday), and thereafter throughout the year.
- From September 1966 the Pwllheli portion was replaced by a diesel multiple unit (DMU) connection from Dovey Junction.

No. 5035 *Coity Castle* oozes steam at the northern end of Birmingham's Snow Hill station, while the fireman brings coal forward in the tender, 3 January 1957. In the shelter of the canopy, two young spotters (presumably) admire the warmth of the footplate. *(Michael Mensing)*

Same headboard, but here in the more rural setting of Portmadoc (as it was then spelt). The BR Mk 1 coaching stock in regional colours forms the Pwllheli portion of the southbound train that will unite with the Aberystwyth portion at Dovey Junction. The tank engine, then allocated to Machynlleth, has been preserved, being bought originally by Patrick Whitehouse. Note how on smaller-boilered engines the headboard is carried totally proud of the boiler. *(B.K.B. Green Collection/Initial Photographics)*

Further down the coast and entering Barmouth station, 12 September 1958, the portion from Pwllheli is this time powered by the unusual combination of a 'Dukedog' 4–4–0 leading BR Standard 2–6–0 No. 78006. Owing to the severe axle load restriction on the long Barmouth bridge over the Mawddach estuary, relatively small lightweight locos were the only steam engines allowed to cross it. *(R.J. Buckley/Initial Photographics)*

THE CORNISHMAN

Wolverhampton (Low Level)–Penzance
Sheffield (Midland)–Penzance from 10 September 1962
Bradford (Forster Square)–Penzance from 14 June 1965
Bradford (Exchange)–Penzance from 1 May 1967

Inaugural titled run	30 June 1952
Last titled run	3 May 1975

(a) 1st style headboard	Introduced 30 March 1953 but superseded by style (b) BR Type 3 with black background.
(b) 2nd style headboard	Introduced Summer 1957 and used on both steam and diesel traction until at least 1962 Brown letters on cream background surmounted by a Cornish pixie leaping a toadstool. 40in wide, pixie 12¼in above the top of main headboard, itself 10in deep centrally.

- Until the re-routing in 1962 this service operated via Stratford-upon-Avon.
- In the privatised era, Virgin Trains applied this title to a Glasgow–Penzance HST service (see Colour Section).

The northbound train calls at Exeter (St Davids) on 11 June 1960, double-headed by *Clifford Castle* and a 'County' class 4–6–0. Despite the date, the Type 3 headboard remains in use. *(B.K.B. Green Collection/Initial Photographics)*

'Castle' class No. 5070 *Sir Daniel Gooch* has covered the dozen or so miles from Wolverhampton and now awaits departure from Birmingham Snow Hill, next stop Stratford-upon-Avon, 27 May 1958. *(Frank Ashley)*

PEMBROKE COAST EXPRESS

Paddington–Pembroke Dock

Inaugural titled run	8 June 1953
Last titled run	7 September 1963
(a) 1st style headboard	Introduced Summer 1953, superseded by style (b) BR Type 7 with black background.
(b) 2nd style headboard	Introduced Summer 1958 and used until the end of this service Brown letters on cream background incorporating two shields, with the arms of Tenby (left) and Pembroke, radially aligned, both without mottos or crests (see back cover).

- The arms of Tenby comprise three martlets in the upper section (from the arms of the Earls of Pembroke) and three cinquefoils (from the arms of the See of St David's) in the base.
- The arms of Pembroke comprise a border of twelve martlets, containing within this a shield of six red chevrons.
- Chocolate and cream stock was allocated from February 1957. A Swindon headboard may have been received earlier than the period quoted, but the author has not found photographic evidence to confirm this.

In the early days of the service, and with apparently only nine vehicles in tow, all of GWR design, Old Oak Common's No. 70015 *Apollo* speeds westbound. The London shed never really liked 'Britannias', as can be inferred from the loco's dirty state, and all its allocation were later transferred to Cardiff's Canton shed, whose men did like them. *(NRM/SSPL)*

THE SOUTH WALES PULLMAN

Paddington–Swansea (High Street)

Inaugural titled run	27 June 1955
Last titled run	8 September 1961

Only headboard	Introduced 27 June 1955 and used throughout the period of service, including final day
	BR Type 7 with black background.

- The ASLEF rail strike caused a fortnight's delay in the introduction of this service, as the summer timetable had been due to commence on 13 June.
- Upon withdrawal of the steam-hauled service, a 'Blue Pullman' DMU took over from 11 September 1961. This ran until 4 May 1973 but did not of course carry headboards.
- The only previous use of Pullman cars on Paddington services had been the TORQUAY PULLMAN LIMITED during 1929/30.
- A trial run was held on 21 June 1955, hauled in the Down direction by No. 5016 *Montgomery Castle*, which also powered the inaugural Up working.

The Western Region's only Pullman car service, at Paddington on 4 July 1955 headed by No. 4074 *Caldicot Castle*. Just a week after its introduction the train's Pullmans fairly glisten and the almost brand-new headboard shows the title to advantage despite being in the shadows. Most of the Pullman cars used in this formation had seen previous service on THE DEVON BELLE (see Southern Section), which had ceased to run at the end of the summer timetable of 1954. *(The Stephenson Locomotive Society)*

CAPITALS UNITED EXPRESS

Paddington–Cardiff/Swansea (High Street)

Inaugural titled run	6 February 1956
Last titled run	12 June 1965

(a) 1st style headboard	**Introduced 6 February 1956, superseded by style (c)**	
	BR Type 7 with black or red background.	
(b) 2nd style headboard	**Introduced 1956 and used only until style (c) became available**	
	As (a) but with colours reversed, i.e. dark letters on light-coloured background.	
(c) 3rd style headboard	**Introduced late 1959 but rarely carried after 1961**	
	Brown letters on cream background with two shields offset at each side showing the arms of London (left) and Cardiff, with crests but without mottos. 44in wide, 16½in deep overall.	
(d) 4th style headboard	**Introduced 22 November 1961, for inspection purposes**	
	Experimental only, not used in traffic. Made in fibreglass and designed for diesel traction (see also THE RED DRAGON). The shields mounted centrally are the arms of London (left) and Cardiff, as in (c). Again not flat with a 2½in bow front to back.	

- Cardiff became the official capital of Wales on 20 December 1955 and the service was titled in recognition of this. Hence the mid-timetable introduction date.
- The arms of Cardiff comprise a red dragon holding a banner with three chevrons, a leek to the left of this. The crest has three ostrich feathers emanating from a Tudor rose.
- The title was bestowed on the 8 a.m. ex-Cardiff and the 3.55 p.m. return service from Paddington.

One of Canton's 'Castles', No. 5020 *Trematon Castle*, passes its home shed westbound on 19 June 1956 wearing the short-lived 'reversed-colour' headboard type noted earlier. *(John Hodge)*

Canton's No. 4073 *Caerphilly Castle* is in charge of the Up train near Reading and passing beneath a fine gantry of lower quadrant signals that give the crew a 'clear road ahead' indication. This engine was the doyen of the class, being built in 1923 and exhibited in the British Empire Exhibition in 1924. On withdrawal in 1960 it was preserved and placed on display at the Science Museum in London for many years before moving to the GWR Museum at Swindon, finally transferring to the Steam Museum, also at Swindon, where it currently resides. *(John Ashman, courtesy Mike Esau)*

Swindon Works yard again, showing the proposed replacement headboard. Rectangular headboards were of course widely used on Southern Region steam locos, though only one of these displayed any armorial device (see THE MAN OF KENT). Note the low-tech oil lamp and the 'Warship' in the background. Swindon Works itself closed completely in 1985. *(NRM/SSPL)*

A wooden pattern for the Cardiff shield on the 3rd style headboard. *(Author, courtesy Adrian Crafer)*

Opposite, bottom: Swansea (High Street) station is pictured here in 1962 with No. 4099 *Kilgerran Castle* at the head of the Down service. Beneath the largest headboard WR steam regularly carried, the three-character train description panel has now changed to the one-letter-two-numerals style adopted in 1960, whereby F denotes a South Wales destination, and 15 describes the train itself, the 8.55 a.m. from Paddington. *(John Hodge)*

CHELTENHAM SPA EXPRESS

Paddington–Cheltenham Spa (St James)

Inaugural titled run	11 June 1956
Last titled run	4 May 1973

(a) 1st style headboard	Introduced 11 June 1956, superseded by style (b) BR Type 1 with black background.
(b) 2nd style headboard	Introduced late 1957 and in use until 1962 Brown letters on cream background surmounted by the arms, crest and motto of Cheltenham Spa.

- See CHELTENHAM FLYER (page 6) for pre-war equivalent working.
- The title was bestowed on the 8 a.m. ex-Cheltenham and the 4.55 p.m. return working from Paddington.
- The arms displayed comprise a red chevron with two pigeons above this and an oak tree below, topped by a border showing a silver cross between two open books. The crest has another pigeon, perched on a roundel, flanked by two sprays of oak. The motto reads *Salubritas et eruditio* ('Health and learning'). All were granted in 1887, the year of Queen Victoria's Golden Jubilee.

A close-up of the headboard and the arms, crest and motto described above. It will also be seen that no fewer than ten bolt-heads are showing among the lettering, denoting significant repairs to this board at some stage. *(Roy Denison)*

The London-bound express near Pangbourne on 25 August 1956 has 'Hall' class 4–6–0 No. 5907 *Marble Hall* in charge instead of the more usual 'Castle'. Unique to this service on the Western Region, full-size Type 1 headboards were otherwise confined to the Eastern and Scottish regions. *(D.M.C. Hepburne-Scott/Rail Archive Stephenson)*

No. 4088 *Berkeley Castle* (like No. 5907 a Gloucester (85B) engine) heads the train near Reading (West Junction) in this classic shot of a 'Castle' at speed. Note the multitude of telegraph wires. *(John Ashman, courtesy Mike Esau)*

THE MAYFLOWER

Paddington–Plymouth (North Road)

Inaugural titled run	17 June 1957
Last titled run	12 June 1965

(a) 1st style headboard	Introduced 17 June 1957, superseded by style (b) BR Type 3 with black background.
(b) 2nd style headboard	Introduced late 1957, but not carried later than summer 1963 Brown letters and edging on a cream background surmounted by a curved-edge pentagon containing a depiction of the Pilgrim Fathers' ship Mayflower of 1620. 10in deep at centre and 38½in wide, pentagon height 12½in. (See also Colour Section)

- The title was bestowed on the 8.30 a.m. ex-Plymouth and the 5.30 p.m. return working from Paddington, chocolate and cream stock being provided on naming.
- Although running from the start of the summer timetable, no mention of the title was made until the winter timetable, commencing 16 September 1957.
- The title was briefly reinstated between 4 May 1970 and 30 April 1971 to commemorate the 350th anniversary of the original sailing. No headboard was carried, however.

As a late entry in the WR headboard story, THE MAYFLOWER rather surprisingly gained two styles of headboard. Here the short-lived early version has been in use for about six weeks as No. 6008 *King James II* carries it along the sea wall at Teignmouth towards Exeter on 31 July 1957. *(Ray Hinton)*

An extract from the winter timetable 1961/2. *(BRB (Residuary) Ltd)*

Table 6

THE MAYFLOWER

RESTAURANT CAR SERVICE

LONDON, TAUNTON, EXETER

NEWTON ABBOT and PLYMOUTH

(Also conveys Through Carriages to and from Torquay, Paignton, Kingswear and Truro—see Table 81)

WEEK DAYS

	pm			am
London (Paddington) .. ..dep	4A30	Truro .. ..dep		6A30
Reading General .. .. ,,	5 10	St. Austell .. .. ,,		6 52
Westbury .. ..arr	6 8	Par.. .. .. ,,		7 1
Taunton .. .. ,,	7 0	Bodmin Road .. .. ,,		7 14
Exeter (St. David's) .. .. ,,	7 35	Liskeard .. .. ,,		7 32
Newton Abbot .. .. ,,	8 5	Menheniot .. .. ,,		7 39
		St. Germans .. .. ,,		7 48
Torquay .. .. ,,	8 28	Saltash .. .. ,,		7 56
Paignton .. .. ,,	8 39	St. Budeaux (F.Rd.) .. .. ,,		8 2
Churston (for Brixham) .. .. .. ,,	8 50	Keyham . .. . ,,		8 6
Kingswear .. .. ,,	8 59	Devonport (A.Rd.) .. .. ,,		8 10
		Plymouth.. .. .. ,,		8A30
Plymouth .. .. ,,	9 2	Totnes. .. .. ,,		9 10
		Kingswear .. .. ,,		8A35
Liskeard .. .. ,,	9 41	Churston (for Brixham) .. .. .. ,,		8A45
Bodmin Road .. .. ,,	9 58	Paignton .. .. ,,		8A55
Lostwithiel .. .. ,,	10 5	Torquay .. .. ,,		9 A 5
Par.. .. .. ,,	10 16	Torre .. .. ,,		9 11
St. Austell .. .. ,,	10 28	Newton Abbot . .. . ,,		9 36
Truro .. .. ,,	10 50	Teignmouth .. .. ,,		9 45
		Dawlish .. .. ,,		9 53
		Exeter (St. David's) . .. . ,,		10 15
		Taunton .. .. ,,		10 51
		Newbury .. ..arr		pm 12 15
		London (Paddington) .. .. ,,		1 20

A—Seats can be reserved In advance on payment of a fee of 2s. 0d. per seat (see page 23).

Just over three years later, on 22 August 1960, the first of the original 'Warship' class, D600 *Active*, stands ready to depart from Paddington. This small class of five was supplied to BR by the North British Locomotive Co. Ltd and rated at 2000hp with a top speed of 90mph. They were, however, not that successful, and all had been withdrawn by December 1967. *(John Hodge)*

THE ROYAL DUCHY

Paddington–Penzance

Inaugural titled run	28 January 1957
Last titled run	12 June 1965

Only headboard   **Introduced 28 January 1957, but not carried after 1962**
Brown letters and edging on cream background, embodying the arms of the Duchy of Cornwall, namely a blue shield containing fifteen golden bezants in five decreasing rows. 48in wide, 13in deep at centre with a shield 6in × 6¾in, letters 3¾in high.

- The consent of Her Majesty the Queen was required for the use of this title.
- As a rake of new (or newly repainted) rolling stock in the chocolate and cream livery became available, this service was titled in mid-timetable, using this rake.
- The title was bestowed on the 11 a.m. ex-Penzance and the 1.30 p.m. from Paddington.

In the early days of the service No. 5006 *Tregenna Castle* rounds the curve past Reading shed heading for the Berks & Hants line and the West of England. The fifteen golden roundels (or bezants) originated in the arms of King John's second son, Richard, Earl of Cornwall, and have been associated with Cornwall for centuries. *(NRM/SSPL)*

CATHEDRALS EXPRESS

Paddington–Worcester/Hereford

Inaugural titled run	16 September 1957
Last titled run	12 June 1965
Only headboard	**Introduced 16 September 1957** 'Curved rectangle' with blue background, gold–coloured lettering in Gothic style; capitals 5in high, lower case 3½in surmounted by bishop's mitre in red with gold flowing ribbons. 46½in wide, mitre extends 8½in above top edge. 6⅞in between curved edges. (See also Colour Section)

- Although running from the start of the winter 1957/8 timetable, no mention of the title was made until the summer timetable of 1958.
- The title was bestowed on the 7.45 a.m. ex-Hereford and the 4.45 p.m. working from Paddington, chocolate and cream stock being provided on naming.
- Except for a very short-lived Southern Region title, this headboard is unique in respect of this style of lettering.

The last headboarded express to be introduced connected Hereford, Worcester and London with their first titled service, though the schedule was not demanding and between Hereford and Worcester the train was at best a semi-fast. Here No. 7013 *Bristol Castle* makes the northbound Oxford stop, with the BR Mk 1 coaching stock now painted maroon. The engine itself is in reality No. 4082 *Windsor Castle*, the pair having exchanged identities in 1952. No. 4082 had been allocated the duty of drawing the funeral train of King George VI from London to Windsor, but was being overhauled at Swindon at the time, whereas No. 7013 had recently outshopped from the Works and was in first-class condition. Hence the switch, which was never reversed. *(David Anderson)*

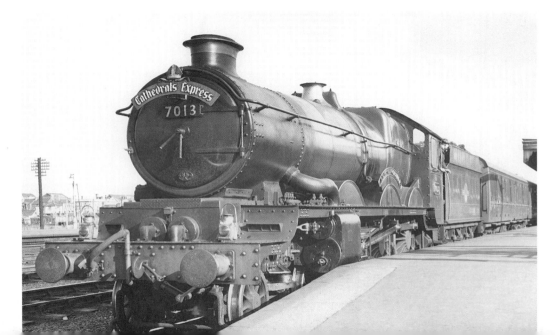

ADDITIONAL TITLES

GOLDEN HIND

Paddington–Plymouth (North Road)

Inaugural titled run	15 June 1964

• No headboard was ever carried, but surprisingly (as none had been used previously on WR expresses) a tailboard was fitted. Exactly when this happened, however, is difficult to say. How long this continued in use is also unknown, but it is thought to have been for only a short duration.

NORTH WALES RADIO LAND CRUISE

Pwllheli–Pwllheli circuit via Harlech, Corwen, Rhyl, Caernarvon and Barmouth

Inaugural titled run	9 July 1957
Last titled run	8 September 1961
Only headboard	Large, circular. Brown letters on a light-cream background. See photograph below right for 1958 variation.

• Typical timings (1959 season) were: Pwllheli dep. 10.10 a.m. arrive back 8.18 p.m. with approximately 1½ hours stop over in Rhyl (early afternoon) and 2 hours in Barmouth in the evening. The train ran Tuesdays and Thursdays 7–23 July, then Saturdays excepted 27 July–4 September (not bank holiday Monday).
• See London Midland Section Additional Titles for details of their similar, but more extensive, services for North Wales holiday-makers.

In response to the North Wales cruise trains operated by the LMR since 1951, the WR (in conjunction with the LMR) also began running their own tours in 1954. The services were aimed purely at holiday-makers and both regions ran their trains over much the same circuit, the LMR running clockwise, the WR anticlockwise. When public address systems were fitted to the coaching stock in 1957, the WR service acquired the title NORTH WALES RADIO LAND CRUISE and an engine headboard. Here BR Standard No. 75026 has the southbound train at Harlech during the summer of 1957. *(Norman Simmons, courtesy Photos of the Fifties)*

The well-worn tailboard at the back end of the express awaiting departure from Paddington. 'Corporate identity' livery has been applied to the BR Mk 1 BFK (Brake–First–Corridor) and the train's title and Inter-city branding display both capital and small-case lettering. As the branding was introduced in 1965, the photograph's date is probably about 1967. *(NRM/SSPL)*

In the lower photograph, a pair of 2251 class 0–6–0s have arrived back at Pwllheli in 1958. This variation on the standard headboard is the only headboard ever to include any words in Welsh. *(Milepost 92½/A.W.V. Mace)*

It's 4 March 1967, the very last day of the CAMBRIAN COAST EXPRESS. To suit the occasion BR Standard 4–6–0 No. 75033 has been given a shine, with repainted buffers and oil lamps being a nice touch. Of the total mileage run by headboarded trains only a small percentage was on single track, and here No. 75033 blasts uphill at Talerddig (about 12 miles east of Machynlleth) with the final London-bound service, though it will give way to diesel traction at Shrewsbury. Thus ended the carrying of headboards on Western Region titled trains. *(Gavin Morrison)*

Titled Expresses of the Southern Railway and BR (SR)

INTRODUCTION TO 'SOUTHERN' HEADBOARDS 1946–80

The loco headboards of the Southern Railway and the Southern Region of BR were both distinctive in themselves and distinctly different from those of other railways or regions. No one else, for instance, had large headboards with and without cut-away corners designed to be displayed on the loco buffer beam. No one else had rectangular headboards carried across the centre of the smokebox door. No one else covered these smokebox doors with circular headboards using embellishments such as arrows and flags. Wingplates were also confined entirely to the Southern. That said, you could certainly see a Southern titled train approaching, and whichever style of headboard was employed, each was noticeably larger than those of other regions and dominated the loco front to an unsurpassed extent. The headboards were therefore effective in attracting the public's attention, and exploited the publicity potential of the device to the full.

'West Country' class Light Pacific No. 21C140 departs Victoria in 1947. The loco carries the full regalia of headboard, flags, and large arrows along the boiler casing. Even the Pullman cars advertised the name on the lower body sides, reading FLECHE D'OR at one end and GOLDEN ARROW at the other, both accompanied by further arrows. This boiler casing arrow was 12ft 7½in long, but there was also a longer version of some 15ft. The engine was less than two years old and had yet to be named *Crewkerne* (which it was on 20 October 1948) but had already received an additional lengthening to the smoke-deflector plates. The white discs indicate the route 'Victoria to Dover via Tonbridge & Ashford'. *(NRM/SSPL)*

At no time were Southern headboards carried in the 'standard' position, adopted throughout the rest of British Railways, i.e. centrally on the top lamp iron immediately below the chimney.[1] The reason for this was dictated by the design of the locomotives hauling virtually all the titled expresses of the time, namely the 'Merchant Navy' and 'West Country'/'Battle of Britain' classes.[2] All these engines (in their unrebuilt form) had, as part of their air-smoothed outline, a hood or cowl that protruded forwards beyond the chimney and overhung the smokebox to some extent. If any headboard, of any design, were to be placed on the top lamp iron, it would be rendered almost invisible by the cowl, and the impact on the public would be lost. It was therefore as a consequence of this cowl that larger than usual headboards could be carried in less restrictive lower positions — much to the public's benefit.[3]

After the early wooden or steel headboards, the rectangular versions were of cast aluminium. In the diesel and electric era a further change of material took place, this time to fibreglass, for the last of the GOLDEN ARROW and NIGHT FERRY headboards. Usage of loco headboards gradually declined as services were withdrawn, re-routed, dieselised or electrified, and by the late 1960s only the Dover ferry services boasted the carrying of headboards on anything like a regular basis. Although the NIGHT FERRY was the last titled train to be withdrawn and on its final runs carried a replica headboard made at Stewarts Lane depot, use of the original had ceased long before 1980, though which date was the very last occasion is unknown.

1. The exception, the inter-regional PINES EXPRESS, carried a BR standard headboard in the period 1962–6, though by no means always.
2. All thirty 'Merchant Navy' and sixty of the 'West Country'/'Battle of Britain' classes were rebuilt between 1956 and 1961. This rebuilding removed the restricting cowl, so that the 'standard' position became available, but no change in headboard policy took place to take account of this.
3. The Southern headlamp (or disc) code for route indication demanded six lamp irons on the loco front, including two at either side of the smokebox door. This provision facilitated the use of the rectangular type of headboard in this position, as it could be easily fixed onto these two lamp irons.

THE HEADBOARD TYPES DESCRIBED

(1) Southern Railway types
      (a) those carried on the buffer beam (three varieties)
      (b) those carried on the smokebox (circular)

(2) Southern Region types
      (a) those carried on the smokebox (rectangular, BR Type 8)
      (b) those carried on the smokebox (circular)
      (c) those made in fibreglass for electric/diesel locos
      (d) others

Details of some of the above are as follows.

(1)   (a)   *1st variety*
                Unique to THE BOURNEMOUTH BELLE. For a description see the text for this train.

2nd variety

Confined to THE DEVON BELLE (initially) and THE BOURNEMOUTH BELLE only. Rectangular steel plates with all four corners cut away. 60in wide overall, 32in deep. Positioned on the central lamp iron and secured by two locking screws onto the outer faces of the engine's frames about 5in above the buffer beam. The steel plates were made rigid by attaching angle frames to the rear, these having two horizontal support bars welded to them. The lower of these had the locking screws at each end. Drawings specify eight headboards for THE DEVON BELLE and only two for THE BOURNEMOUTH BELLE. However, the SR route indication system for Waterloo–Exeter required that the lower central lamp be illuminated in hours of darkness. As the design obscured this lamp, it was unacceptable for THE DEVON BELLE but fine for the Bournemouth service, as that route did not require this particular lamp to be lit. Although at least one headboard of this design was used (see illustration page 48, top left), to avoid this problem THE DEVON BELLE soon acquired the 3rd variety. All the 2nd variety examples were then allocated to THE BOURNEMOUTH BELLE, although how many this amounted to is uncertain.

3rd variety

Rectangular steel plates with the top two corners cut away. 60in wide overall, 26½in deep. They were positioned on the central lamp iron, secured by two locking bolts, and made rigid in a manner similar to the 2nd variety. Drawings specify the following details.

	No. of boards	Colours: lettering/background
ATLANTIC COAST EXPRESS	6	Old gold/green
THE DEVON BELLE	8	Cream/Devon Red
THE ROYAL WESSEX	4	Old gold/green
THE THANET BELLE	3	Old gold/green
THE KENTISH BELLE	1	Old gold/green

Old gold was replaced by off white after 6 December 1948.

All these 3rd variety headboards were pierced by a 4in diameter hole in line with the central lamp so that this could be seen, as necessary, during hours of darkness. Two further pieces were cut from the bottom edge to clear the engine's frames.

(1) (b) These headboards were for the GOLDEN ARROW and NIGHT FERRY services only. For a description see the text for these trains.

(2) (a) These are described as BR Type 8 in the Eastern Section, where the dimensions of all the standard BR cast-aluminium headboards are listed. These were 51in wide, 15in deep, rectangular with rounded corners and polished, beaded edges. If the 4½in lettering was cast integral with the headboard, the raised letters were also polished, and in this case the background was normally green (exceptions to this are noted in the text). For the Southampton boat trains, however, both the background and lettering were painted on, to suit the various shipping lines.

This also applied to the short-lived GOLDEN ARROW and NIGHT FERRY headboards of this type used in 1954 and 1955. Additionally, the headboards came in both 'modified' and 'unmodified' varieties. The modified variety was denoted by the letters MOD cast on the rear, and was further identified by the fact that the lamp irons at either side were separately bolted on and not cast, one-piece, with the rest of the headboard, this feature defining unmodified headboards. These headboards were the only cast-aluminium ones to be seated on two separate lamp irons at the extremities, all others having one central bracket only.

(2) (b) (c) (d) See the texts of individual trains for these.

THE SR HEADCODE SYSTEM FOR ROUTE IDENTIFICATION

This system was unique to the Southern Railway/Region and involved the provision of six lamp irons on the front of steam locomotives. Onto these lamp irons, one, two or three lamps (at night) or white discs (during the day) would be placed in various combinations. Some of these are illustrated below, together with their route descriptions. These were used solely within the Southern system, and any inter-regional services would only adopt these codes on crossing into Southern territory. An entirely different, numerical system of route identification applied to the third-rail suburban network worked by electric multiple units. When steam was superseded this numerical system was then extended to cover all Southern routes.

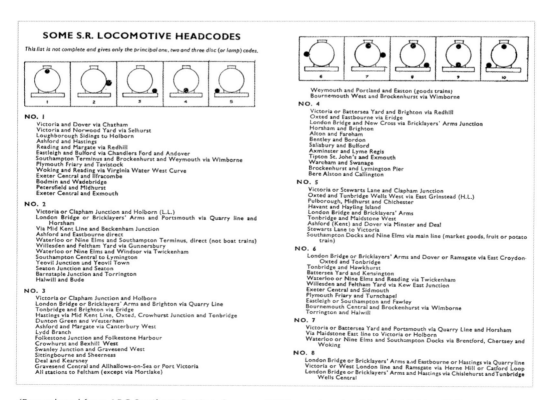

(*Reproduced from* ABC Southern Region, Summer 1956, *courtesy Ian Allan Publishing Ltd*)

THE TITLED EXPRESSES

In approximate order of destination, working west to east. This sequence is repeated in the pages following.

1. ATLANTIC COAST EXPRESS
2. (THE) DEVON BELLE
3. THE ROYAL WESSEX
4. (THE) BOURNEMOUTH BELLE
5. (THE) PINES EXPRESS
6. BRIGHTON BELLE/THE REGENCY BELLE
7. THE THANET BELLE
8. (THE) KENTISH BELLE
9. THE MAN OF KENT
10. GOLDEN ARROW
11. NIGHT FERRY

For Nos 12–27 see Additional Titles (page 72).

- (THE) indicates that the title included the definite article on one style of headboard, but omitted it from another.
- Expresses 4 and 7 also ran, for some part of their careers, with tailboards displaying the title at the rear of the train. No. 2 had the title painted on the rear of the observation car.
- The BRIGHTON BELLE did not carry a headboard, but the name was painted on the front and rear driving cabs, and along the carriage sides, post-December 1968.

Headboard dumping ground, Eastleigh Works, 30 October 1954. An interesting trio. Firstly the NIGHT FERRY with painted lettering as used by No. 10202 during its week-long trial in February of that year. It would probably be used again by No. 10203 in 1955. Secondly THE PINES EXPRESS – very rare – cannibalised at both ends of the unmodified board. Thirdly a heavily riveted ATLANTIC COAST EXPRESS, again broken, cannibalised or both. Others are, unfortunately, face down. (E.W. Fry, courtesy R.K. Blencowe)

ATLANTIC COAST EXPRESS

Waterloo–Padstow/Ilfracombe/Bude and others

Inaugural titled run	19 July 1926
Title withdrawn	10 September 1939
Reintroduced	6 October 1947
Last titled run	5 September 1964

(a) 1st style headboard	Introduced 6 October 1947; superseded by (c)
	Buffer beam, 3rd variety. First red, then green background.
(b) Experimental style	Introduced 1952, inspection only
	Similar in shape to a station 'totem' sign, but slightly deeper. Painted steel, with white letters on a green background. Attached centrally across smokebox door. Not used in traffic.
(c) 2nd style headboard	Introduced Summer 1953
	BR Type 8
	1st version First A of ATLANTIC leading the A in COAST.
	2nd version First A of ATLANTIC trailing (slightly) the A in COAST, with other letters subsequently realigned.

- Although more than twenty years separated the two events, the Southern Railway (like the GWR before it) decided to hold a competition for the best name to bestow upon its principal West of England service from Waterloo. The competition (and the rules for it) were announced in the *SR Magazine* for July 1925 – it was to be for SR employees only – and the chosen name applied on and from 19 July 1926. One of Waterloo's guards was declared the winner and received the prize of 3 guineas, while three others who had made the same suggestion received *King Arthur* paperweights. Again, like others before them, these three had cause to be aggrieved, since 'rule 3' had stipulated that the prize would be divided equally if the winning suggestion was duplicated.

At the time of the 1948 Locomotive Exchanges, the ATLANTIC COAST EXPRESS was the only express in the comparative trials to be running with a headboard. A4 *Mallard*, while being tested on this train on 8 June 1948, did carry, just below the chimney, an LNER-style headboard with the ACE wording, but only between Nine Elms depot and Waterloo, where it was replaced by a white route indicator disc. This, the rarest of all headboards, is not, unfortunately, illustrated. *(NRM/SSPL)*

On show in Eastleigh Works yard in 1952, No. 35010 *Blue Star* displays the experimental painted-steel headboard for evaluation. Although this shape and painted steel were rejected, the idea of a horizontal fixing across the smokebox door and the method of so doing were taken forward. *(NRM/SSPL)*

Standard type, 2nd version, No. 34058 *Sir Frederick Pile* at Wadebridge with the westbound portion for Padstow on 17 April 1954, with the route discs correctly displaying 'between Exeter Central and Padstow'. This loco was subsequently rebuilt. Close examination of the headboard reveals a substantial repair job has been required at some stage, with a large top-to-bottom weld down the centre. *(B.K.B. Green Collection/ Initial Photographics)*

The Southern Region's standard type, 1st version, seen on shed with No. 34015 *Exmouth*. As the headboard was held in place by the two smokebox door lamp brackets, replacements for these had to be attached to the headboard backing plate so that the route indicator discs could still be displayed as necessary. Here the two white discs indicate 'Exeter Central–Exmouth Junction'. The large box placed centrally on the buffer beam above the draw-hook contains the battery for the AWS apparatus. Note that electric lighting is fitted. Exmouth Junction depot, 20 September 1960. *(M.J. Jackson)*

THE DEVON BELLE/DEVON BELLE

Waterloo–Ilfracombe (and Plymouth until 25 September 1949) (Pullman car train)

summers only

Inaugural titled run	20 June 1947
Last titled run	19 September 1954

(a) 1st style headboard	Introduced 9 June 1947
	Buffer beam, 2nd variety with white letters on a red background, plus 'SR' within a circle. Probably used for pre-service trials only.
(b) 2nd style headboard	Introduced 20 June 1947; superseded by (d)
	Buffer beam, 3rd variety with red background.
(c) Experimental style	Introduced *c.* 1951–2; inspection only
	Larger version of a BR curved headboard, but in painted steel. Cream lettering on a green background. For possible fixing onto top lamp iron, but unsuited for use with Pacifics due to over-hanging cowl. Not used in traffic. 41in by 10in. (See also Colour Section)
(d) 3rd style headboard	Introduced Summer 1953
	BR Type 8 without the definite article.

- Also carried 'wingplates' on the smoke deflectors until September 1952.
- Two observation cars were provided for this service, with DEVON BELLE painted on a separate board within a panel beneath the rear window. These cars were a unique feature among SR titled trains. (See also Colour Section)

Waterloo again, this time in 1947 with No. 21C20 *Bibbly Line* in full Southern Railway livery. The route discs indicate 'between Waterloo and Plymouth' and the first four Pullmans will go right through to Plymouth, the train dividing at Exeter Central. The smoke deflector wingplate has serrations painted on it. The leading vehicle is – a sign of the times – for third-class passengers, though a supplement will of course still be payable. *(NRM/SSPL)*

Above left: Before public running began, the style of headboard originally intended for use was displayed for 'official' approval. A Lightweight Pacific was provided for the purpose, complete with whitewashed buffers, and this DEVON BELLE board was the only one to contain a 'Southern Railway' designation. Probably photographed at Nine Elms, 9 June 1947. *(NRM/SSPL)*

Above right: Another experimental headboard that did not see service. This time in green and, unlike the ACE version, not designed to be worn across the smokebox door. As such it had no influence on SR headboard policy. Here, *Orient Line* wears the headboard for a 'visual inspection' at Nine Elms, 16 May 1951. *(NRM/SSPL)*

Left: Unusually, the DEVON BELLE ran through Salisbury non-stop, but changed engines a couple of miles further on at Wilton. Here, an unidentified 'Merchant Navy' waits to take over the westbound train and clearly has the plain-edged wingplates. *(Robin Russell)*

The engine change at Wilton has been completed and 'Merchant Navy' class No. 35009 *Shaw Savill* is about to take the train on to Exeter. This had been brought in by sister engine No. 35013 *Blue Funnel*, which will now run backwards to Salisbury for servicing and turning before coming back to Wilton to take over the Up service later in the day. The familiar wingplates are no longer being carried, but the cast headboard is, so the picture must date from either 1953 or 1954, the last two summers of operation. The batten that previously had the wingplate attached to it can clearly be seen a few inches below the top of the smoke deflector plate on No. 35009. *(Robin Russell)*

The Pullman observation car at the rear of the train was on the Ilfracombe portion. Here it had to be detached, taken to the turntable at the small engine shed and turned before being reattached to the rear of the return service. One car, though without the DEVON BELLE insignia, later saw further use in North Wales (see page 147) and later still in Scotland. The other car went to the USA as part of the *Flying Scotsman* tour train in 1969 but has since been repatriated. *(Robin Russell)*

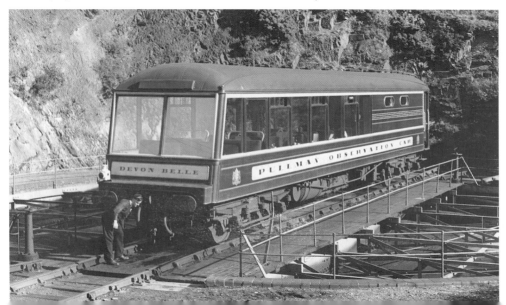

THE ROYAL WESSEX

Waterloo–Weymouth / Swanage / Bournemouth (West)

Inaugural titled run	3 May 1951
Last titled run	8 July 1967

(a) 1st style headboard	**Introduced 3 May 1951; superseded by (b)**
	Buffer beam, 3rd variety.
(b) 2nd style headboard	**Introduced Summer 1953**
	BR Type 8.

- This express was named specifically for the Festival of Britain and was re-equipped with brand-new BR Mk 1 coaching stock in carmine and cream livery.
- The title was bestowed on the regular 7.38 a.m. from Weymouth and the 4.35 p.m. return service from Waterloo.

THE ROYAL WESSEX
UP

Weekdays Only			Summer 1951 Up to June 16 a.m.	Commencing June 18 a.m.
WEYMOUTH ..	..	dep.	7.38	7.34
Dorchester South ..	..	,,	7.53	7.49
Wool ..	..	,,	8.5	8.1
SWANAGE ..	..	dep	7.A47	7.36
Corfe Castle ..	..	,,	7.A57	7.47
Wareham ..	..	,,	8.14	8.13
Poole ..	..	,,	8.25	8.25
BOURNEMOUTH WEST	dep.		8.20	8.20
BOURNEMOUTH CENTRAL	dep.		8.40	8.40
SOUTHAMPTON CENTRAL	,,		9.16	9.16
Winchester City ..	,,		9.38	9.38
WATERLOO ..	..	arr.	10.54	10.50

Note. A—Change at Wareham.

THE ROYAL WESSEX
DOWN

Weekdays Only			Summer 1951 Up to June 16 p.m.	Commencing June 18 p.m.
WATERLOO ..	..	dep.	4.35	4.35
Winchester City ..	..	,,	5.58	5.50
SOUTHAMPTON CENTRAL	..	,,	6.18	6.10
Brockenhurst ..	..	,,	6.41	6.33
BOURNEMOUTH CENTRAL	,,		7.5	6.57
BOURNEMOUTH WEST	arr.		7.21	7.13
Poole ..	..	dep.	7.18	7.10
Wareham ..	..	,,	7.31	7.23
Corfe Castle ..	..	dep.	7.50	7.42
SWANAGE ..	..	arr.	8.0	7.52
Dorchester South ..	..	dep.	7.50	7.43
WEYMOUTH ..	..	arr.	8.3	7.55

Festival TRAINS

THE ROYAL WESSEX

BRITISH RAILWAYS

Of the five 'Festival' expresses that gained new titles, it is believed that only two were provided with their own advertising literature (see also THE RED ROSE). 'Britannia' Pacifics, depicted here, would not, however, normally work this train, though No. 70009 certainly did, if only on a few occasions. *(BRB (Residuary) Ltd)*

Right: 'West County' class Light Pacific No. 34105 *Swanage* rests on Bournemouth shed, its home depot, coded 71B, 1 July 1951. Although the headboard is barely two months old, the steel plate is already noticeably scratched. The two lamp brackets on the lower smokebox door, the fixing points for the later rectangular headboards, can be clearly seen. The engine itself still exists, being preserved at the Mid-Hants Railway. *(Philip J. Kelley)*

Below: Bournemouth Central station, *c.* 1954, with the eastbound express ready to depart behind No. 34107 *Blandford Forum*, which had been simply *Blandford* until October 1952. The spired church of St Paul, on the left, was demolished in about 1986 to make way for new development. *(Norman Lockett, copyright David Lockett)*

THE BOURNEMOUTH BELLE/BOURNEMOUTH BELLE

Waterloo–Bournemouth (West) until 3 October 1965
Waterloo–Bournemouth (Central) from 4 October 1965, on closure of West. (Pullman car train)

Inaugural titled run	5 July 1931
Title withdrawn	10 September 1939
Reintroduced	7 October 1946
Last titled run	9 July 1967

(a) 1st style headboard   **Introduced 7 October 1946, superseded by (b)**
Buffer beam, 1st variety. Rectangular wooden headboard edged yellow with rounded corners. 39in wide, 32in deep. Yellow letters, shaded black on a dark green background.

(b) 2nd style headboard   **Introduced Summer 1948, with later lettering differences**
Buffer beam, 2nd variety.
1st version   Low 'dip' to letter M, yellow letters, shaded black.
2nd version   High 'dip' to letter M, white letters.
3rd version   Intermediate 'dip' to wide letter M.

(c) 3rd style headboard   **Introduced Summer 1953**
BR Type 8, without the definite article. (See also Colour Section).

- As 7 October 1946 was after the winter timetable had started, the train was first shown titled in the next summer timetable, effective 16 June 1947.
- One of only two expresses on the Southern to have a 'tailboard' (without the definite article) on the rear car.

Opposite: The 1st version of the four-corners-cut-away type, a shape first seen briefly on the DEVON BELLE in 1947. Indeed, it may well be that these were, at least initially, prepared from blanks made for the DEVON BELLE but not used. In service the shape is unique to this title. No. 35013 *Blue Funnel* stands at Waterloo with trainspotters and 4-COR unit No. 3103 for company. *(A.G. Forsyth/Initial Photographics)*

Below: The inaugural run of the postwar service. No. 21C18 *British India Line* leaves Waterloo at 12.30 p.m., first stop Southampton, then Bournemouth (Central and West). Supplementary fares to Bournemouth were 5s (first class) and 3s 6d (third class). On this day No. 21C18 also worked the return train, the 7.15 p.m. from West, with a two-hour run from Central to Waterloo, 7 October 1946. *(Topfoto)*

During 1951 one of the new 'Britannia' Pacifics had a short spell working from Nine Elms depot (70A). Here, *Alfred the Great* displays a 2nd version headboard before setting off for Bournemouth West, where it will be turned and serviced on Branksome shed, 6 June 1951. *(NRM/SSPL)*

Stranger in the camp, 20 May 1953. Doncaster's V2 class 2–6–2 was drafted in to cover a motive power shortage during a period when Bulleid's 'Merchant Navy' Pacifics were temporarily withdrawn. This followed a fracture of a driving axle at speed on 24 April 1953 on loco No. 35020, and the whole class was then examined as a precaution. Commendably clean, No. 60896, complete with 36A shedplate and an additional lamp bracket provided for the disc on the smokebox door, sets off from Waterloo carrying the 3rd version of the 2nd style headboard. *(Philip J. Kelley)*

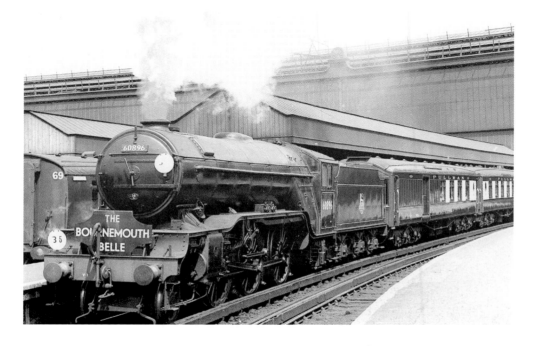

Only two months or so since its rebuilding No. 35018 *British India Line* starts the Up service from Bournemouth West terminus, 21 April 1956. The smoke deflector hand-rails were not included in the rebuilding specification and have been added since leaving Eastleigh Works. *(Colin Boocock)*

The Pullman Car Company's tailboard, which was fixed to the rear of the train. The company's arms included devices for England, Scotland, Ireland and Wales, though it operated in Ireland for only a few years. *(NRM/SSPL)*

THE PINES EXPRESS/PINES EXPRESS

Manchester (London Road)–Bournemouth (West) until 8 September 1962[1]
Manchester (Piccadilly)–Bournemouth (West) until 3 October 1965[2]
Manchester (Piccadilly)–Poole from 4 October 1965[3]

1.   Via Bath and the Somerset & Dorset line.
2.   Via Oxford and Southampton. London Road was renamed Piccadilly on 12 September 1960. From 6 September to 3 October 1965 (inclusive) rail services between Central and West stations were replaced by buses due to engineering works for the Bournemouth electrification.
3.   On closure of Bournemouth West on 4 October 1965, the service was extended to Poole by arrangement with the local Transport Users Consultative Committee.

Inaugural titled run	7 May 1928
Title withdrawn	9 September 1939
Reintroduced	23 May 1949
Last titled run	4 March 1967

(a) 1st style headboard	**Introduced Summer 1953 for a few weeks only**
	BR Type 8.
(b) 2nd style headboard	**Introduced Summer 1962**
	BR Type 3 without the definite article. Uniquely, this headboard had a composite bracket on the rear, the casting combining both the WR offset bracket and the BR standard central bracket.

•   This inter-regional train, while travelling via the S&D, only ever carried a headboard south of Bath, and then only rarely.
•   The Type 3 headboard was the very last 'new' headboard of this cast-aluminium style anywhere on BR.

Although the main engine shed for Bournemouth was directly opposite Central station, for trains using the West station there was a subshed in the triangle of lines at Branksome. Here, No. 34042 *Dorchester*, still in its original form (it was rebuilt at Eastleigh in January 1959), is being serviced after bringing in the southbound train in summer 1953. It has an unmodified headboard. *(Author's collection)*

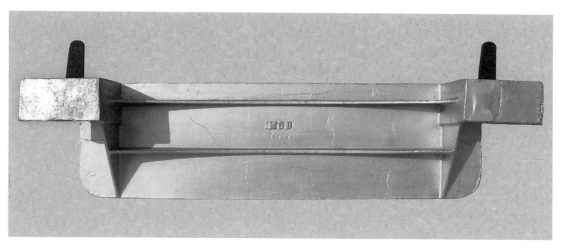

The reverse of a typical cast-aluminium headboard. The small initials MOD in the centre refer to 'Modified'. Whereas, originally, the replacement lamp irons were cast integral with the backing plate, later castings were modified to omit these, provision being made by bolting on more robust iron or steel individual ones. *(Tony Deller)*

The very last day of the train's routing over the Somerset & Dorset was Saturday 8 September 1962. On this day, appropriately, the very last steam engine built by BR, No. 92220 *Evening Star*, named at Swindon in March 1960, heads the southbound twelve-coach load through Midsomer Norton and receives farewell waves from the local population. The 9F 2–10–0 was specially allocated to Bath (S&D) shed, coded 82F at the time, and the four-character headcode is displayed on the buffer beam, in which the letter O denotes an inter-regional train from the Western Region to the Southern Region. *(Ivo Peters, courtesy Julian Peters)*

The Southern Region's responsibility for loco provision began and ended at Oxford, from where rebuilt 'Battle of Britain' class No. 34085 *501 Squadron* is about to set out for Bournemouth (West), summer 1963. While running on Western Region territory, the white discs will not denote a Southern 'route', simply 'express passenger'. At Basingstoke the fireman will (in theory) move the disc nearest the camera so that the code for 'Waterloo and Bournemouth' is displayed. *(David Anderson)*

Immediately after the re-routing via Oxford, the section between here and Wolverhampton was still steam-hauled. This gave the WR the brief opportunity of carrying this headboard over its own main line. Birmingham (Snow Hill) therefore sees the arrival of the northbound service behind No. 7029 *Clun Castle* in late 1962. The engine is seen in its final BR form with four-row superheater and double chimney, and is preserved in this form. M04 denotes an inter-regional service with a London Midland destination (M), train number 04. *(NRM/SSPL)*

BRIGHTON BELLE

Victoria–Brighton (Pullman car train)

Inaugural titled run	29 June 1934
Title withdrawn	10 September 1939
Reintroduced	6 October 1947
Last titled run	30 April 1972

These three famous five-car train sets (the only electric Pullman sets ever to run) did not carry headboards, but the name appeared on both ends of each unit from 19 December 1968 onwards, and also along the carriage body sides. This latter feature recalled similar pre-war practice on the CORONATION and WEST RIDING LIMITED streamlined trains (see LNER Section). Only these three expresses ever carried their titles in this position, and the electric units were definitely the slowest of the three. (The bilingual GOLDEN ARROW carriage nameboards were hardly in the same league.) The title BRIGHTON BELLE referred to all of the several services per day formed by these units.

THE REGENCY BELLE

Victoria–Brighton (Pullman car train)

Inaugural titled run	28 March 1964
Last titled run	19 April 1964

It was reported at the time that the SR would be hiring a BRIGHTON BELLE unit to an organiser of luxury weekend evening excursions from London to a Brighton casino, and that passengers would get a champagne supper for their 7 guineas all-in fare, which included a return to London in the small hours. However, when this stock was unavailable, or diversions were in force, a steam loco plus Pullman cars were employed. This charter service was very short-lived, running on four weekends only, and it is astonishing that a headboard was even created, much less carried for so few occasions, particularly as the return journey was always in the dark. The circular headboard was the last new title headboard to be officially introduced on the Southern Region, and featured the arms of Brighton (two black dolphins and six gold martlets) together with the motto *In deo fidemus* ('In God we trust').

The pristine headboard complete with Gothic-style lettering in both upper and lower cases, and displaying the arms of Brighton, rests on No. 34088 *213 Squadron* at Nine Elms. The fixing bolts on the smoke deflectors are evidence of former GOLDEN ARROW work.
(*J.G. Walmsley/ Transport Treasury*)

Renaming day, Friday 29 June 1934. The SOUTHERN BELLE had been the London, Brighton & South Coast Railway's prestige Pullman train to Brighton since 1908, and was continued in this elevated position by the Southern Railway. However, when the Brighton line was electrified, this steam-hauled service was replaced by brand-new five-car electric units as from 1 January 1933, though still under the title SOUTHERN BELLE. The name change celebrated the opening (in Brighton) on that day of the largest covered sea-water swimming pool in the world. Here, the 11 a.m. departure from Victoria receives special treatment for the camera, and is complete with a headboard showing Brighton's coat of arms and motto: *In deo fidemus* ('In God we trust'). *(Getty Images)*

Thirty-six years on, 5-BEL unit No. 3052 has a full yellow front end complete with the legend BRIGHTON BELLE, Brighton, 27 September 1970. Now that the Pullman Car Company has been bought by British Railways, the old livery has gone (replaced by two-tone blue/grey) and the train's title has been painted additionally on the body sides where the car's name (if first class) or number (if second class) were once displayed. *(T.J. Edgington)*

THE THANET BELLE

Victoria–Ramsgate (Pullman car train); summer only

Inaugural titled run	31 May 1948
Last titled run	24 September 1950
Only headboard	Introduced 31 May 1948
	Buffer beam, 3rd variety.

- As with THE BOURNEMOUTH BELLE, this service also carried a 'tailboard' (without the definite article) on the rear car.

THE KENTISH BELLE/KENTISH BELLE

Victoria–Ramsgate (and Canterbury, 1951 only) (Pullman car train); summer only

Inaugural titled run	2 July 1951
Last titled run	14 September 1958
(a) 1st style headboard	Introduced 2 July 1951; superseded by (b)
	Buffer beam, 3rd variety.
(b) 2nd style headboard	Introduced Summer 1953
	BR Type 8 without the definite article.

- The 1951 summer timetable was due to commence on 18 June, but was delayed by two weeks.
- The inclusion of Canterbury as a destination for 1951 caused THE THANET BELLE service to be renamed as above. Despite ceasing to run to Canterbury after Festival of Britain year, the service did not revert to its former title.

A close-up of the Pullman Car Company's tailboard, probably at Ramsgate, *c.* 1949. These were provided by the company's works at Preston Park, Brighton. *(J.C. Flemons/Transport Treasury)*

On the first day of the new service, 31 May 1948, it's six 'Belles' for the price of one. Miss Ramsgate shakes hands with the driver while Misses Margate, Broadstairs, Whitstable and Herne Bay look on. Victoria's stationmaster oversees proceedings. (*Topfoto*)

Herne Bay in the summer of 1951, with No. 34084 heading for Faversham with a light load of five cars. Here the three-coach Canterbury portion will be attached before heading for Victoria. Although the engine entered traffic on 4 November 1948, it had yet to receive its name. This turned out to be *253 Squadron* (which was actually the Hyderabad State Squadron), which was affixed at Eastleigh Works in September 1951. *(NRM/SSPL)*

No. 34068 *Kenley* brings ten cars upgrade out of Victoria in 1954. Some, but by no means all, trains were banked from the terminus up the initial rise. Not so here, however, as the 'Battle of Britain' 4–6–2 has the task well in hand. *(NRM/SSPL)*

THE MAN OF KENT

Charing Cross–Margate

Inaugural titled run	8 June 1953
Last titled run	10 June 1961

(a) 1st style headboard   Introduced 8 June 1953; used alongside (b) but eventually superseded by it
BR Type 8 with black background.

(b) 2nd style headboard   Introduced *c.* 1954–5
As above, but including two identical shields depicting the White Horse of Kent (i.e. the steed of Odin) and the legend *Invicta* ('Unconquered') below these. This style came with both black and green backgrounds, with different colours and letter spacings on the hand-painted embellishments, between the black and green versions.

- The only BR Type 8 headboard to receive decorative shields in this manner.
- The white horse was said to have been displayed on the standard of the Saxon chieftains who first invaded Kent (Hengist and Horsa).

Above, right: The 2nd style headboard with black background. Each shield measured 4½in by 5½in with a 7in scroll beneath. *(Author, with the permission of NRM)*

Below: A 1954 shot of the plain headboard being carried by No. 34077 *603 Squadron* (later rebuilt). The title itself is somewhat misleading, as 'Men of Kent' would be more appropriate. Customarily a train name would refer to one service running both ways. In this case, however, by 1956 both the 1.15 p.m. and 4.15 p.m. departures from Charing Cross (and their return workings at 9.40 a.m. and 12.40 p.m. from Margate) were known by this name. Neither were the timings particularly quick, since, although running 'express' to Folkestone, thereafter the train became a stopping service and took nearly three hours to reach Margate from London. *(NRM/SSPL)*

GOLDEN ARROW

Victoria–Dover (Marine) for Calais (Maritime) and Paris (Nord) (Pullman car train)

Inaugural titled run	15 May 1929
Title withdrawn	3 September 1939
Reintroduced	15 April 1946 (public)
Last titled run	30 September 1972

(a) 1st style headboard — Introduced 13 April 1946 and carried until steam locos ceased to operate the service, 11 June 1961

Painted, circular; 33in diameter with 67in-long arrow running NW to SE across the circle and piercing the two letter Os. Early versions were wood, later versions steel. Malachite green, later Brunswick green background, black rim, gold letters and arrow. Also blue background for short period in 1952. Letters edged/shaded black, sometimes neither. (See also Colour Section).

(b) 2nd style headboard — Variation of (a) with crossed flags of UK and France painted above GOLDEN. Rarely seen, since the tricolour was wrongly painted, with red (rather than blue) against the flagpole. October 1951 only.

(c) 3rd style headboard — Only used from 8 to 13 February 1954 when No. 10202 was on trial on this service

BR Type 8 with gold or yellow painted lettering and arrow, which ran SW to NE between the wording. Green background.

(d) 4th style headboard — Only used from 13 to 19 March 1955 when No. 10203 was on trial on this service

As (c) but with arrow running NE to SW.

(e) 5th style headboard — Introduced late 1960

Narrow fibreglass rectangle with rounded corners. Both words on single line, no arrow. Gold letters on a black background, edged gold. Board curved outwards with a 4¾in bow front to back, 68½in long, 9½in deep, letters 4in.

- A press run on 13 April 1946, on which the headboard was also carried, preceded the inaugural run postwar. As this run occurred with only three weeks of the winter timetable remaining, the train was first shown titled in the summer timetable commencing 6 May 1946.
- From 11 June 1951 the train received ten brand-new Pullman cars as part of the Festival of Britain refurbishment programme.
- The service used Folkestone (Harbour) for two periods:
  Northbound from Boulogne between 6 October 1935 and 3 September 1939
  Southbound to Calais between 15 September 1952 and 28 May 1960.
- The onward service to Paris (Nord) was also headboarded. Again this was by a circular headboard with diagonal arrow and the legend FLECHE D'OR (steam engines only; a different design was used for electric locos).

- On 11 March 1929 Major (later Sir) Henry Segrave set a new world land speed record of 231mph in a car named *Golden Arrow* on Daytona Beach, Florida. It is therefore presumed that the Southern Railway's Publicity Office picked up on this, and caused the train to be thus named. In the USA the Pennsylvania Railway followed suit, naming its twenty-hour New York–Chicago 4 p.m. express THE GOLDEN ARROW.

'Britannia' Pacific No. 70004 *William Shakespeare* was one of the star exhibits at the Festival of Britain and stands in immaculate condition at Victoria on 11 October 1951. Originally allocated to the Eastern Region at Stratford depot, No. 70004 and sister engine No. 70014 *Iron Duke*, were drafted to Stewarts Lane at the end of the Festival and remained there for seven years, mainly working the ARROW and other boat trains to Dover or Folkestone. Here, No. 70004 has the short-lived 'extra flags' headboard, and a comparison with the tricolour on the buffer beam quickly reveals the error. The flags were laundered daily at the time. The route discs have been freshly painted (4 was the Stewarts Lane duty number), the loco has red-backed chromed nameplates and builder's plates, burnished cylinder covers and silvered buffers – a real 'exhibition' finish. The side arrows have been moved to the smoke deflector plates, a position they also occupied on the rebuilt Bulleid Pacifics. *(Getty Images)*

Although instigated by the Southern Railway in 1946, a pilot scheme of main-line diesel-electric locos (for the Southern Region) was eventually put in hand by British Railways in 1950. Nos 10201/2 were built at Ashford Works in 1951 and were 1,750hp machines with English Electric power units and a 1 Co–Co 1 wheel arrangement. A third loco, No. 10203, was completed in 1954, incorporated various improvements and was uprated to 2,000hp. In 1954, No. 10202 was set to work for a trial period of a week in February on GOLDEN ARROW and NIGHT FERRY duties, and is seen here with its train-heating boiler making much smoke at Victoria. *(Author's Collection)*

A year later, in March 1955, No. 10203 was employed on the same duties and is seen here on the Bickley Junction to Petts Wood Junction connection with the London-bound service. As the arrow had, on earlier headboards, pointed downwards, the 1954 version was replaced with an arrow in the conventional direction for 1955. *(Arthur Tayler)*

The scene at Dover Marine station in 1962 with class 71 Bo-Bo electric No. E5015. Having brought in the nine-coach load, the engine has uncoupled and drawn forward before running round its train. The fibreglass headboard suits the loco well. The twin flags are still displayed and no fewer than four arrows are carried near the cab doors. Doncaster-built in 1960 with a rated horsepower of 2552 and maximum speed of 90mph, this third-rail 750V dc design was also equipped with a pantograph (see centre of roof) for working to and from freight yards where the power supply was from overhead wires. Despite this 'modern traction' image, note the continued reliance on oil lamps. *(NRM/SSPL)*

The last steam-hauled GOLDEN ARROW ran on 11 June 1961, and at the end of the last run the various adornments are removed at Victoria. This would normally have taken place at Stewarts Lane depot, but this platform scene gives a good idea not only of the shape of the fixing bracket to which the circular headboard was attached, but also of the strengthening bar running along the rear of the arrow for the full length. Earlier arrows tended to bend or break without it. Note also the black rim to the headboard, and that the letters are either shaded or edged. The crew of No. 34100 *Appledore* are in the process of removing the hardwood gold-painted arrow, secured by four bolts, for the final time. *(Empics)*

NIGHT FERRY

Victoria–Dover (Marine)–Dunkerque (Maritime)–Paris (Nord) (Sleeping car train)

Inaugural titled run	14 October 1936
Title withdrawn	25 August 1939
Reintroduced	14 December 1947 (ex-Paris); 15 December (ex-London)
Last titled run	31 October 1980 (ex-London); 1 November (ex-Paris)

(a) 1st style headboard	Introduced 14 December 1947; superseded by (c) Painted steel, circular with white rim. Title within a central horizontal black band superimposed over a yellow crescent moon. 'London' curved below the upper circumference, 'Paris' curved above the lower. All letters white on a dark blue background 40in diameter.
(b) 2nd style headboard	Used only between 8 and 13 February 1954 and 13 and 19 March 1955 when Nos 10202/3 operated the service on a trial basis (see also GOLDEN ARROW) BR Type 8 with painted lettering (yellow or white) on a dark blue background.
(c) 3rd style headboard	Introduced 2 June 1957; last used 14 June 1959, when steam was replaced by electric traction Similar to (a) but with a different wording, 'Brussels' being added to the right of 'Paris' when that city was included as a destination. Three stars also appear between place names. Black band now above centre. Rim is now black, other colours same. At least one had a light blue background.
(d) 4th style headboard	Introduced 15 June 1959(?) BR Type 8 with black background. For use on electric locos.
(e) 5th style headboard	Introduced c. 1960 Narrow fibreglass rectangle with rounded corners. Both words on single line. Gold letters on a black background, edged gold. Board curved outwards with a 4¾in bow front to back. 68½in long, 9½in deep, letters 4in.
(f) 6th style headboard	As 3rd style (see below).

- This train-ferry service between London and Paris uniquely brought continental Wagons-Lits sleeping cars onto Britain's railways on a daily basis. The cars had, of course, to be built to the British loading gauge and were therefore dedicated to this service only.
- The onward service to Paris was also headboarded with a circular board and titled PARIS LONDRES FERRY BOAT DE NUIT.
- The service to Brussels was via Lille and Tournai.
- Around 1963 this was the heaviest passenger train on BR, conveying up to ten Wagons-Lits coaches and weighing some 800 tons in all.
- For the last week of service in October 1980, Stewarts Lane depot made a replacement headboard, based on the original of 1957. This replacement now resides in the NRM.

Stewarts Lane depot in Battersea prepared all the engines for NIGHT FERRY duties as well as GOLDEN ARROW turns. A sunny day in 1953 sees No. 35030 *Elder-Dempster Lines* simmering on shed alongside either No. 10201 or No. 10202, since at this time the final unit had yet to be built. No. 35030 itself was rebuilt in April 1958 and had the dubious distinction of hauling the last passenger train of the (Southern) steam era, this being the 2.07 p.m. Weymouth–Waterloo on 9 July 1967. It was scrapped in South Wales in November 1968, outliving the diesel-electric by two years. *(NRM/SSPL)*

Now with the three-cities headboard, L1 class 4–4–0 No. 31753 pilots No. 34087 *145 Squadron* with the London-bound service, April 1959. The location is St Mary Cray Junction on the Chatham line and Kent Coast electrification is only two months away from being inaugurated. *(Derek Cross, courtesy David Cross)*

No. E5002 has seventeen vehicles in tow (not all in shot) passing Stewarts Lane with the inbound train, but the gang of three (right) are too busy to notice. Route 74 is 'Dover via Tonbridge and the Catford loop'. The photo is undated, but is likely to be about 1961. *(Arthur Tayler)*

Below, left: The Up train approaches Catford on 10 August 1959 behind No. E5006, carrying the rarely seen cast-aluminium headboard. Although these locos also carried a pantograph, this too was rarely seen, usage being confined to a small number of freight marshalling yards. *(NRM/SSPL)*

Below, right: The penultimate departure from Victoria's No. 1 platform on 30 October 1980 has Birmingham Railway Carriage & Wagon 1,550hp diesel-electric No. 33043 as motive power. Stewarts Lane's replica old-style headboard enhances the front end, as the steam-age original had gone out of use some twenty years earlier. *(Author's collection)*

ADDITIONAL TITLES

Boat Train Expresses to Southampton Docks

PART ONE: pre-1952

12.	IMPERIAL AIRWAYS	–	Flying Boat Specials
13.	CUNARD WHITE STAR	–	Maiden Voyage Specials
14.	OCEAN TERMINAL EXPRESS	–	Opening Day Special

PART TWO: 1952–67

15.	THE CUNARDER	–	Cunard Line
16.	'STATESMAN'	–	United States Line
17.	HOLLAND AMERICAN	–	Holland–America Line
18.	UNION-CASTLE EXPRESS	}	
19.	SPRINGBOK	} –	Union Castle Line
20.	UNION-CASTLE SAFMARINE	}	
21.	THE SOUTH AMERICAN	–	Royal Mail Lines
22.	GREEK LINE		
23.	SITMAR LINE		
24.	ORIANA	} –	Cruise Liners for P&O
25.	CANBERRA	}	
26.	BRITTANY EXPRESS	–	Continental Ferry Services
27.	CHANNEL ISLANDS BOAT TRAIN	–	to Weymouth Quay

- No photograph of a headboard for No. 19 has yet come to light, though it is known to have existed.
- Of those listed above, only Nos 15, 16 and occasionally 17 regularly used the Ocean Terminal.
- The Old (or Eastern) Docks – berths 22–50 – accommodated Nos 21, 22, 26 and usually 17. Also Union Castle until 1960 when they transferred to the Western Docks and a dedicated berth (104).
- The New (or Western) Docks – berths 101–110 – accommodated Nos 12, 24 and 25, P&O having a dedicated berth (106).

It was not until 1952 that some of the boat trains running to Southampton Docks began to display loco headboards on a regular basis. However, a number of earlier special trains, significant in themselves and germane to what happened post-1952, have also been included both to enhance the record and to provide some background for what happened later. These trains form Part One, i.e. named trains 12, 13 and 14.

The Ocean Terminal was opened on 31 July 1950 and within a few years the Southern Region was operating a whole series of 'on demand' headboarded boat train expresses to connect with the arrival and departure of the many large passenger ships then offering worldwide scheduled sailings. These trains form Part Two, i.e. named trains 15–26.

Although these services were not in the same category as the timetabled expresses detailed in the previous section, they formed a large group of non-stop mainline expresses. Many had at least some Pullman cars and most had dining or refreshment facilities, and of course distinctive headboards specific to the shipping lines. As a group, therefore, all these services are worthy of inclusion, though, like their timetabled counterparts, not always was the headboard carried. Indeed, as the years passed, the use of headboards became less and less frequent, and by the completion of the electrification to Southampton in 1967 few if any of these were still in evidence. By this time ocean passenger sailings had largely been superseded by the jet airliner, and although cruise ships were replacing some lost trade, almost all the regular sailings had stopped by the early 1970s. The Ocean Terminal itself eventually fell into disuse and was razed to the ground in April 1983.

The type of headboards used for these services mirrored the two styles commonly in use on the Southern Region for other titled expresses. The first to be carried, those for the Cunard and the United States shipping lines, were circular – Cunard having two different designs. Both these lines' trains then changed to the rectangular pattern, consistent with the other shipping companies' trains, for the duration of these services. The latter headboards were of cast aluminium with a beaded edge, as per those for timetabled expresses, but the titles and embellishments were hand-painted. The headboard for the Holland–America Line was unique in having the legend in script. With the elimination of steam traction in 1967, the use of loco headboards on these services ceased. Even before the end of steam some boat trains were being diesel hauled, and as the dock area was not electrified, during 1967 some electric locos of class 71 were converted to become electro-diesels (redesignated class 74) in order to work these services into the docks.

It is also worth noting that the headboarded expresses detailed here did not, by any stretch of the imagination, represent the sum total of boat trains using Southampton Docks. Many other shipping lines also had their own connecting boat trains. These services were distinguished by the provision of carriage roofboards only, and these trains formed the bulk of the passenger traffic entering the docks. Headboarded services did of course carry roofboards in addition to the engine headboard. Only eight of the twenty-five shipping companies that ran special trains (in 1963), shown in the table below, had headboarded services.

SHIPPING COMPANY	DOWN TRAINS				
	Special Attachments		Passengers		
	Trains	to regular Services	1st class	2nd class	Total
Bergen Line	9	1	310	329	639
British India Steam Nav	-	-	-	-	-
Canadian Pacific	1	1	202	51	253
Clipper Line	-	2	40	15	55
Cogedar Line	8	-	73	1,280	1,353
Cunard Line	123	4	10,215	15,026	25,241
Elders & Fyffes	2	16	386	369	755
Europe/Australia Line	1	-	32	299	331
Europe/Canada Line	-	-	-	-	-
French Line	46	18	3,940	3,787	7,727
Gydnia America Line	2	-	140	142	282
Greek Line	28	-	1,944	2,609	4,553
Grimaldi Line	14	-	157	3,095	3,252
Hamburg/America Line	3	12	182	384	566
Holland/Africa Line	1	10	138	223	361
Holland/America Line	34	20	2,072	3,948	6,020
Home Line	7	-	168	810	978
Mocre McCormack	1	-	170	-	170
Nederland Line	7	-	319	1,031	1,350
New Zealand Line	-	-	-	-	-
North German Lloyd	6	20	351	656	1,007
P&O	69	4	3,993	10,277	14,270
Royal Mail Lines	13	-	1,776	401	2,177
Royal Netherland Line	-	19	93	239	332
Royal Rotterdam Lloyd	10	-	392	1,353	1,745
Shaw Savill	16	-	566	4,028	4,594
Sitmar Line	42	-	201	2,567	2,768
Spanish Line	13	4	87	2,342	2,429
Transocean	-	1	-	105	105
Union Castle S S Co	88	-	4,182	9,141	13,323
United States Lines	42	-	3,548	3,441	6,989
	586	132	35,677	67,948	103,625

Ocean liner trains, 1963.
(Table courtesy D.W. Winkworth)

It is 6 June 1939 at Victoria station and T9 class 4–4–0 No. 338 is ready to leave the new Imperial Airways Terminus (Platform 17) bound for Southampton Docks. This was the first Imperial Airways express to convey passengers for the Empire Flying Boat services. At first these aircraft would be moored a couple of hundred yards away from the docks, out on the Solent, and their passengers would be transferred by launch from the shore. Later a quayside landing stage was provided for flying boats. In November 1939 Imperial Airways merged with British Airways to form British Overseas Airways Corporation (BOAC), and from 1940 BOAC's flying boat services were transferred to Poole Harbour until 1948. Services recommenced from Southampton that year, but BOAC ceased to operate flying boats in 1949. *(Getty Images)*

Opposite, top: Having put in yeoman service as a troopship during the Second World War, the liner *Queen Elizabeth* was refitted and made its maiden peacetime voyage from Southampton on 16 October 1946. On that day, the Southern Railway turned out 'Merchant Navy' No. 21C4 *Cunard White Star* to take the first-class passengers to the docks. The close similarity between this headboard and the 1952 version will be noted. Unlike its sister ship *Queen Mary*, the *Queen Elizabeth* ended its days ignominiously, being destroyed by fire in Hong Kong Harbour, where it had been used as a floating university, in January 1972. *(Getty Images)*

More than ten years earlier, on 27 May 1936, the maiden voyage (to Cherbourg, then New York) took place of the original superliner *Queen Mary*. Here 'Lord Nelson' class 4–6–0 No. 852 *Sir Walter Raleigh* leaves Waterloo with one of the many special trains for the occasion. The liner itself still exists as a floating hotel and convention centre and may be visited at Long Beach, California, having cruised for the last time in September 1967. *(NRM/SSPL)*

THE CUNARDER

Inaugural titled run   2 July 1952

The liners *Queen Mary* and *Queen Elizabeth* were withdrawn from transatlantic duties in 1967 and 1968 respectively. Last usage of headboards is unlikely to be later than these dates.

(a) 1st style headboard	Introduced 2 July 1952; superseded by (b) and (c)
	Painted steel, circular, with large shield containing the title and the company symbol below. Shield surmounted by stylised crown. Two sizes: 38in/39in for use on Pacifics, and 57in/58in diameter for use on 'Lord Nelson' class.
(b) 2nd style headboard	Introduced 1952/3; superseded by (c)
	Painted steel, circular, with single large raked funnel in company colours with the title between bands. OCEAN LINER EXPRESS in lowest band. Large size only, 57in/58in diameter.
(c) 3rd style headboard	Introduced Summer 1953
	BR Type 8 with painted face. Gold lettering superimposed over a raked funnel (with smoke) in red with black upper section. Blue background. Lettering running uphill, left to right, the only headboard to feature this style of lettering.

No. 35001 *Channel Packet* heads the twelve-car Pullman train specially provided for the official opening of the Ocean Terminal on 31 July 1950. The train is seen here at the new terminal, with the 'Southampton Docks' clock showing nearly 11.45 a.m. The then prime minister, Mr Clement Attlee, performed the ceremony and was conveyed from and returned to Waterloo by this train. *(ABP Collection/Southampton Archive Services)*

It was to be nearly two years after the opening of the Ocean Terminal before any of the regular boat trains were actually titled. First off the mark (but only just) was THE CUNARDER when No. 35004 *Cunard White Star*, seen here on the inaugural run, left Waterloo on the evening of 2 July 1952 for the following day's sailing of *Queen Mary* for New York. The train itself was practically all-Pullman and conveyed first-class passengers only. During the previous year, 1951, no fewer than 146 special trains left Waterloo in conjunction with sailings of the two great 'Queen' liners alone, with 115 meeting their arrivals. *(Topfoto)*

A 'Lord Nelson' class 4–6–0 sets off from the Ocean Terminal carrying the large-diameter headboard and protected, as always, by flag-bearers. *Queen Mary* lurks in the smoky background. *(Topfoto)*

Opposite, top: In 1953 many guests for the Coronation of Her Majesty the Queen arrived by sea and completed their journey to London by train. On 30 May of that year the 19-year-old Crown Prince Akihito of Japan arrived at Waterloo on board THE CUNARDER boat train hauled by No. 30855 *Robert Blake*. *(Getty Images)*

Opposite, bottom: Having taken its boat train to the Ocean Terminal, No. 34004 *Yeovil* has returned light engine to Eastleigh depot for servicing and is seen here alongside the coaling plant, April 1964. Note the oil lamp atop the electric lighting, the heaps of ash and clinker and the deplorable external condition of an engine allocated to a high-profile prestige service. *(Barry Eagles)*

This time it is the *Queen Elizabeth* that is berthed alongside the Ocean Terminal, while the doyen of the class No. 30850 *Lord Nelson* (now preserved) handles the Pullmans. When opened, the original designation was 'British Railways Ocean Terminal', changing to 'Southampton' in about 1952/3. *(ABP Collection/Southampton Archive Services)*

'STATESMAN'

Inaugural titled run	8 July 1952

The final sailing of the liner *United States* from Southampton was in November 1969. It is unlikely that headboards were still in use as late as this.

(a) 1st style headboard	Introduced 8 July 1952; superseded by (b)
	Painted steel, circular, with wide roped border. Lettering centrally placed within this, top and bottom. American eagle as main symbol, with outstretched wings cutting across roped border. About 39in/40in diameter.
(b) 2nd style headboard	Introduced Summer 1953
	BR Type 8 with painted face. Title horizontal on brick-red background between two roundels containing eagles (as above). Shipping line named below this in black. Eagles also black.

• The only headboard to frame the title within quotation marks.

'West Country' class Pacific No. 34012 *Launceston* (later rebuilt) stands on Eastleigh shed bearing the 1st style headboard. Note the batten on the upper part of the smoke deflector plate where DEVON BELLE wingplates could be attached if necessary. *(J. Fry Collection)*

Rebuilt 'West Country' No. 34098 *Templecombe* being serviced in Southampton Western Docks. The date is about 1966 and the headboard is looking a bit worse for wear. Indeed, the loco nameplate has already been removed to reveal the naked backing plate. *(Roger Sherlock)*

HOLLAND AMERICAN

Inaugural titled run   15 July 1953

Regular sailings of Holland America Line ships had ceased by 1970.

Only headboard   **Introduced 15 July 1953**
BR Type 8 with painted face. Central vertical ellipse containing superimposed depictions of ancient and modern vessels. Wording to left and right of this.

• The only headboard to contain the title in script.

A close-up of the unique headboard at Waterloo, carried by No. 34007 *Wadebridge*. This headboard would appear to be unmodified, in that the lamp bracket on the left (looking at the photo) is cast integral with the backing plate. Again the engine has the tell-tale batten (just visible on the extreme left) for DEVON BELLE workings. No. 34007 never did undergo rebuilding and still exists in preservation. *(Robin Russell)*

The earliest of the three varieties of headboard carried by Union Castle Line boat trains, at the front of a line-up of others at Nine Elms. *(J. Oatway)*

UNION CASTLE
Shipping Line

Union Castle sailed to South Africa on a regular weekly basis, and as such its trains had scheduled departures from Waterloo that were not 'conditional'. The last arrival from South Africa was in September 1977, though the carrying of headboards had ceased long before that. Over the years three different wordings were used on these headboards.

(a) 1st variety	**Introduced 16 July 1953** UNION-CASTLE EXPRESS BR Type 8 with painted face. Two company flags either side of EXPRESS, both flagpoles outermost. White background, black letters, flags blue/red.
(b) 2nd variety	**Introduced c. February 1958** SPRINGBOK No photograph of this headboard has yet been found, though it is believed to be BR Type 8 with painted face. Evidence of its existence is provided by the extract from the February 1959 issue of the Working Timetable shown overleaf. In this, note that the 9.21 departure is not a Q (conditional) path.
(c) 3rd variety	**Introduced 2 February 1966** UNION-CASTLE SAFMARINE As (a) with SAFMARINE replacing EXPRESS, and the flags now absent.

The headboards for some of the services listed above. Partially visible are two for THE CUNARDER, plus 'STATESMAN', ORIANA and CANBERRA. Tantalisingly there are others as well: perhaps SPRINGBOK was one of them. Nine Elms depot, 22 January 1967.
(Barry Fletcher)

In later years diesel locos did occasionally work into the docks area with titled boat trains. Here, Sulzer-engined diesel No. D6546 stands outside the Union Castle Line terminal against a background of cranes. *(ABP Collection/ Southampton Archive Services)*

THURSDAY, 26th MARCH

No. 12—Train Alterations, etc.—continued

Time	From	To	Remarks	Service No.
a.m.				
8 40	Andover Jct.	Eastleigh	Formed Diesel Unit and form 9.40 a.m. Eastleigh to Portsmouth & Southsea.	—
8 53	Portsmouth & S'sea	Eastleigh	Form 9.40 a.m. Eastleigh to Andover Jct.	—
8 54 Q	Waterloo	So'ton Old Docks (Ocean Terminal)	Will run. 'Queen Elizabeth.' Train No. B.64. 'The Cunarder.'	—
(Boat)				
9 ‖ 0	Brockenhurst	Bournemouth Ctl.	Will not run.	
9 3	Bristol	Bournemouth West	Depart Poole 12.47 p.m. and run 3 minutes later thence.	—
9 20	Birkenhead	Bournemouth West	Revised	28
9 21	Waterloo	So'ton New Docks	Will carry Train No. B.65. 'Winchester Castle'. 'The Springbok'. 'Union-Castle Line'.	—
(Boat)				
9 40	Eastleigh	Portsmouth & S'sea	Formed of Diesel Unit off 8.40 a.m. Andover Jct.	—
9 40	Brighton	Bournemouth West	Will run at suspended times	—
9 40	Eastleigh	Andover Jct.	Formed Diesel Unit off 8.53 a.m. ex Portsmouth & Southsea. Headcode 67.	—
9 45	Bournemouth West	Manchester Mayfield	Will run to Sheffield	—
9 55 Q	Bournemouth West	Liverpool and Manchester	Will run	—

No photograph of the SPRINGBOK headboard has come to light. However, its existence is implied by this extract from the Working Timetable issued in February 1959. Note that THE CUNARDER runs in conjunction with the *Queen Elizabeth* to the Old Docks on a Q (i.e. conditional) path, whereas SPRINGBOK ran to the New (or Western) Docks on a regular booked path, as *Winchester Castle* sailed weekly for South Africa. *(BRB (Residuary) Ltd)*

It is 12.36 p.m. by the dock gate clock, and although the date on which the photograph was taken is unknown, the notice board behind the pillar box says 'British Railways Southern Region'. The Southern Railway invested heavily in both the Old and New docks, the latter dating from 1933. The docks themselves had been railway-owned since 1892, when they were bought by the London & South Western Railway. *(ABP Collection/Southampton Archive Services)*

THE SOUTH AMERICAN

Inaugural titled run	9 October 1953

This service ran in conjunction with the Royal Mail Line sailings to Buenos Aires, the last of which took place in February/March 1969.

Only headboard	BR Type 8 with painted face. Light blue background with two rectangular flags (no poles) either side of THE. Flags have red diagonal crosses, running into central crown.

GREEK LINE

Inaugural titled run	May 1954

Although regular sailings ceased as early as 1959, occasional departures continued until October/November 1966.

Only headboard	BR Type 8 with painted face. White superstructure of ship with large funnel coloured yellow/light blue/black (from base). Dark brown lettering.

SITMAR LINE

Inaugural titled run	c. 1960

The Sitmar Group owned the Fair Line Shipping Co. of Monrovia, who operated the *Fairsky* between Southampton and Sydney from June 1958. This ship was replaced by the *Fairstar* from 1964 onwards, which before renaming had previously been *Oxfordshire*, the last troopship ordered by HM Government.

Only headboard	BR Type 8 with painted face. Title below ship's flag, large V within.

'Lord Nelson' class 4–6–0 No. 30860 *Lord Hawke* speeds along the South Western main line near Basingstoke in the early days of the titled service. *(Author's Collection)*

Rebuilt 'West Country' 4–6–2 No. 34009 *Lyme Regis* crosses Canute Road into Southampton (Eastern) Docks with a Down train in September 1963, prominently displaying the correct route discs for the Northam approach to the Old Docks. *(A. Sainty Collection/Colour Rail/BRS 1043)*

Waterloo, 14 March 1967: quite late for Southern main-line steam (it finished completely on 9 July of that year), and very late to see headboarded steam. Nevertheless, No. 34108 *Wincanton* still has its nameplates, though the headboard itself has suffered damage to its top right-hand corner. The carriage roofboards read 'Southampton Sitmar Line Australia', and the V on the shipping line flag denoted the Vlasov Group (of companies). The route discs show the train to be bound for the New (Western) Docks via Millbrook. *(R.K. Blencowe Collection)*

ORIANA

Inaugural titled run	1960

Cruise liner traffic did begin to compensate for the loss of the transatlantic trade, but only slightly. P&O contributed two late entrants to headboarded boat trains, outlined below.

Only headboard	BR Type 8 with painted face. ORIANA in white on a black strip, orange background. Shipping company name below strip, on which, either side of the title, are superimposed back-to-back capital Es surmounted by a stylised crown (see also the line drawing).

On the headboard, the devices on either side of the word ORIANA closely resemble the ship's logo. The Es were for Elizabeth I who styled herself 'Gloriana' – a name used in inner circles only – of which the ship's name (and the train's) is a contraction. *(P&O History & Archives)*

The ship's logo, again duplicated on the engine headboard. *(P&O History & Archives)*

CANBERRA

Inaugural titled run	May 1961

Only headboard	Similar to ORIANA. Light blue background instead of orange. Devices to left and right of CANBERRA comprise Australia embraced by a capital C together with a black ring to indicate the position of Canberra, plus some 'wavy' sea (see also line drawings).

It was not usual for 'Merchant Navy' class engines to work the Southampton Docks boat trains, since although non-stop, the schedules were not quick, and the locomotive work relatively undemanding. To find Salisbury shed's No. 35006 *Peninsular & Oriental S.N.Co.* at the head of such a train therefore denoted an important occasion. In this case it is likely to be a pre-maiden voyage trip for special guests in May 1961 (though on which date is uncertain) on the new cruise ship. *(NRM/SSPL)*

Eastleigh depot, August 1961, with No. 34022 *Exmoor* appearing commendably clean and in good condition. (Exactly where, in 1961, this loco would run beneath overhead electrification is something of a mystery, but at least four (two each side) white 'flash' panels have been added.) The ORIANA referred to on the headboard was the last liner built for the Orient Line, entering service in 1960 and ending its days with P&O in 1986. *(T.J. Edgington/Colour Rail/BRS 853)*

No. 30854 *Howard of Effingham* about to depart on the 8.05 a.m. from the Eastern Docks via Millbrook to London, 7 July 1957. *(Frank Hornby)*

BRITTANY EXPRESS

St Malo service; summer only

Inaugural titled run	June 1954
Last titled run	27 September 1964

This service operated only from the end of June to the end of September, southbound on Monday/Wednesday/Friday (the 6.35 p.m. Waterloo–Southampton Docks) and northbound on Wednesday/Friday/Sunday. On nine Wednesdays during 1964 the sailing was to and from Weymouth. Not a Q train – not subject to Special Traffic procedures.

Only headboard	BR Type 8 without definite article.

OTHER HEADBOARDED SERVICES

Before air travel became widely used, it was customary for visiting royalty, heads of state, prime ministers, etc. to arrive in the UK by sea, mostly at either Portsmouth or Dover. Special trains (usually Pullman) then carried such dignitaries up to London. These trains were frequently supplied, either by the Southern Railway or by British Railways, with appropriate specially designed headboards. One example is illustrated below, and again in the Colour Section.

In later years special trains also ran to and from the major airports. Here, electro-diesel No. E6036 has just arrived back at Victoria from Gatwick, having taken the Soviet prime minister Mr Kosygin and his party there at the end of his visit to Great Britain, 13 February 1967. *(NRM/SSPL)*

CHANNEL ISLANDS BOAT TRAIN

Waterloo–Weymouth (Quay)

Inaugural titled run	*c.* 1981– 2
Last titled run	1988

This might be termed an 'authorised private venture', and the headboard was usually carried only between Bournemouth and Weymouth and return. Very occasionally it appeared at Waterloo on a class 33. First painted white with black letters and red edging, it was later repainted green with yellow letters and small quarter circles (also yellow) in the corners.

The time-honoured procedure at Weymouth, where boat trains had to traverse the streets to reach the ferry terminal. The train itself follows sedately well behind the police vehicle, which is complete with flashing light and a large roofboard. The latter can still be seen on display in the Weymouth Museum. *(NRM/SSPL)*

The repainted version, now in private hands. *(Author)*

Further down the road towards the quay, No. 33111, also displaying a flashing light, plus bell, plus headboard, slowly passes the Royal Oak Inn on 22 June 1983 on the 9.40 a.m. from Waterloo. *(Graham Chinn)*

Chapter Three

TITLED EXPRESSES OF THE LMS, BR (LMR) AND BR (SCR EX-LMS LINES)

INTRODUCTION TO 'MIDLAND' HEADBOARDS 1950–75

When the first London Midland Region headboard appeared in 1950 it was an eye-catching device. It had a bright red background, white lettering for ROYAL SCOT, and incorporated a yellow shield depicting, in red, a Scottish lion rampant. That, however, was the end of innovation for seven years. The red background soon gave way to an appropriate, though less highly visible, Hunting Stewart tartan, but it was to be 1957 before a headboard similar in profile to, and as striking as, the original ROYAL SCOT headboard was introduced, for the CALEDONIAN. This new service, together with THE ROYAL SCOT, were of course the prestige London–Glasgow daytime services, and it was totally fitting for them to have highly individual headboards.

Ocean passengers were also conveyed between London and Liverpool, from where many liners departed, rather than Southampton. One of Edge Hill's 'Black 5s' is entrusted with the Down train at Euston in the early 1950s. The train reporting number varied over the years. *(NRM/SSPL)*

As for the rest of the expresses titled in the public timetable, and there were a substantial number of them, the headboard provided was 'standard' in the extreme, with no variation in design throughout the era in which headboards were carried. The sole timetabled exception was the shield-embellished MASTER CUTLER, itself a late (1969) re-routed import from the Eastern Region, where such additions had been commonplace.

One well-known express not to be found in the following pages is the PINES EXPRESS, which famously ran from Manchester to Bournemouth for many years. This train, however, never carried a headboard north of Bath when running over the Somerset & Dorset line. Even when working via Oxford, it again never carried a headboard over 'main-stream' LMR metals. It is therefore described in the Southern Section.

The standard two-line or three-line headboards provided were in cast aluminium with a polished beaded border, polished letters and a painted background. This background was usually red, sometimes maroon, and occasionally black with one wild excursion into green. Scottish Region light blue could also be seen on some Anglo-Scottish services' headboards. These came in four basic sizes, described in the table below as BR Types 2, 3, 6 and 7. (Again, as with the corresponding table in the Western Section, the 'Type' designation is for convenience only; it is not a BR description.)

Dimensions are in inches	Type 2	Type 3	Type 6	Type 7
Length of top arc	24	24	28	35
Distance between lowest points	28	31	28	31
Distance between top/bottom edges	9⅞	9⅞	12½	14⅜

(For a full listing of all the various BR headboard sizes, see the Eastern Section.)

These sizes were carried on the London Midland Region expresses as follows:

Type 2	Type 6	THE WELSH CHIEFTAIN
THE COMET	THE ROYAL SCOT	CUNARD SPECIAL
THE MANXMAN	THE MID-DAY SCOT	EMPRESS VOYAGER
THE IRISHMAN	THE ROYAL HIGHLANDER	CONDOR
	THE MANCUNIAN	
Type 3	THE LANCASTRIAN	Type 7
THE MIDLANDER	THE RED ROSE	THE NORTHERN
THE RED ROSE	THE SHAMROCK	IRISHMAN
THE IRISH MAIL	THE WELSHMAN	THE MERSEYSIDE EXPRESS
THE DEVONIAN	THE LAKES EXPRESS	THE ULSTER EXPRESS
THE BON ACCORD	THE WAVERLEY	THE EMERALD ISLE
THE GRANITE CITY	THE PALATINE	EXPRESS
THE SAINT MUNGO	THE ROBIN HOOD	THE THAMES–CLYDE
	THE MASTER CUTLER	EXPRESS
	THE DEVONIAN	CAMBRIAN RADIO CRUISE

Unlike on the Southern, LMR headboards were mostly carried in the 'standard' position on the top lamp iron just below the chimney. They were, however, also occasionally to be seen displayed centrally on the buffer beam, though this was not visually advantageous as they were partially obscured by the vacuum piping in this position.

Five of the headboards listed in the Additional Titles represented services introduced at the instigation of the LMS and BR's Chester Division for summer-only operation in North Wales. Although not appearing as titled trains in the public timetable, they were regularly scheduled excursions with interesting itineraries, were well advertised locally, and popular with holiday-makers. They deserve inclusion for the initiative alone. Two further services excluded from the public timetable were the 'as required' boat train expresses that ran to Liverpool (Riverside). Here they connected with Cunard and Canadian Pacific ocean liners plying transatlantic routes. Liverpool, however, could not match Southampton in respect of titled boat trains.

In common with other regions, the reduced usage of headboards came in parallel with the declining numbers of steam-hauled expresses, though diesels did prolong the tradition for a while by carrying those steam-style headboards that still existed. The only concessions in the way of newly designed headboards specifically for diesel traction were a reworking of both the (tartan) ROYAL SCOT and THE CALEDONIAN headboards, neither of which were carried for any length of time, and the circular ORCADIAN – again short-lived. Electric locos, in their turn, rarely carried headboards at all, though a new version of the ROYAL SCOT headboard was tried for a short while in both 1970 and 1974 and, much later, Virgin Trains trialled yet another not long before withdrawing the title altogether.

This account covers the period from 1950 to the mid-1970s,[1] by which time new names were being introduced to replace the old – 'The Night Limited' and 'The Clansman' for instance. But the era of regular headboard-carrying had passed, and these titles and other later names are not relevant here. On the LMR it was ironically THE MASTER CUTLER that closed the 'headboard' chapter, though the date of the final carrying is unknown.

1.   Two short-term instances lie outside this range but are included for interest: the LMS's GOLDEN SANDS EXPRESS (1931) and Virgin Trains' ROYAL SCOT, mentioned earlier. Also, the LMS's THE ROYAL SCOT (1933–50) permanently attached to engine No. (4)6100.

THE TITLED EXPRESSES

(a) *Services using Euston*
   (THE) ROYAL SCOT   (ii) (iii)
   THE MID-DAY SCOT   } Anglo-Scottish services
   THE CALEDONIAN   (ii)
   THE NORTHERN IRISHMAN
   THE ROYAL HIGHLANDER
   THE MIDLANDER
   THE MANCUNIAN   (iii)
   THE LANCASTRIAN   } Manchester services
   THE COMET
   THE MERSEYSIDE EXPRESS
   THE RED ROSE   (ii)   } Liverpool services
   THE MANXMAN
   THE SHAMROCK
   THE IRISH MAIL
   THE EMERALD ISLE EXPRESS
   THE WELSHMAN   } Other services
   THE ULSTER EXPRESS   (iii)
   THE LAKES EXPRESS

(b) *Services using St Pancras*
   THE THAMES–CLYDE EXPRESS   (iii)   } Anglo-Scottish services
   THE WAVERLEY
   THE PALATINE
   THE ROBIN HOOD
   THE MASTER CUTLER   (i)

(c) *Inter-Regional Services*
   THE DEVONIAN
   PINES EXPRESS (see the Southern Section for this service)

(d) *Internal Scottish Services*
   THE IRISHMAN
   THE BON ACCORD   (iii)
   THE GRANITE CITY   } Aberdeen services
   THE SAINT MUNGO
   THE ORCADIAN

(i)   This service was transferred from King's Cross.
(ii)   These services also carried tailboards.
(iii) These services also carried a 1953 Coronation commemorative headboard

ADDITIONAL TITLES

(e) THE ELECTRIC SCOTS
    EMPRESS VOYAGER } Euston services
    CUNARD SPECIAL
    CONDOR Freight train
    TRANS PENNINE
    CTAC SCOTTISH TOURS EXPRESS

    GOLDEN SANDS EXPRESS
    THE WELSH DRAGON
    NORTH WALES LAND CRUISE } North Wales holiday–makers trains
    CAMBRIAN RADIO CRUISE
    THE WELSH CHIEFTAIN
    STRATHPEFFER SPA Highland Railway

An official Crewe Works photo of the 'pointed head' lion painted-steel board, 1957. *(NRM/SSPL)*

(See page 95): English Electric diesel No. D222 heads THE LANCASTRIAN through Nuneaton, around 1960. Note the multiplicity of tracks and sidings to the right and the absense of any yellow warning panel on the front of the loco. *(G.W. Sharpe)*

Before the National Railway Museum was established at York in 1975, most exhibits resided in the Museum of British Transport, Clapham, London. Part of the headboard display, seen here in October 1968, features five LMR titles, the bottom two having rarely been seen in service. *(G.R. Mortimer)*

(THE) ROYAL SCOT

Euston–Glasgow (Central)

Inaugural titled run	11 July 1927
Title withdrawn	9 September 1939
Reintroduced	16 February 1948
Last titled run	1 June 2002

(a) 1st style headboard	Introduced 1933, removed 1950
	LMS, cast-iron narrow rectangle with rounded corners, three words on one line. Permanently attached to the central smokebox of No. (4)6100 until rebuilding.
(b) 2nd style (1st version)	Introduced 5 June 1950, superseded by 2nd version
	Rectangular wooden board with semicircular ends surmounted centrally by a shield depicting a Scottish lion rampant, facing left. Yellow letters, edged black. Red background edged black. Lion red on yellow background. Two words only.
(2nd version)	Introduced 3 May 1951
	As 1st version but with red background replaced by a Hunting Stewart tartan design.
(3rd version)	Introduced October 1953
	Similar to 2nd version but in painted steel. Later replacements had lions with 'pointed heads'.
(4th version)	Introduced c. 1961
	Similar to 2nd version but in cast aluminium with letters riveted from rear. Shield tapers to slightly lower point. NB: There are many detailed differences in the ways in which the tartan background is applied.
(c) 3rd style (1st version)	Introduced c. 1951–3, order unknown
	BR Type 6 with black, red, maroon or light blue backgrounds. Small lettering (3½in). Three words.
(2nd version)	Similar to 1st version with larger (4in) lettering.
(3rd version)	Similar to 2nd version but with lettering on bottom line slightly inset, and near-vertical alignment of E with S.
(d) 4th style headboard	Rectangular with lower wing extensions for fixing to class 86 electric locos. Two words only, with red lion rampant within isolated yellow shield above legend. Blue board with white letters. 4 May 1970.
(e) 5th style headboard	As 4th style but with upper wing extensions for fixing to class 50 diesel electric locos. 4 May 1970.
(f) 6th style headboard	Virgin Trains' short-lived equivalent of the 1950 headboard. White raised letters on a maroon background. Shield white with highly stylised red lion. (See also Colour Section).

- Sunday 15 February 1948 was the centenary of the opening, by the Caledonian Railway, of the last stretch of its main line over Beattock summit, thus creating a through London–Glasgow rail route. The title was restored the following day in commemoration of this event.

- One of only three LMR expresses to be provided with a tailboard, two versions of which were used over the years.
- (THE) indicates that some styles of headboard included the definite article, while others did not.
- One of the four LMR expresses to carry the extra Coronation crown and cypher headboard.

The scene at London's Euston station on Friday 15 December 1933, with No. 6100 *Royal Scot* being piped to a halt. The engine was in fact No. 6152 *The King's Dragoon Guardsman*, with which No. 6100 had swapped identities for the purposes of its exhibition at the 1933 Chicago World Fair, and the subsequent 11,000-mile tour of the USA and Canada. The loco, and the brand-new rolling stock forming the ROYAL SCOT service, had been unloaded at Tilbury on the 5th from the Canadian Pacific steamer *Beaverdale*. The entire eight-coach train plus engine then proceeded on an exhibition tour within the UK, visiting Southend, Euston, Leeds (Wellington) and Glasgow (Central), among others. The electric headlight (fitted at Derby) was compulsory for the overseas running, and the large hand-operated warning bell was acquired on its arrival in Canada before proceeding to Chicago. The two white angle brackets either side of the headlight held white marker flags, denoting an 'extra' train while abroad. *(Topfoto)*

At the same time that No. 46100 was losing its permanent headboard because of rebuilding, the LMR introduced its first home-spun headboard for its crack train. Whether this timing was coincidence or deliberate is unknown, but No. 46220 *Coronation* stands at Euston on 5 June 1950 with the brand-new headboard. A legacy of its streamlined days, the elliptical upper smokebox was not made circular until December 1955. *(NRM/SSPL)*

No. 46245 *City of London* displaying the early painted-steel version of the tartan headboard with the rounded-head lion, Euston, 29 October 1953. A former streamlined engine, it retained the elliptical upper smokebox until December 1957. *(NRM/SSPL)*

Below: Engine-changing at the south end of Carlisle station. No. 46257 *City of Salford* has just taken over from No. 46230 *Duchess of Buccleuch*. Amazingly, both the steel headboards (pointed-head variety) appear to have their tartan striping identically applied. Note how the electric lighting fitted to No. 46257 is off-set from the top lamp iron. Probably taken in 1957. *(NRM/SSPL)*

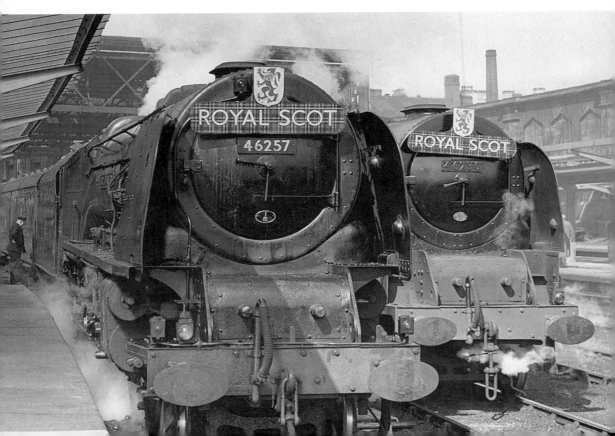

Class 40 No. D378 at Carlisle's Upperby depot, 1 September 1963. This time the tartan headboard is in cast aluminium with raised letters. Note the coarser moulded lion in comparison with the painted versions. The four-character train reporting panel indicates express passenger/Scottish Region (destination region)/two-digit train number 57, the northbound ROYAL SCOT. No. D378 will have hauled the Euston–Carlisle sector (299 miles). *(Martin S. Welch)*

Two for the price of one. Polmadie's No. 46231 *Duchess of Atholl* carries the 3rd style, 3rd version headboard, No. 46244 a later, pointed-head steel tartan headboard. No. 46231 will take over from Camden's No. 46244 *King George VI* for the Carlisle to Glasgow Central section of the journey. *(NRM/SSPL)*

Two for the price of one – again. For a couple of weeks or so either side of the Queen's Coronation on 2 June 1953, an extra regal embellishment was carried on certain services. These were THE ROYAL SCOT, THE MANCUNIAN, THE THAMES–CLYDE EXPRESS and THE ULSTER EXPRESS. Seen here at its home depot of Camden (1B), No. 46245 *City of London* displays this 'extra' together with the cast-aluminium version with small (3½in) letters. (See also Colour Section). *(NRM/SSPL)*

The 2nd version of the Type 6 board. Note the displacement of the E and S in comparison with the 3rd version. *(Author, courtesy Frank Burridge)*

Train No. 1S57 again, this time in the process of being headboarded at Euston on 4 May 1970. Class 86 electric No. E3182 will haul the express on its new 354-minute schedule as far as Crewe, where diesel power will be substituted. Note that 'E3182' is in raised aluminium characters. *(NRM/SSPL)*

Another 158 miles further on, two English Electric class 50 diesels (No. D437 leading No. D447) wait to take over. On the platform, a film and audio crew wait for interviews. *(NRM/SSPL)*

The short-lived Virgin Trains version of the classic headboard on a class 87 No. 87008 at Euston on 1 December 1998. *(Darren Ford)*

Bringing up the rear of the northbound train at Euston is a BR Mk 1 BFK, tidily finished off by a tailboard. Despite electrification, a standard oil lamp shows the train to be complete. *(NRM/SSPL)*

Now to Glasgow Central, with a BR Mk 1 BG as first coach together with a recently painted tailboard covering the vestibule doors. The train is the Up service, and with ten minutes to go before departure at 10 a.m. the loco has yet to back on. 29 June 1956. *(J.D. Gomersall Collection)*

Until THE CALEDONIAN was introduced in 1957 there were only two titled expresses between Euston and Glasgow – THE ROYAL SCOT and THE MID-DAY SCOT. On this historic stretch of line No. 46210 *Lady Patricia* restarts the southbound service from a water stop at Beattock summit, 1,015ft above sea level and the highest point on the Euston–Glasgow route. The photo is undated, but as the stock is in carmine and cream and includes at least two ex-LMS vehicles it is likely to be around 1953/4. Since the load is a mere ten coaches, it is also probable that this is the winter timetable. *(NRM/SSPL)*

THE MID-DAY SCOT

Euston–Glasgow (Central)

Inaugural titled run	26 September 1927
Title withdrawn	9 September 1939
Reintroduced	26 September 1949
Last titled run	13 June 1965

Only headboard	Introduced Summer 1951
(1st version)	BR Type 6 with a red or light blue background (this page).
(2nd version)	Similar, but with E and Y overlapping (see page 98).

• One of only eight cast–aluminium headboards to include a hyphenated name.

The sole BR class 8 Pacific No. 71000 *Duke of Gloucester*, stands in the centre road at Crewe ready to take over the northbound train, which it will also strengthen with extra carriages. After its introduction in 1954 No. 71000 was a frequent performer on this service from its home depot, Crewe North (5A). This loco, fitted with British Caprotti rotary-cam poppet valves, was an 'accountant's replacement' for the Pacific No. 46202 *Princess Anne*, which was written off after the Harrow & Wealdstone accident in 1952. The BR1E tender was unique to this loco. On its withdrawal in 1962 BR placed the loco in store for preservation, but five years later decided to scrap it, except for the left-hand cylinder, which was removed and put on display in the Science Museum in London. The *Duke* arrived at Barry for cutting up in October 1967, but never was, and left again in April 1974 to be preserved, and finally restored to working order on the Great Central Railway at Loughborough. The engine was officially recommissioned by HRH Prince Richard the Duke of Gloucester in November 1986 and remains based at Loughborough. *(NRM/SSPL)*

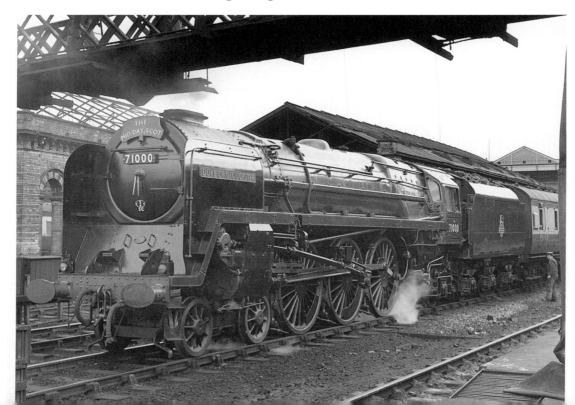

THE CALEDONIAN

Euston–Glasgow (Central)

Inaugural titled run	17 June 1957
Last titled run	4 September 1964

(a) 1st style headboard		Introduced 17 June 1957
	(1st version)	Painted steel, rectangular with semicircular ends. Surmounted by two touching shields (St Andrew, left, and St George) side by side, angled but centrally placed. Red background, edged grey with white italicised lettering. 60in wide.
	(2nd version)	Similar to 1st version but in cast aluminium. White painted letters riveted from rear.
	(3rd version)	Introduced 1958–61, order unknown between 2nd and 3rd versions
		Similar to 2nd version but with lettering differences and the bottom of the left shield pointing to the gap between A and L, rather than the top of A.
(b) 2nd style headboard		Introduced *c.* 1962
		Two-line variant of 1st style, deeper and only 36in wide. Wooden. Intended for use with diesel traction.

- One of only three LMR expresses to be provided with a tailboard.
- Introduced as an additional Anglo-Scottish service on a 400-minute schedule, this service was 'doubled-up' from 9 June 1958 to give a morning and afternoon departure from both terminals (7.45 a.m. and 4.15 p.m. ex-Euston, 8.30 a.m. and 4 p.m. ex-Glasgow). This arrangement was not successful and the practice ended on 12 September 1958 (see also THE TALISMAN, Eastern Section).

Inauguration day. No. 46242 *City of Glasgow* is appropriate motive power for the non-stop Euston–Glasgow run. Successor to the streamlined pre-war CORONATION SCOT, the service is piped away by the Royal Caledonian School band. No. 46242 had also been severely damaged in the Harrow accident and spent more than a year out of traffic while extensive repairs were carried out at Crewe Works. *(NRM/SSPL)*

Euston's Platform 6 hosts the arrival (at 10.40 p.m. if it was on time) of the 4.00 p.m. ex-Glasgow. Suitcases, fur coats and porters complete the period scene. No. D308 has a 1B (Camden) shedplate below the number but 9A (Longsight, Manchester) stencilled below the buffers, while the 1st cast-aluminium version of the headboard graces the communication doors. The gentleman in the cab wearing a bowler hat was probably an inspector, so this may have been a special occasion of some sort. *(NRM/SSPL)*

The slightly later and even more italicised 3rd version of the cast headboard with narrow shields. *(Courtesy Sheffield Railwayana Auctions)*

Above: The two-line, 2nd style headboard in close-up. *(Graham Kelsey, courtesy Sheffield Railwayana Auctions)*

Left: No. D298 has the less conspicuous two-line headboard as it climbs out of Euston, passing Primrose Hill signal-box in the background. Note the output from the train heating boiler being wasted from the front end. Undated photo. *(Roger Holmes, courtesy Photos of the Fifties)*

Below: The last coach on the northbound service on 20 June 1958 passes under Hest Bank footbridge, with the water troughs in the distance. The eight-coach 'limited load' formation concluded with an ex-LMS brake and sported a very distinctive tailboard comprising the Saltire on a red background, the English flag on blue. Lettering was cream or off-white in a black panel. *(R. Butterfield/ Initial Photographics)*

THE NORTHERN IRISHMAN

Euston–Stranraer Harbour (Sleeping car train)

Inaugural titled run	30 June 1952
Last titled run	17 April 1966

Only headboard	Introduced; unknown, rarely photographed
	BR Type 7 with a red or green background – the only LMR headboard with this colour. (See Colour Section).

- This service was operated in conjunction with sailings to and from Larne Harbour, with connections to Belfast (York Road).
- Before 14 June 1965 this service had operated over the direct route (73¾ miles) from Dumfries to Stranraer via Newton Stewart. With the closure (on this date) of the direct route, an enforced detour via Mauchline, Ayr and Girvan was thereafter undertaken, increasing the distance travelled by nearly 60 miles.

A rare headboard on a class that rarely bore headboards. This is Kingmoor shed, Carlisle, to which No. 72009 *Clan Stewart* was allocated, on 20 January 1958. The engine clearly has damage to its front buffer beam. As the tender is full and the headboard is fitted, perhaps a 'rough shunt' immediately before working the service was the cause. *(N.L. Browne, courtesy Frank Hornby)*

THE ROYAL HIGHLANDER

Euston–Inverness (Sleeping car train)

Inaugural titled run	26 September 1927
Title withdrawn	10 September 1939
Reintroduced	17 June 1957
Last titled run	12 May 1985

Only headboard	Introduced 17 June 1957
(1st version)	BR Type 6 with a red, maroon or light-blue background, with inset lettering. (See also Colour Section).
(2nd version)	Introduced c. 1961
	Similar but with slightly wider letter spacing.

- In 1957 the title was bestowed on the 7.20 p.m. ex-Euston and the 5.25 p.m. ex-Inverness.
- The last title in this book to include ROYAL on the headboard, the only four with this distinction being:

ROYAL DUCHY	(WR)	(THE) ROYAL SCOT	(LMR)
THE ROYAL WESSEX	(SR)	THE ROYAL HIGHLANDER	(LMR)

Above, right: The 2nd version of the headboard, in ex-loco condition. The alignment of the lower L with the space between THE and ROYAL is the most noticeable difference. *(Author, with permission of NRM)*

Below: No. 46205 *Princess Victoria* on the inaugural northbound headboarded run near Watford on 17 June 1957. The engine carries the 'inset lettering' headboard and an Edge Hill shedplate (8A). All the visible coaching stock is ex-LMS. *(NRM/SSPL)*

THE MIDLANDER

Euston–Wolverhampton (High Level)

Inaugural titled run	25 September 1950
Last titled run	11 September 1959

Only headboard	Introduced *c.* 1951
	BR Type 3 with a red background.

- As a result of BR granting greater autonomy to the regions, this train, together with the ROYAL SCOT, MANCUNIAN and MERSEYSIDE EXPRESS services, was the first to receive refurbished Mk 1 stock painted in the LMR's chosen colour of maroon lined in black and yellow, on 11 June 1956. New, distinctive carriage roofboards were also introduced for these services at the same time.

The same location as for THE ROYAL HIGHLANDER but somewhat earlier on the evening of 17 June 1957. The principal business train to and from the Midlands heads north behind Bushbury's No. 45733 *Novelty*. (NRM/SSPL)

THE MANCUNIAN

Euston–Manchester (London Road)/(Piccadilly, from 12 September 1960)

Inaugural titled run	26 September 1927
Title withdrawn	9 September 1939
Reintroduced	26 September 1949
Last titled run	15 April 1966
Only headboard	Introduced *c.* 1951
	BR Type 6 with a red background.

- Diverted from 25 April 1960 to Manchester (Exchange) during the rebuilding of London Road. Reverted to the new Piccadilly on and from 12 September 1960, to be electrically hauled as far as Crewe, at least initially.
- One of the four LMR expresses to carry the extra Coronation crown and cypher headboard (not illustrated).

No. 46162 *Queen's Westminster Rifleman* climbs Camden Bank out of Euston. As the entire visible coaching stock is ex-LMS painted in the early BR colours of carmine and cream, the date must be in the early 1950s. *(NRM/SSPL)*

THE LANCASTRIAN

Euston–Manchester (London Road)/(Piccadilly, from 12 September 1960)

Inaugural titled run	1 February 1928
Title withdrawn	9 September 1939
Reintroduced	16 September 1957
Last titled run	8 September 1962

(Author, with permission of NRM)

Only headboard	Introduced 16 September 1957(?). BR Type 6 with a red background.

- In 1957 the title was conferred on the 7.55 a.m. ex-Euston and the 4 p.m. return working from Manchester. (See illustration on page 95).
- Diverted, like both the other titled expresses running to Manchester, to Exchange station between April and September 1960.

THE COMET

Euston–Manchester (London Road)/(Piccadilly, from 12 September 1960)

Inaugural titled run	12 September 1932
Title withdrawn	9 September 1939
Reintroduced	26 September 1949
Last titled run	7 September 1962

Only headboard	Introduced c. 1951 BR Type 2 with a red background.

- Diverted, like the MANCUNIAN, between April and September 1960 to run to and from Exchange station.
- COMET is a contraction of 'Cottonopolis' (for Manchester) and 'Metropolis' (for London). It has the distinction of having the shortest of all named passenger express titles to be carried on a headboard.

An eleven-coach set of ex-LMS stock trails No. 70044 in the vicinity of Manchester (London Road), 26 June 1953. Both this loco and No. 70043 were fitted from new with Westinghouse air pumps and were extensively tested on freight trains. The equipment was later removed, smoke deflector plates added, and Nos 70043/4 were then named *Earl Kitchener* and *Earl Haig* respectively. *(B.K.B. Green Collection/Initial Photographics)*

THE MERSEYSIDE EXPRESS

Euston–Liverpool (Lime Street)/Southport (Chapel Street)

Inaugural titled run	1 March 1928
Title withdrawn	9 September 1939
Reintroduced	26 September 1949
Last titled run	16 April 1966

Only headboard	Introduced *c.* 1951
(1st version)	BR Type 7 with a red background.
(2nd version)	Introduced *c.* 1961
	Similar to first, but with noticeably inset lettering on second and third lines.

The 2nd version, with the inset lettering.
(Author, with permission of NRM)

- Originally styled 'The London and Merseyside Express' from 26 September 1927. Changed to the shorter title in 1928, hence the mid-timetable introduction date.
- The prototype 'Deltic' made its first public-service run on this train on 12 December 1955 (on the Up service).

No. 46164 *The Artists' Rifleman* exits Euston and begins the climb of Camden Bank in the early 1950s. This time BR Mk 1 stock is in carmine and cream and the leading two coaches carry roofboards. Note that the steam-operated sanders are in use. *(NRM/SSPL)*

THE RED ROSE

Euston–Liverpool (Lime Street)

Inaugural titled run	3 May 1951
Last titled run	16 April 1966

(a) 1st style headboard	Introduced 3 May 1951
	BR Type 3 with black or red background.
(b) 2nd style headboard	Introduced *c.* 1961
	BR Type 6 with red background.

- This express was named specially for the Festival of Britain, so its titled running coincided with the opening of the Festival rather than the beginning of the summer timetable.
- The title was conferred on the (already running) 12.05 p.m. ex-Euston and the 5.25 p.m. return working from Liverpool.
- This was one of only three LMR expresses to carry a tailboard as well as a headboard; indeed, it probably carried this feature longer than the headboard.

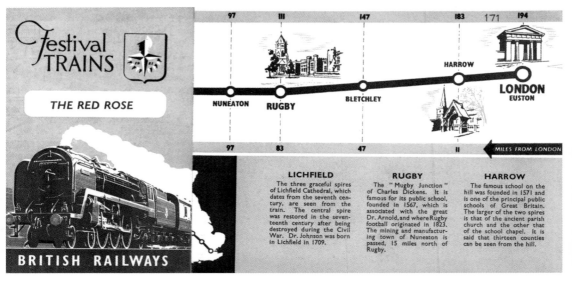

One of only two closely similar pieces of advertising literature specific to the newly titled 'Festival' trains, the other being for THE ROYAL WESSEX. Like its Southern Region counterpart, this train rarely saw 'Britannia' haulage, with 'Princess Royal' power being the norm. *(BRB (Residuary) Ltd)*

Only twelve days after the title was introduced, Mold Junction's 'Black 5' No. 45288 is captured at Euston on 15 May 1951, at the head of the northbound train. *(NRM/SSPL)*

No. 46207 *Princess Arthur of Connaught* enters Crewe from the south in August 1961 beneath the newly erected 25kV ac overhead wiring. Not only are the coaches now in BR maroon, but so is the Stanier Pacific, which was withdrawn three months later and cut up at Crewe in May 1962. The rare 2nd style headboard is being carried. *(G.W. Sharpe Collection)*

Another early shot at Euston, this time of the first version of the tailboard, 24 May 1951. Colours unknown (though the rose is probably red) and the letters are edged. The BTK (Brake Third Corridor) is part of a new rake of Mk 1s in carmine and cream allocated to this Festival train. Third class was abolished in 1956, and a trolley of milk churns would not be a common sight much longer either. *(NRM/SSPL)*

In later years, a rake of maroon stock heads north under the gantries. A tailboard is again fitted, but of a different variety on which the rose does not appear to be very red. *(NRM/SSPL)*

THE MANXMAN

Euston–Liverpool (Lime Street)

Inaugural titled run	11 July 1927
Title withdrawn	9 September 1939
Reintroduced	2 July 1951
Last titled run	16 April 1966

Only headboard	Introduced Summer 1951
	BR Type 2 with a red background.

- This service operated in the summer timetable only, and ran in conjunction with sailings from Pier Head to the Isle of Man.

The Up MANXMAN about to leave Rugby behind No. 46114 *Coldstream Guardsman* in July 1959. *(M.J. Jackson)*

THE SHAMROCK

Euston–Liverpool (Lime Street)

The 1st version of the headboard.
(Author, with permission of NRM)

Inaugural titled run	14 June 1954
Last titled run	16 April 1966

Only headboard	Introduced 14 June 1954(?)
	BR Type 6 with a red background.
(1st version)	Lettering close to bottom edge.
(2nd version)	Lettering raised above bottom edge.

- This service operated in conjunction with sailings from Liverpool to Belfast (by the Belfast Steamship Co.) and to Dublin (by the British & Irish Steam Packet Co.).
- The title was conferred on the (already running) 8.10 a.m. ex–Liverpool and the 4.55 p.m. return working from Euston. On the inaugural day No. 46205 worked the Up service, No. 46153 the Down.

In a classic combination of sun and shadow, No. 46208 *Princess Helena Victoria* threads the tunnels between Lime Street and Edge Hill. Again note the use of steam sanders to improve adhesion on the 1 in 93 gradient. *(NRM/SSPL)*

THE IRISH MAIL

Euston–Holyhead

Inaugural titled run	26 September 1927
Title withdrawn	10 September 1939
Reintroduced	31 May 1948
Last titled run	12 May 1985

Only headboard	Introduced Summer 1951
	BR Type 3 with a red background.

- Although the title became official in 1927 (when carriage roofboards were also displayed), the service had been called this unofficially since 1848 – the earliest known 'title' of any train in the UK. It had also been named in some LNWR timetables, and in LMS timetables, before 1927.
- At the outbreak of the Second World War the train's name disappeared from the public timetables, only to reappear intermittently at various intervals during the hostilities.
- This service was operated in conjunction with sailings to Dun Laoghaire, with onward connections to Dublin (Kingsbridge).

The south end of Rugby again with Holyhead (6J) 'Britannia' No. 70045 *Lord Rowallan* ready to depart. 'SC' means 'self-cleaning' and consists of a wire-mesh device fitted inside the smokebox that causes most of the char drawn through the boiler tubes to be thrown out of the chimney, rather than collecting in a heap in the smokebox. July 1959. *(M.J. Jackson)*

THE EMERALD ISLE EXPRESS

Euston–Holyhead

Inaugural titled run	20 September 1954
Last titled run	3 May 1975

Only headboard	Introduced 20 September 1954(?)
	BR Type 7 with a red background.

* This service was operated in conjunction with sailings to Dun Laoghaire, with onward connections to Dublin (Kingsbridge).
* The name was bestowed on the 5.35 p.m. ex-Euston and the 7.30 a.m. return working from Holyhead.

The old Euston, with English Electric diesel No. D382 at the buffer stops. Whether the mountain of parcels alongside the loco has been unloaded from this service is unclear, but there's another, smaller pile on the adjacent platform also. Note that the 'light engine' lamp has already been placed above the left buffer in preparation for the move to Camden depot. *(NRM/SSPL)*

THE WELSHMAN

Euston–Holyhead/Portmadoc/Pwllheli

Inaugural titled run	11 July 1927
Title withdrawn	10 September 1939
Reintroduced	5 June 1950
Last titled run	30 August 1963
Only headboard	Introduced c. 1951, rarely carried
	BR Type 6 with a red background.

- This service operated during the summer timetable only.

No. 45531 *Sir Frederick Harrison* (rebuilt 'Patriot' class) heads north through the London suburbs in July 1962. *(NRM/SSPL)*

THE ULSTER EXPRESS

Euston–Fleetwood (from 11 July 1927)
Euston–Heysham (from 30 April 1928)

Inaugural titled run	11 July 1927
Title withdrawn	10 September 1939
Reintroduced	26 September 1949
Last titled run	6 April 1975

Only headboard	Introduced *c.* 1951
	BR Type 7 with a red background.

- This service was operated in conjunction with sailings to Belfast (Donegal Quay).
- This service also carried the Coronation crown and cypher headboard during the period 22 May to 14 June 1953.

THE LAKES EXPRESS

Euston–Windermere / Workington

Inaugural titled run	11 July 1927
Title withdrawn	9 September 1939
Reintroduced	5 June 1950
Last titled run	28 August 1964

Only headboard	Introduced *c.* 1951, rarely carried
	BR Type 6 with a red background.

- The Windermere portion was detached at Oxenholme. The remaining train then went on to Penrith, before reversing direction towards Workington via Keswick.
- This service operated during the summer timetable only.

The old Euston again, with No. 46168 *The Girl Guide* at the buffer stops on Platform 3, while foot-plate staff chat with, possibly, the guard. *(Martin S. Welch)*

Unknown engine, unknown location, but the date must be close to 2 June 1953 (Coronation Day), as the LMR's crown and cypher headboard is being carried. *(H.N. James Collection/Ipswich Transport Museum)*

Watford embankment on 26 August 1959 sees the southbound passage of the sixteen-coach ULSTER EXPRESS. No. 46256 *Sir William A. Stanier FRS* was the penultimate 'Princess Coronation' class Pacific and the last to be built by the LMS, entering traffic in December 1947. Although introduced by Stanier in 1937, the two postwar examples were built in H.G. Ivatt's time as chief mechanical engineer and embodied many detailed improvements. *(NRM/SSPL)*

THE THAMES–CLYDE EXPRESS

St Pancras–Glasgow (St Enoch)
St Pancras–Glasgow (Central) from 27 June 1966 on closure of St Enoch

Inaugural titled run	26 September 1927
Title withdrawn	9 September 1939
Reintroduced	26 September 1949
Last titled run	3 May 1975

Only headboard (1st version)	Introduced Summer 1951 and usage continued alongside the 2nd version
	BR Type 7 with a black or red background.
(2nd version)	Introduced *c.* 1961 but rarely seen in comparison with the 1st version
	Similar to 1st version but letter spacing on the bottom line is inset from the sides.

• The fourth of the LMR expresses to carry the Coronation crown and cypher headboard.

Left: The 2nd version, with the word EXPRESS noticeably inset from each side. *(Author, with permission of NRM)*

Below: Over the Coronation period this express also ran with the LMR's crown and cypher device in celebration, which dates the photo to between 22 May and 14 June 1953. An unidentifiable 'Black 5' 4–6–0 sets off with two headboards, that on the buffer beam having, most likely, a black background. Both the 'Mickey' (local slang for a 'Black 5') and 2P 4–4–0 No. 40351 shunting the carriage sidings were part of Holbeck's (20A) allocation. *(NRM/SSPL)*

THE WAVERLEY

St Pancras–Edinburgh (Waverley)

Inaugural titled run	17 June 1957
Last titled run	28 September 1968

Only headboard (1st version)	Introduced 17 June 1957 and usage continued alongside the 2nd version BR Type 6 with a red, maroon or light blue background.
(2nd version)	Introduced *c.* 1961 Similar to 1st version but letter spacing on the lower line is inset from the sides.

- In 1957 the title was bestowed on the 9.15 a.m. ex-St Pancras and the 10.05 a.m. ex-Waverley.
- From 1965 to 1968 inclusive the service ran during the summer timetable only.
- Before the Second World War this service was known as the 'Thames–Forth Express' and was named in the timetables from 26 September 1927. Over the LNER route from Carlisle to Edinburgh the engine carried North British-style destination boards reading 'St Pancras' when heading south and 'Edinburgh' northbound, but no 'Thames–Forth Express' headboard was ever carried (see the Additional Titles to the pre-war LNER Section).

The 2nd version of the headboard.
(Courtesy Sheffield Railwayana Auctions)

Another ex-Midland Railway 2P 4–4–0 this time Kentish Town's (14B) No. 40421, has the headboard as pilot engine to a 'Jubilee' 4–6–0 at St Pancras, *c.* 1958. *(Martin S. Welsh)*

THE PALATINE

St Pancras–Manchester (Central)

Inaugural titled run	4 July 1938
Title withdrawn	9 September 1939
Reintroduced	16 September 1957
Last titled run	13 June 1964

Only headboard (1st version)	Introduced 16 September 1957(?) and usage continued alongside the 2nd version
	BR Type 6 with a red or maroon background.
(2nd version)	Introduced *c.* 1961
	Similar to 1st version but with lettering on lower line inset from the sides.

• In 1957 the title was bestowed on the 7.55 a.m. ex–St Pancras and the 2.25 p.m. from Manchester. (See also Colour Section).

Left: The 2nd version of the headboard. *(Author, with permission of NRM)*

Below: The Manchester-bound express rolls to a halt at its Miller's Dale stop in 1960. Motive power is provided by Trafford Park's 'Britannia' No. 70042 *Lord Roberts*. The spacious station closed on 6 March 1967 when the through route via Peak Forest and Matlock was deemed superfluous. *(J.M. Bentley)*

THE ROBIN HOOD

St Pancras–Nottingham (Midland)

Inaugural titled run	2 February 1959
Last titled run	7 September 1962

Only headboard	Introduced 2 February 1959(?), both versions
(1st version)	BR Type 6 with a red or maroon background.
(2nd version)	Similar to 1st version but with slightly different letter spacing.

* In 1959 the name was bestowed on the 8.15 a.m. ex-Nottingham and the 4.45 p.m. from St Pancras.
* Note the mid-timetable introduction date.

The 2nd version, on which the T is noticeably further to the left. *(Author, with permission of NRM)*

No. D100 has brought the train Up from Nottingham and stands, symmetrically placed, under William Barlow's magnificent arch at St Pancras on 26 September 1961. The Sulzer-engined 1 Co–Co 1 2,500hp diesel has the split-panel reporting number indicators and a Derby (17A) steam-age shedplate. The electrification warning flash rather spoils the symmetry. The clutter of platform trolleys, still usual at the time, is again evident. *(NRM/SSPL)*

THE MASTER CUTLER

St Pancras–Sheffield (Midland)

Inaugural titled run	6 January 1969
Last titled run	10 May 1985

Only headboard	Introduced 6 January 1969 with 1st and 2nd versions that had been used previously on the Eastern Region. Overlapping usage of the four versions (probably not all at the same time) lasted until at least the mid-1970s
	BR Type 6 with two shields on either side of the definite article. On the left (facing the headboard), the arms of the Company of Cutlers in Hallamshire; on the right the arms of the City of Sheffield. Although superficially similar, there were four versions of this headboard.
(1st version)	Lettering and shields in stainless steel (supplied by Firth-Vickers Stainless Steels), each individually attached to the cast-aluminium plate. Dark blue background (see Colour Section).
(2nd version)	Lettering and shields cast integral with the plate (as per common practice). Dark blue background.
(3rd version)	As 2nd version but in fibreglass. Again with dark blue background (not illustrated).
(4th version)	Reversed colours, i.e. lettering dark against a light-coloured background. Precise colours unknown.

- It is not known whether the 4th version was 'new', or a repainting of the 2nd or 3rd versions.
- The service commenced running to and from St Pancras on 7 October 1968 but was untitled up to 3 January 1969 inclusive.
- The service continued to operate from 13 May 1985, unnamed, when High Speed Train sets took over the operation. The title was again reintroduced from 29 September 1986 (as MASTER CUTLER PULLMAN) and continued to run titled in the timetable until at least the mid-1990s. No headboard was carried in this period, however.
- During its headboarded years this service, uniquely, used no fewer than five terminals on a regularly scheduled basis, as below.

Sheffield (Victoria)	– Marylebone	6/10/47 to 13/9/58
	– King's Cross	15/9/58 to 1/10/65
(Midland)	– King's Cross	4/10/65 to 4/10/68
	– St Pancras	7/10/68 to 10/5/85

- See the Eastern Section for details of workings from 6 October 1947 to 4 October 1968.

St Pancras in the spring of 1969 sees the Down service ready to depart behind Brush Sulzer class 47 No. D1568. The headboard is looking a bit tatty and the depot allocation (41A, Sheffield Tinsley) is now painted on the cabside below the number. The train's Pullman status had ceased when the service was transferred to St Pancras in October 1968. *(David Percival)*

In June 1973 No. D1575 heads south near Kibworth with a neat rake of eight Mk 1 coaches, now in the corporate blue livery. The headboard carried is of the 'reversed colours' variety. *(J.H. Cooper-Smith)*

Whether by legal agreement or by tacit understanding is unknown, but the practise had been established that whoever was elected Master Cutler had the right, during his term of office, to travel up to London once a year in the cab of the locomotive. (See also page 18). A number of incumbants exercised this privilege and during his 1974/5 period as Master Cutler, Mr Norman Hanlon, pictured wearing his chain of office also availed himself of his right, and is pictured beside an unidentified Sulzer-engined class 45 or 46. The headboard is that with stainless-steel lettering and shields. Note that by this date the four-character train description system was no longer being used. *(Courtesy Sheffield Newspapers Ltd)*

The appointment of Mr Stanley Speight to the position of Master Cutler in 1977 probably gave rise to this photograph. As he was also a director of Sheffield Wednesday at the time, the opportunity was taken to celebrate both at once. In all probability, this is the team coach about to leave Hillsborough for the away match against Preston North End on 4 October, Wednesday losing 2–1. Players of the day Paul Bradshaw (left) and Rodger Wylde help to hold the 1st version headboard. *(Courtesy Sheffield Newspapers Ltd)*

The Type 6 headboard was also manufactured in fibreglass resin and, from a distance, was indistinguishable from that above. However, an entirely new design in fibreglass had also been prepared and approved by BR. The fibreglass designs for THE FLYING SCOTSMAN and QUEEN OF SCOTS had already appeared, and that for THE MASTER CUTLER was to be the third of this type. Sadly this headboard never materialised but was to feature a pair of crossed swords (coloured silver) and several ears of wheat (in gold).

THE DEVONIAN

Bradford (Forster Square)–Paignton
Bradford (Exchange)–Paignton (from 1 May 1967)
Leeds (City)–Paignton (from 3 May 1971)

Inaugural titled run	26 September 1927
Title withdrawn	10 September 1939
Reintroduced	23 May 1949
Last titled run	3 May 1975

(a) 1st style headboard	Introduced Summer 1951
	BR Type 3 with a black or red background.
(b) 2nd style headboard	Introduced *c.* 1961
	BR Type 6 with a red background (see Colour Section).

- See also the Western Section for this inter-regional service, since headboards were changed at Bristol.
- At 8.30 a.m. on 1 June 1874 the first-ever scheduled British Pullman car train left Bradford (Market Street, as Forster Square was then called) for St Pancras. This event is Bradford's only claim to fame, railway-wise.

Another of Holbeck's 'Black 5s' leaves what was then Platform 5 at Leeds City for Paignton on 28 September 1953. At the time the train was the 9.45 a.m. departure (after reversal), due at its final destination at 7.25 p.m. The LMS's Queen's Hotel fills the space to the left of the smokebox and is still there, largely unchanged (externally at least), whereas Leeds City has been remodelled completely twice in the intervening years. *(Philip J. Kelley)*

THE IRISHMAN

Glasgow (St Enoch)–Stranraer Harbour
Glasgow (Central)–Stranraer Harbour (from 27 June 1966 on closure of St Enoch)

Inaugural titled run	17 July 1933
Title withdrawn	10 September 1939
Reintroduced	23 May 1949
Last titled run	5 March 1967

Only headboard	Introduced Summer 1951, rarely seen
	BR Type 2 with black or red background.

THE BON ACCORD

Glasgow (Buchanan Street)–Aberdeen
Glasgow (Queen Street)–Aberdeen (from 7 November 1966 on closure of Buchanan Street)

Inaugural titled run	5 July 1937
Title withdrawn	8 September 1939
Reintroduced	23 May 1949
Last titled run	4 May 1968

Only headboard	Introduced Summer 1951, used in 1950s only
	BR Type 3 with a black or red background.

• The train's title is the motto of the city of Aberdeen, and the Granite City's official guide describes the meaning thus: 'which doth safely come to Common-Wealth'.

THE GRANITE CITY

Glasgow (Buchanan Street)–Aberdeen
Glasgow (Queen Street)–Aberdeen (from 7 November 1966 on closure of Buchanan Street)

Inaugural titled run	17 July 1933
Title withdrawn	9 September 1939
Reintroduced	23 May 1949
Last titled run	4 May 1968

Only headboard	Introduced Summer 1951, used in 1950s only
	BR Type 3 with a black or red background.

• This service also carried the ScR's Coronation headboard for a couple of weeks either side of 2 June 1953.

Corkerhill (67A) 'Jubilee' No. 45645 *Collingwood* basks in the evening sun at its home shed before working the southbound service, mid-1950s.
(J.L. Stevenson, courtesy Hamish Stevenson)

The two locos that were later that day to double-head BR's eighteen-coach 'Grand Scottish Tour' onwards to Aberdeen. The Scottish Region's 'Coronation' headboard sees the light of day for the first time in fourteen years, and this was to be the last run of No. 60009 before retiring to the Lochty Private Railway for preservation. Perth shed, Easter Saturday, 25 March 1967. (See also Colour section) (*Transport Treasury*)

The northbound service (1.35 p.m. from Buchanan Street at the time) gets into its stride as it passes St Rollox shed behind one of Perth's numerous 'Black 5s' on 25 June 1955. Note the 'webbed' or 'flared' protrusion of the fixing bracket – see the next two photos also. *(J. Robertson/Transport Treasury)*

Ex-LMS Compound 4P 4–4–0 No. 41125 pilots BR Standard 5MT 4–6–0 No. 73005 southbound out of Aberdeen, July 1951. Note 'British Railways' in full on the tender. Perth shed (63A) provided both engines. *(Campbell Lawson Kerr/Mitchell Library, Glasgow)*

THE SAINT MUNGO

Glasgow (Buchanan Street)–Aberdeen
Glasgow (Queen Street)–Aberdeen (from 7 November 1966 on closure of Buchanan Street)

Inaugural titled run	5 July 1937
Title withdrawn	8 September 1939
Reintroduced	23 May 1949
Last titled run	4 May 1968

Only headboard	Introduced *c.* 1951, used in 1950s only
	BR Type 3 with a black background.

- The train's title commemorates St Kentigern (popularly St Mungo, died AD 603), who founded a monastery on the site of the present Glasgow Cathedral, and whose tomb resides beneath it. St Mungo is the patron saint of Glasgow.
- In April 1961 NBL Type 2 diesels, working in pairs, took over these Glasgow–Aberdeen services. However, these units proved to be unreliable and so an accelerated three-hour steam-hauled service, using A3 and A4 Pacifics drafted in for the purpose, was reintroduced from Monday 10 September 1962. A fourth title was added to the list, and the trains were advertised as below:

8.25 a.m.	7.10 a.m.
Glasgow–Aberdeen, THE GRAMPIAN	Aberdeen–Glasgow, THE BON ACCORD
5.30 p.m.	5.15 p.m.
Glasgow–Aberdeen, THE SAINT MUNGO	Aberdeen–Glasgow, THE GRANITE CITY

Note that each individual title was used in one direction only, and that no headboards were carried during the period 10 September 1962 to Saturday 3 September 1966, when steam finally gave way to (un-headboarded) diesels.

The Glasgow-bound service takes the right fork away from the Edinburgh line at Hilton Junction, south of Perth, 29 September 1953. *(W.J.V. Anderson/Rail Archive Stephenson)*

THE ORCADIAN

Inverness–Wick/Thurso

Inaugural titled run	29 June 1962
Last titled run	5 September 1964

Only headboard	**Introduced 29 June 1962. In use for three Summers only** Circular, 15in diameter, wooden, painted; a Viking longboat at sail on the open sea depicted in a large (12in) central disc. Title in black letters (2½in) on a white background around the upper circumference, as an integral part of the whole.

- The title was allocated to the 9.05 a.m. northbound service and the 1.15 p.m. return working from Wick – a tight turnround on a four-hour schedule.

Left: A close-up of the unusual wooden board. *(Courtesy Sheffield Railwayana Auctions)*

Below: July 1962, and Wick station is about to witness the departure of the most northerly titled train. The Inverness-based Sulzer diesel No. D53xx will work the entire 161½ miles to the Highland capital. Note the tablet-exchange apparatus, recessed into the cabside. *(Roger Holmes, courtesy Photos of the Fifties)*

ADDITIONAL TITLES

THE ELECTRIC SCOTS

Glasgow (Central)–Euston   *(ScR initiative)*

Headboard   **Introduced 6 May 1974**

Large wooden headboard in ScR light blue with white lettering on three lines; destinations above, the only headboard to display both terminal points. Used for a very brief period – perhaps only on 6 May – when the new timetable began and heralded the introduction of full electric working over the entire West Coast Main Line.

The Scottish Region of British Railways celebrated the inauguration of through electric working to Euston by introducing a short-lived (but large) headboard that covered both the 'Royal Scot' and 'Clansman' workings. Here the 'Royal Scot' is soon to depart from Glasgow (Central) behind a class 87 5,000hp Bo-Bo electric with the very prominent pristine headboard on 6 May 1974. The London Midland Region made no equivalent gesture. *(NRM/SSPL)*

The Type 6 headboard. Surprisingly these came both with and without a full stop, and were the only boards to include this – at the end, rather than to abbreviate.
See CTAC. *(Author, with permission of NRM)*

THE LIVERPOOL (RIVERSIDE) BOAT TRAINS

Euston–Liverpool (Riverside)

These were not expresses that appeared in the public timetable, but ran as and when required, in similar manner to the Southampton Docks boat trains (see Southern Section). Riverside station was the property of the Mersey Docks & Harbour Board, and as such did not appear in any BR timetable. It closed on 1 March 1971, having opened on 10 July 1895 for the LNWR boat trains.

EMPRESS VOYAGER

Title introduced	12 May 1953
Title withdrawn	1966
Headboard	BR Type 6 with red background.

These were run to connect with Canadian Pacific sailings, and initially ran northbound on Tuesdays, southbound on Fridays.

CUNARD SPECIAL

Title introduced	1956
Title withdrawn	1966
Headboard	BR Type 6 with red background.

These were run to connect with Cunard sailings, the last being the departure of Sylvania for New York on 24 November 1966.

- Only five LMR cast-aluminium headboards did not contain the definite article: these two, the diesel version of ROYAL SCOT, CAMBRIAN RADIO CRUISE and CONDOR.
- EMPRESS VOYAGER and CUNARDER boat trains also ran between Glasgow (St Enoch) and Greenock (Princes Pier) – returning to Glasgow (Central) – for much the same period as the Liverpool trains. Although both these services carried roofboards, neither was headboarded.

Euston again, with the 1950s CUNARD SPECIAL roofboard, enclosed by company images in house colours. *(NRM/SSPL)*

Although the LMS did not confer headboards on its engines, it did make extensive use of carriage roofboards. In this mid-thirties scene at Euston CANADIAN PACIFIC roofboards are being removed from a recent arrival from Liverpool (Riverside). Note the 'finger pointers' on the platform numbers and the CUNARD roofboard on the left-hand trolley, July 1935. *(NRM/SSPL)*

No. D210 has just been named *Empress of Britain Canadian Pacific Steamships* at Euston on 12 May 1960. The naming ceremony complete, No. D210 has moved to the platform end and awaits departure for Camden. The appropriate headboard adorns the rear nose, on which folding indicator discs are prominent. *(NRM/SSPL)*

CONDOR

(London) Hendon–Gushetfaulds (Glasgow) (Overnight freight service)

First run	16 March 1959
Last run	26 October 1967

(Birmingham) Aston–Gushetfaulds

First run	7 January 1963
Last run	About a month after the Hendon service

Headboards	Hendon service – split lettering (vertically). Aston service – solid lettering (not illustrated). Both BR Type 6 with left-hand half LMR red, right-hand half ScR blue, colours reversed on bracket stem.

- CONDOR is a contraction of 'containers-door-to-door'.
- The service ran five nights per week, taking ten hours for the 400 miles from Hendon. Fully loaded, the twenty-seven wagons grossed 550 tons, all wagons having roller-bearing axleboxes, and the train was vacuum-braked throughout.
- After their last runs under this title both trains became 'Freightliner' services.

TRANS PENNINE

Headboard	Introduced 2 January 1961 A large rectangular board with rounded corners on which was painted TRANS PENNINE within a horizontally 'stretched' pentagon, letter size reducing from the centre outwards. The only headboard to feature tapered lettering.

Swindon-built Cross-Country sets each of six cars operated this service. Initially it comprised ten trains per day each way between Leeds (City) and Manchester (Exchange), of which five trains per day extended through to Hull (Paragon) and Liverpool (Lime Street).

CTAC SCOTTISH TOURS EXPRESS

Throughout the 1950s and in conjunction with BR the CTAC (Creative Tourist Agents Conference) ran tours of Scotland for rail staff on an 'all inclusive' basis. For instance in 1954 every Sunday from 5 June staff from the Lancashire/Yorkshire/Stoke/Leicester/Nottingham/Birmingham regions could book a (reduced charge) week's tour for £15 7s 6d per person. Travel was by special train throughout (though some bus tours and steamer cruises were included) and hotel accommodation was provided overnight.

Headboard	Non-standard. Strongly resembled BR Type 7 but with more noticeable 'shoulders'. Background colours varied, blue, red and grey being noted, the latter also having twin 'Scotland' badges on either side of CTAC. Cast aluminium.

The Hendon service headboard. No other board had two regional colours, nor split lettering. *(Author, with permission of NRM)*

A close-up of the well laid-out cast headboard complete with the rarely seen 'Scotland' badges on the top line. *(Courtesy Sheffield Railwayana Auctions)*

THE NORTH WALES HOLIDAY TRAINS

GOLDEN SANDS EXPRESS	CAMBRIAN RADIO CRUISE
THE WELSH DRAGON	NORTH WALES LAND CRUISE
THE WELSH CHIEFTAIN	NORTH WALES RADIO LAND CRUISE

When THE WELSH DRAGON was introduced in July 1950 to run as a shuttle service between Rhyl and Llandudno, it was not the first service of this type to operate along that stretch of the North Wales coast. Back in the summer of 1931 (for all these and subsequent trains ran summer only) the LMS had put on the GOLDEN SANDS EXPRESS between the same points. This made three return trips per day that were not advertised by this name in the timetable, but nevertheless displayed the title on a loco headboard. This local initiative was backed by the then LMS authorities, and later BR's Chester District management repeated the enterprise.

THE WELSH DRAGON went on to become quite long-lived, its final season being summer 1970, though it had been a diesel multiple unit service (named on roofboards only) since 1956. Its success, however, spawned a whole series of 'Land Cruise' trains taking holiday-makers on full-day circular tours of scenic North Wales. 1951 saw the introduction of the 'Festival Land Cruise' train, and although no headboard was carried in that year, it was advertised locally under this name and performed a 152-mile circuit from Rhyl. In the following year it was re-titled as the NORTH WALES LAND CRUISE, and was joined by a second train that started and finished at Llandudno. The Rhyl train (only) was headboarded under this name from 1952 to 1958, despite being advertised as the 'Coronation Land Cruise' in 1953. Both trains followed each other clockwise round the circuit (for route, see page 148).

In 1954 the two LMR NWLC trains were joined by a third, this time from Llandudno Junction, which ran anticlockwise. Additionally, the WR commenced running its own 'Cruise' train, using Pwllheli as a departure point, also covering the circuit anticlockwise. These four were continued in season 1955 unchanged, but in 1956 the train from Llandudno became the CAMBRIAN RADIO CRUISE and in 1957 the WR train was named NORTH WALES RADIO LAND CRUISE. As the names imply, both services were equipped with public address facilities throughout the trains, and a descriptive commentary was broadcast to passengers. The Rhyl train remained advertised as a NWLC, but the Llandudno Junction train was dropped. A further attraction came the following year (1958) when an ex-DEVON BELLE Pullman observation car was included at the rear of the Rhyl NWLC. This train then gained the new title THE WELSH CHIEFTAIN in 1959 and

Opposite, upper: The northbound container train from Hendon heads down the four-track Midland main line with the overnight service to Glasgow. Motive power is provided by two of Derby (17A) depot's 1,200hp Co-Bos, which were regularly diagrammed for this service at the time. The folding-disc code indicates a class 4 train, i.e. express freight vacuum-fitted throughout. *(NRM/SSPL)*

Opposite, middle: Those travelling first class would enjoy the forward view towards Liverpool (Lime Street) as the six-car unit leaves Manchester (Exchange) on a through working from Hull. Note the carriage symbol on the body side and the (not-in-use) four-character headcode panel. The second car displays a TRANS PENNINE roofboard. *(NRM/SSPL)*

Opposite, lower: 'Jubilee' 4–6–0 No. 45719 *Glorious* takes water at Dillicar troughs (in the Lune Valley) while heading north with special working C380, 7 June 1952. The C denoted a Central Division originating station (i.e. broadly ex-Midland Railway stations). *(Author's collection)*

reversed its running direction to complete the Rhyl–Rhyl cycle anticlockwise. These titled trains then ran as a trio during 1959, 1960 and 1961 but all three ceased for good in September 1961 (though the observation car went on to see further use in Scotland on the Inverness to Kyle of Lochalsh route).

The above account covers mostly those holiday trains that, for some part of their existence, bore headboards. Others, although advertised as 'named,' did not. The 'Snowdonian', for instance, carried roofboards only and ran Rhyl–Llanberis and back between 1954 and 1964, when the branch line to Llanberis was closed completely (having lost its passenger service in 1930). This train, like the GOLDEN SANDS EXPRESS mentioned above, had been an LMS excursion in the 1930s. In addition, the 'Clwyd Ranger' performed out and back excursions between Llandudno and Corwen (via Rhyl) twice a week in 1959/60, though as a DMU it also carried only roofboards.

Route: (LMR trains, clockwise): Rhyl–Denbigh–Ruthin–Corwen–Dolgelley–Barmouth–Harlech–Portmadoc–Afon Wen–Caernarvon–Bangor–Llandudno Junction–Rhyl (1950s spellings used here).

It should be noted that large parts of this 152-mile circuit were single track, and that from February 1953 the Ruthin–Corwen Section was nominally freight only. This was also true of the line between Rhyl and Denbigh from September 1955, so that for the last six years of operation the 'Cruise' trains used about 30 miles of freight-only railway in their itineraries.

Headboard details are as follows.

GOLDEN SANDS EXPRESS	Rectangular wooden board, with dark painted letters on a light-coloured background; three lines. Carried on smokebox door, centrally in upper half. Used 1931 only(?).
THE WELSH DRAGON	Similar in outline to the ROYAL SCOT headboard of 1950. Rectangular wooden board (49in × 9¼in) surmounted by a shield (16in × 16in overall) containing a depiction of a left-facing dragon. Letter size 3in for THE, otherwise 4in high. White letters on a red or maroon background. Used 1950–5 and intermittently afterwards if the roofboarded DMU set was unavailable.
NORTH WALES LAND CRUISE	Rectangular wooden board. Left-facing dragon (red) in central dark green circle. Cream lettering around circumference. Background red or maroon. Used 1952–8 inclusive.
CAMBRIAN RADIO CRUISE	BR Type 7 with a maroon background. Decorative shield on lower line between RADIO and CRUISE. Shield 6in wide, 7½in high, top half white, bottom dark green with a left-facing dragon straddling both halves. The only Type 7 board to feature two lines only. Used 1956–1961.
THE WELSH CHIEFTAIN	BR Type 6 with a red or maroon background. Used 1959–61.

• For the NORTH WALES RADIO LAND CRUISE, see the Additional Titles of the Western Section.

The scene at Rhyl on the day of introduction of the service. Four young girls in national costume grace the buffer beam of an Ivatt 2–6–2 tank engine before its 17-mile run to Llandudno. The elaborate framework necessary to secure the headboard between the outer lamp irons is well seen. Note also 'British Railways' in full along the side tank, 3 July 1950. *(Jim Parry)*

A 1931 shot of this locally named, headboarded, LMS train at Colwyn Bay. An ex-LNWR 'George the Fifth' class 4–4–0 provides the motive power. *(Milepost 92½/A.W.V. Mace)*

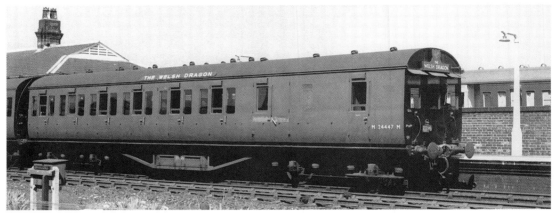

Being a push-pull service (sometimes two-car, sometimes three-car), the headboard could, with advantage, also be placed on the leading vehicle when running backwards. This unique arrangement is seen here at Abergele, the driving coach being complete with roofboards. *(R.S. Carpenter Photos)*

Caernarvon No. 1 signal-box is passed by No. 46428 returning the NORTH WALES LAND CRUISE towards Rhyl in July 1953. A neat rake of six ex-LMS coaches in carmine and cream is in tow, the cafeteria car being the fourth vehicle. The engine carries the headboard on the smokebox door, the only LMR services to do so. *(W.G. Rear)*

Since privatisation Virgin has been the only Train Operating Company to venture into headboard provision, albeit briefly. Two contrasting applications are seen here, with a highly positioned 'sticker' on HST power car No. 43068 at Reading in 1999, and a rare view on 1 December 1998 of class 87 No. 87008 at Euston with a cast board bearing a passing resemblance to the original 1950 version but with a modernised lion. (*Both photographs courtesy Darren Ford*)

1

5

2

6

3

7

4

8

1 & 2   (Author, with permission of NRM)   5   (Author's collection)
3   (Author, courtesy Paul Tilley)   7   (Author, courtesy Frank Burridge)
4, 6 & 8   (Courtesy Sheffield Railwayana Auctions)

1

4

2

5

3

1 & 4   *(Author, courtesy Steam Museum of the GWR)*
2, 3 & 5   *(Author, with permission of NRM)*
6   Enlargement of the arms, crest and motto of
           the Society of Merchant Venturers. *(Author,*
           with permission of NRM)

6

The London-bound train at Newport in June 1961 with No. 6028 *King George VI* in charge. This engine name was also being carried by No. 46244 at the time, a rare instance of dual naming. (*Courtesy the late D.C. Tritton/Colour Rail/BRW 1856*)

A month earlier, May 1961, sees No. 46143 *The South Staffordshire Regiment* about to leave Manchester Central with the Up service. Nowadays the express would be standing inside the GMEX centre, itself served by a modern tramway system. (*Colour Rail/BRM 1623*)

June again, but this time BR is only eighteen months old as No. 34011 *Tavistock* is serviced at Exmouth Junction shed. The engine wears the experimental apple green livery. Note the painted serrations on the red wing-plate. (The late W.H.G. Boot/Colour Rail/ BRS 164)

No. D9001 *St Paddy* rushes north near Brookman's Park with train 1N24 and displays the rarely seen 3rd style headboard. It's May 1962 and most (but not all) Pullman cars have been replaced by new vehicles from Metro-Cammell, riding on Commonwealth bogies, at least six of which can be seen here. (*The late C.R. Gordon Stuart/Colour Rail/DE 2366*)

1

4

2

5

3

6

Note the different angles to the vertical of the flagpoles. The Dutch disc has probably been refixed at some stage, therefore. (*Courtesy Sheffield Railwayana Auctions*)

(*Courtesy Sheffield Railwayana Auctions*)

(*Courtesy Sheffield Railwayana Auctions*)

A wooden pattern. (*Courtesy Sheffield Railwayana Auctions*)

(*Author, courtesy Sheffield Railwayana Auctions*)

For further details of all the headboards in this colour section, see the text for each individual title.

Holbeck 'Jubilee' No. 45566 *Queensland* heads the southbound train at Gloucester Eastgate, 12 May 1961. The rarely seen Type 6 headboard adorns the upper lamp bracket. (*B.J. Ashworth*)

Double headboarding was extremely unusual, but here at Crewe North *City of Birmingham* has worked in from Perth displaying two boards, 7 September 1958. The engine still exists, appropriately housed in Birmingham Museum. (*Alan Chandler/Colour Rail/BRM 2263*)

Accession year, 1952. Not only is the engine in blue livery, but so is the headboard. The 'Merchant Navy' is No. 35027 *Port Line*, which carried the BR blue from April 1950 until repainted green in November 1953. Photographed at Victoria, the headboard was painted blue for a considerably shorter time than the loco, though the exact period is uncertain. No. 35027 (in its rebuilt form) still exists in preservation. (*S.E. Teasdale/ Colour Rail/BRS 818*)

Silver Jubilee year, 1977. Although not diagrammed to work the train on a regular basis, class 47 locos were nevertheless given the opportunity of carrying the headboard if the need arose. This did, however, entail the provision of an alternative backing frame design suitable for attachment to these locos, as seen here on No. 47527 at York on 22 September. (*Fastline Films*)

Golden Jubilee year, 2002. The Royal Train is steam-hauled again after a lapse of thirty-five years, Holyhead, 11 June. The engine is No. 6233 *Duchess of Sutherland* and the headboard is a modern-day version of the LMR 1953 Coronation headboard, which itself doubled occasionally on Royal trains in the 1950s. Note also the red lamps arranged in the unique Royal Train headcode position. These lamps were specially made for the occasion, a fifth being presented to the Queen at Llandudno Junction. (*Brian Dobbs*)

BR class 4 No. 75054 heads south along the single-track, freight-only railway, but carries both 'express passenger' lamps and a named train headboard. In addition, the station, St Asaph between Rhyl and Denbigh, had been closed for five years when this August 1960 shot was taken. The six diverse coaches used on this train all had interesting histories in themselves. *(W.G. Rear)*

Rhyl shed's Standard class 4 No. 75028 at Portmadoc heading south over the level crossing on 25 August 1959. It has the headboard on the buffer beam between the 'express passenger' headlamp code. The ex-LMS stock is now in maroon, the cafeteria is the third coach and the last (out of sight) will be the observation car. *(Hamish Stevenson)*

STRATHPEFFER SPA

Aviemore—Strathpeffer (Highland Railway)

Headboard

Introduced 1913, Summer only, Tuesday only, northbound only
This was the 2.30 p.m. ex-Aviemore that ran direct to Dingwall – omitting Inverness station – and arrived at the spa town of Strathpeffer (where the Highland Railway had opened a new hotel) at 4.15 p.m. Also ran in 1914 but not thereafter.

- The train was not named as such in the timetable, but an advertisement on the inside rear cover gave details.
- The train ran to connect with the 2.14 p.m. arrival of the train from Edinburgh, Glasgow, Dundee and Perth. The return service from Strathpeffer ran via Inverness station.

Highland Railway 4–4–0 No. 129 *Loch Maree, c.* 1913. Whether or not this qualifies as a true headboard is open to some debate. This is the only known shot of it, and the HR did not headboard any of its other expresses, nor did it follow the North British practice of displaying destination boards in this position. More than ninety years later it is unlikely that the matter will be definitively resolved, but it was an interesting train in its own right, headboarded or not. *(NRM/SSPL)*

Chapter Four

TITLED EXPRESSES OF THE NBR
AND PRE-WAR LNER

INTRODUCTION TO LNER HEADBOARDS 1923–39

The LNER came into being on 1 January 1923 and was a result of the Railways Act of 1921, under which several companies were amalgamated to become what was generally referred to as the East Coast Group. Prominent among these were the Great Eastern, the Great Central, and the three companies that formed the backbone of the Anglo–Scottish east coast route, namely the Great Northern, the North Eastern and the North British. Having absorbed the latter company, the LNER found itself in the unique position (among the 'Big Four' companies created by the 1921 Act) of having inherited a company that already used

As far as is known, THE SILVER JUBILEE, seen here at Doncaster Carriage Works, *c.* 1937, was only the second express (after THE FLYING SCOTSMAN in 1932) to run with a distinctive tailboard. All three of the high-speed streamlined trains also had twin lamps on the rear coach, and it will be noted that the lamp brackets are not in symmetrical positions, one being higher than the other. *(NRM/SSPL)*

loco headboards for two of its titled trains. Granted, there were only two, and even these were confined to summer-only operation in lowland Scotland. However, the LNER did not curtail this practice, and for the first five years of its existence these internal Scottish services were the only services to carry headboards on the LNER, or indeed anywhere in the UK.

From 1927 onwards the LNER developed its express passenger services beyond recognition. In 1927 many expresses were officially named for the first time, these names appearing both in the public timetable and on carriage roofboards. The year 1928 saw the introduction of non-stop running over the 393 miles between London and Edinburgh – a world-record distance. This, however, was only made possible by the invention of the corridor tender. These were unique to the LNER and enabled foot-plate crews to be changed halfway at speed, though they were only used on summer-only non-stop runs by the FLYING SCOTSMAN. This innovation generated huge publicity for the company, and to identify this particular service in the public's eye, the first main-line usage of engine headboards was instituted in the summer of 1928. This was expanded in 1932 when the LNER acknowledged the advertising value of headboards by so equipping twelve of its named services.

A novel wheel arrangement for passenger use was introduced in 1934 when a large 2–8–2 Mikado-type locomotive was built for the difficult Edinburgh–Aberdeen route. At the end of that year the LNER again innovated by having one of these new 2–8–2 engines tested in France at Vitry Testing Station, and out on the (French) main line. The test results proved to H.N. Gresley the value of internally streamlining an engine's steam passages, and in using the Kylchap (Kylala-Chapelon) exhaust system. A further piece in the jigsaw that was to culminate in the SILVER JUBILEE train of 1935 was the development of the wedge-shaped aerodynamic engine front for high-speed running. This shape was based on the Bugatti railcars, then running between Paris and Deauville. A scale model of the 'wedge' was tested in the wind tunnels at both the City & Guilds (Engineering) College and the National Physical Laboratory before being applied to the new A4 class.

Two further streamlined trains entered service in 1937, the CORONATION and the WEST RIDING LIMITED, the former also being streamlined at the rear by having an observation car with the same profile as the engine. Perhaps surprisingly, none of these three 'extra speed' trains sported headboards (tailboards – yes), though with their own specific colour schemes they were pretty distinctive anyway.

And so to 1938, when the Gresley A4 Pacific *Mallard* (with Kylchap double chimney) touched 126 mph on a braking trial – another world record for the LNER. As outlined above, this was only achieved on the back of several years' development work, both at home and abroad, and Gresley's collaboration with André Chapelon in France was instrumental in this success. Although the war years and their aftermath precluded any return to running the streamlined trains, the well-established practice of naming other expresses, and providing them with headboards, was reinstituted in the last two years of the LNER's independent existence.

Some of the 1932–9 standard headboards survived to be reused (presumably repainted first) after the Second World War; indeed, a few made it to well into the nationalised era. Amazingly, one or two (at least) of these originals from the LNER pre- and postwar periods still exist today.

During the war itself the use of headboards, tailboards and roofboards was officially banned, but as the vast majority of train titles also disappeared from the timetables, they

The first four A4 Pacifics, Nos 2509–12, were introduced in 1935 with a silver-grey livery specifically to work the SILVER JUBILEE streamlined train between London and Newcastle. These, however, were not their sole duties, and here No. 2510 *Quicksilver* is about to depart from Newcastle with the southbound FLYING SCOTSMAN. The engine name was painted on the boiler casing from new, and was only replaced by a cast nameplate when the loco gained blue livery in 1938. *(By permission of Hull University Archives)*

were superfluous anyway. Three trains escaped this anonymity, however, as the FLYING SCOTSMAN, NIGHT SCOTSMAN and ABERDONIAN names lived on in all the timetables (except the Emergency Timetable, October–December 1939) throughout the years 1939–45 inclusive. These were the only services, nationally, to do so. Strings were pulled somewhere.

Looking ahead a little, after nationalisation the practice of providing loco headboards for named expresses was not only continued by BR but expanded throughout the country, a direct legacy of the LNER's 1932 policy. It could also be said (with some truth) that BR's successful High Speed Trains (HSTs) were simply a 'dusting-off' of the CORONATION idea forty years earlier (with a change of motive power). It was, after all, not a bad concept to bequeath.

Leeds Central in the early 1930s sees Ivatt C1 Atlantic No. 3280 with the QUEEN OF SCOTS headboard. The 4–4–2 has brought the train in from London, uncoupled, and given the northbound departure a push-start, though only along the platform length, and will stop at the signals. *(The Stephenson Locomotive Society)*

THE HEADBOARDS DESCRIBED

Part 1: Depot-made, 1923–32
Part 2: Works-made, 1932–9
Part 3: Tailboards

Part 1: Depot-made, 1923–32

The situation in 1923 was that the only headboarded services the LNER inherited from its constituent parts were two trains from the North British Railway. These were the LOTHIAN COAST EXPRESS and the FIFE COAST EXPRESS. Both ran summers only and both were introduced, and headboarded, in 1912. Both were withdrawn after three years of operation and reintroduced (by the NBR) in 1920. Until 1 May 1928 only these two, of the several LNER titled expresses, carried loco headboards.

The NBR had initiated the practice of placing destination boards on its engines in about 1908. These consisted of a painted-metal plate in the shape of a curved rectangle, usually contained one word only and were positioned centrally on the front of the engine just below the chimney. They were not, however, placed on the lamp iron but secured by two well-spaced vertical 'pegs' protruding downwards from the board that sank into metal slots attached for the purpose around the rim of the smokebox, above the smokebox door. The boards' lettering was white shaded black, on a red background, and they were double-sided, front and back showing a different destination.

Out of this basic shape grew the three-word single-sided boards for the two titled trains of 1912. These were in two lines, with COAST EXPRESS on the lower, LOTHIAN OR FIFE centrally above these, the boards being 'stepped' to contain the three words fairly closely. These types continued in use throughout the early LNER period with the 'Lothian' version surviving until 1930 (at least), though it is believed both were restricted to usage east of Edinburgh, that is, they are presumed to have been made at Haymarket. However, both trains also used a second type of headboard, which was probably provided by Glasgow (Eastfield) depot, namely the familiarly shaped two-line curved rectangle with rounded corners. These both had EXPRESS (only) on the bottom line, with the lettering cream (?) on a dark blue (?) rather than red background. The method and position of fixing were as described above.

A third variety must also be mentioned. This was a LOTHIAN COAST EXPRESS curved rectangle with the lower line indented at both ends – a unique shape and, significantly, fixed to the top lamp iron by a central bracket on the rear. The lettering was shaded and the background most likely red. This was an LNER board dating from c.1930 and was still in use when the title was withdrawn in 1934.

The familiar black-lettering-on-a-white-background, single-sided curved rectangle headboard with central bracket on the rear, was thus a direct descendant of the earlier NBR boards, and made its appearance, as a Haymarket product, on the inaugural southbound non-stop FLYING SCOTSMAN on Tuesday 1 May 1928. Whether this was one-upmanship on Haymarket's part, a natural extension of a long-standing practice at that depot or lack of communication between King's Cross and Haymarket is of course speculation, but suffice to say that it was to be a fortnight before King's Cross depot had made up its own equivalent headboard ready to go north, thus ensuring that both the non-stops were headboarded for the remainder of that summer. The winter timetable FLYING SCOTSMAN was not, however, non-stop, and neither was it headboarded, so that usage of headboards up to 1932 may be summarised as follows:

Summer only: 1923–7   LOTHIAN/FIFE COAST EXPRESS
Summer only: 1928–31 The above, plus FLYING SCOTSMAN

REFERENCE   5/1   **90**

(5495)
Est. 494—100 bks., 200 lvs.—8/30.

THE LONDON & NORTH EASTERN RAILWAY
(GREAT NORTHERN SECTION.)

LOCOMOTIVE DRAWING OFFICE,

[Stamp: LONDON & NORTH EASTERN RAILWAY / LOCOMOTIVE DRAWING OFFICE / 30 MAY 1932 / DONCASTER.]

Memo. to *Robt. A. Thom Esq*

Train Name Boards on Engines.

Your Reference S.609. dated 28th May.

*Herewith Copy of Drawing Y-1162N
Train name boards on Engines. This
drawing was prepared in reply to
your letter dated May 13th.
It differs from the original boards
made at Kings Cross in being fitted
with a more substantial bracket and
a spring for securing it on to the
Smokebox Lamp iron.*

A. Broughton

A copy of the original letter referred to in the text on page 160. *(By permission of Hull University Archives)*

A rare survivor of an original LNER pre-war headboard, drawing Y1162N. The face is repainted on top of the lettering that was still visible beneath. *(Harwich Railway & Shipping Museum, Bob Clow Collection)*

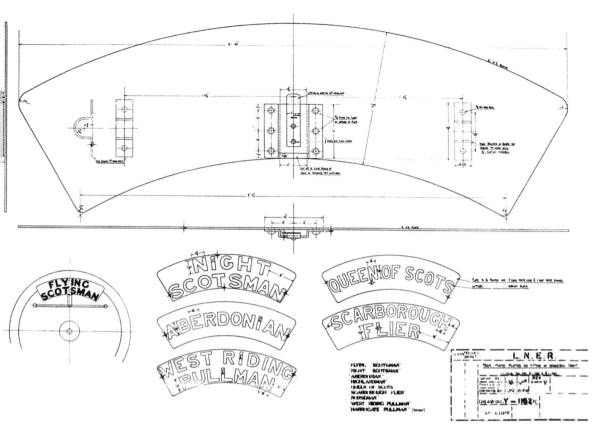

Doncaster drawing Y1162N referred to in the letter of 28 May 1932 (opposite). *(NRM/SSPL)*

These were provided by the depots at Eastfield, Haymarket and King's Cross. In the case of the Anglo-Scottish service, obviously these boards were subject to much greater wear and tear, and it appears (from photographic evidence) that these were regularly repainted before the summer season began. Certainly there were numerous differences of letter form and spacing on these hand-painted boards. One further variation is worthy of note and concerns the two successive days in 1930 when 4–6–4 No. 10000 worked the non-stop, south on 31 July, north the following day. On its arrival at King's Cross the headboard was carried on the upper lamp iron, as was the practice, but on 1 August it was fixed to the handrail across the smokebox access doors. Close inspection of photographs of the occasion reveals that, between the two runs, King's Cross shed must have fitted two extra brackets to the rear so that it could be clipped to the handrail. Evidence of these additions is seen in the two pairs of studs, or bolt heads, visible between the letters F and C (on the left) and G and A (on the right).

As the 4–6–4 did not again work this service (or indeed any other headboarded train pre-war, it seems), these turned out to have been superfluous, but were nevertheless incorporated into the Works Drawing that Doncaster produced for the 1932 issues. The headboard itself continued to see service on A1/A3 locos, as other photos confirm.

Part 2: Works-made, 1932–9

The year 1932 saw the mutual abolition, by the LMS and LNER jointly, of the agreement made between the West Coast and East Coast companies (back in 1900) that the daytime Anglo-Scottish expresses should take a minimum of 8¼ hours. This agreement had been a consequence of the 1895 Race to Aberdeen, and had been overdue for abandonment for some years. The immediate effect was a general acceleration of the LNER's several titled services, and this resulted in the advertising department obtaining sanction for engine headboards to be carried on all these expresses, all year round. This provision was also to be made a 'works' job, and gave rise to the memo to Robert A. Thom (Senior Mechanical Engineer) from H. Broughton (Chief Locomotive Draughtsman), stamped Locomotive Drawing Office, Doncaster, 30 May 1932 (see page 158).

These (single-sided) boards were to be made to the same size and style as before (on FLYING SCOTSMAN) and were available by the start of the summer service on 18 July 1932.

It is presumed that this initial batch (numbers unknown) were sent out to depots already painted by Doncaster Works, but that subsequent re-paintings were carried out by depot signwriters. The drawing also includes the provision of two extra brackets 'on boards for engine No. 10000 only'. It is not thought that any of these works boards actually provided these, however.

Three Liverpool Street services also gained headboards at more or less the same time, though since these were not named on drawing Y1162N it is difficult to be precise as to dates. However, either during the summer or autumn the FLUSHING CONTINENTAL, SCANDINAVIAN and EASTERN BELLE were added to the list, making fourteen headboarded titles in all (twelve English, two Scottish), though five of these ran summer only. 1932 was therefore the year that the loco headboard officially arrived on a noticeable scale on LNER main lines. (Elsewhere, the only headboard being carried at this time was that for the CHELTENHAM FLYER WORLD'S FASTEST TRAIN and this was the GWR's only venture into headboards.)

In 1933 the number of titles sporting headboards increased by one, the NORTHERN BELLE. This title has an interesting prelude in that a 'trial' of five proposed designs of headboard for this train was held in May, and these were made available for inspection in Doncaster Works yard. (Just why, only one year after the introduction of the standard LNER type, it was thought necessary to consider a new version is a good, unresolved, question.) However, a new version was duly adopted for this luxury touring train (first week's tour commenced 16 June) and was subsequently also applied to three other titles, namely the SCARBOROUGH FLIER (year unknown), the QUEEN OF SCOTS (1936) and the YORKSHIRE PULLMAN (1938?), though only in the latter's case was it the sole type of headboard used. No drawing exists for this, the second standard version, but it would appear to have measured approximately 46in wide and 5¾in deep.

The application of this type of headboard to the QUEEN OF SCOTS came in October/November 1936, when Copley Hill received its first allocation of Pacifics. These had not previously been allowed into Leeds (from Doncaster) on a regular basis until the Calder Viaduct at Wakefield had been strengthened. The delay in the provision of any headboard at all for the YORKSHIRE PULLMAN is, however, rather puzzling. The service commenced on 30 September 1935 and was effectively a retitling of the

WEST RIDING PULLMAN, with Hull replacing Newcastle as a destination. Why these redundant headboards were not immediately repainted to say 'Yorkshire' instead of 'West Riding'is unknown, but the author can find no evidence that this happened, or any headboardbeing supplied earlier than July 1938. It may be that, after the WEST RIDING LIMITED began running on 27 September 1937, with the southbound YORKSHIRE PULLMAN re-routed from Harrogate to Doncaster via York in consequence, the headboard wascarried from this earlier date. This again is speculation – can anyone help on this point?

All the headboards of this period were hand-painted, and with the universal adoption by the LNER of the Gill Sans letter face it was inevitable that all the early headboards (not in Gill Sans) would be repainted at some stage to conform. Whether this was entirely true in practice is questionable; the writer has yet to see, for example, a photograph of a Gill Sans FLUSHING CONTINENTAL (can any reader remedy this?). At the other end of the scale, over the period 1928–39 there were at least sixty distinguishable varieties of FLYING SCOTSMAN headboard, though it must be remembered here that King's Cross, Grantham, Gateshead and Haymarket would all be involved in providing headboards for this train. Even the official Gill Sans lettering became vertically stretched on its application to the YORKSHIRE PULLMAN, some QUEEN OF SCOTS and some NORTHERN BELLE headboards.

After its 1932 and 1933 rejections the definite article was again proposed for inclusion in a mock-up of THE SILVER JUBILEE headboard, although this got no further than gracing the full-scale model of an A4 front end. However, considering that the carriage roofboards, certain tailboards (when provided) and the public timetables all declared 'The' to be part of the title, loco headboards were definitely the odd man out in this respect, and it's an interesting question as to whose hand was deciding this pre-war, since this policy was immediately reversed in 1946.

Apart from noting the absence of headboards on the streamlined trains of the period – which cannot therefore be described – no further innovation in respect of headboards took place after 1933.

Part 3: Tailboards

During the 1930s the LNER was unique among the 'Big Four' companies in providing tailboards as a means of 'finishing off' the appearance of certain trains. The first to receive this feature was THE FLYING SCOTSMAN (as it said) in the summer of 1932, when the dedicated train sets for this service received tailboards with white lettering in Gill Sans on three lines on a black background. Until 1935 these remained the only examples, when THE SILVER JUBILEE set was similarly adorned by a silver-grey tailboard with dark blue lettering that was definitely Gill Sans on three lines. The CORONATION was next in 1937, for whereas the beaver-tail observation car displayed the title in stainless steel for about 40 per cent of the year, when this was not in use the train sets were completed by tailboards again in the train's colours, this time garter blue with light (Marlborough) blue lettering, and this time omitting the definite article.

Predictably, the fourth train to be so treated was THE WEST RIDING LIMITED, where again the last vestibule was closed off, this time by a tailboard with the title on four lines. (It is presumed that this was also in the train's colours of two-tone blue, though the only photographic evidence seen of this is somewhat 'murky'.)

On the GE Section, the HOOK CONTINENTAL stock was renewed in October 1938 and this set also displayed a tailboard, again omitting 'The'. The colouring of this is uncertain, but was probably white letters on a black background. Another service believed to have benefited from the provision of a tailboard was the EAST ANGLIAN, though no evidence has come to light to prove this. (If anyone can establish that this was the case, the author would be grateful for news of this via the publisher.)

Readers may be surprised to find no reference to Pullman tailboards, as these were definitely in use postwar, but again, no evidence has been found of their existence before this.

The NORTHERN BELLE was a heavy train and is seen here preparing to leave King's Cross in either 1938 or 1939, as *Wild Swan* did not enter service until February 1938. Note that the lettering is now a vertically stretched version of that introduced originally. Unlike the EASTERN BELLE, or the two Southern Railway BELLES, this was not a Pullman car train. *(NRM/SSPL)*

THE TITLED EXPRESSES

LOTHIAN COAST EXPRESS
FIFE COAST EXPRESS   } Internal Scottish services
FLYING SCOTSMAN
ABERDONIAN
NIGHT SCOTSMAN
HIGHLANDMAN
WEST RIDING PULLMAN
SCARBOROUGH FLIER
QUEEN OF SCOTS   } King's Cross services
HARROGATE PULLMAN
NORSEMAN
YORKSHIRE PULLMAN
(THE) SILVER JUBILEE
CORONATION
WEST RIDING LIMITED
FLUSHING CONTINENTAL
HOOK CONTINENTAL   } Liverpool Street services
SCANDINAVIAN

ADDITIONAL TITLES

EASTERN BELLE
NORTHERN BELLE
THAMES-FORTH EXPRESS

All these services appear in the above order on the following pages.

LOTHIAN COAST EXPRESS

Glasgow (Queen Street)–North Berwick / Gullane / Dunbar

Inaugural titled run	3 June 1912 (by NBR)
Title withdrawn	30 September 1914
Reintroduced	1 June 1920 (by NBR)
Last titled run	15 September 1934

(a) 1st style headboard
Introduced 3 June 1912(?)
LOTHIAN on top line, centrally above COAST EXPRESS. Painted-steel plate shaped to surround these words closely, being 'stepped down' on either side of top word. Dark red background, white lettering shaded black. Two well-spaced fixing pegs.

(b) 2nd style headboard
Introduced 3 June 1912(?)
Painted-steel 'curved rectangle' EXPRESS centrally on bottom line. White/cream lettering on dark-coloured background. Two well-spaced fixing pegs.

(c) 3rd style headboard
Introduced *c.* 1930(?)
EXPRESS below LOTHIAN COAST on larger painted-steel board with indentations at each end pointing towards EXPRESS. Unique shape. White shaded lettering on (probably) red background. LNER design with one central bracket.

- This train ran only during the months June–September.
- For the commencement of the 1923 service on 1 June, newly painted LNER stock was acquired and the entire train ran through to North Berwick, with the Gullane and Dunbar portions replaced by connections at Longniddry and Drem respectively.
- It is likely that (b) and (c) were Eastfield products, whereas (a) probably originated at Haymarket.
- This title was not resumed after the Second World War.

D30 4–4–0 No. 9424 *Lady Rowena* (from Scott's novel *Ivanhoe* of 1819) helps to push the empty stock up Cowlairs Bank out of Queen Street station. Note that the fourth coach behind No. 9424 is a Pullman car and that all the coaches appear to have roofboards. The inclusion of the Pullman restaurant car (a practice begun in 1932) makes the period of the photo 1932–4. *(LCGB: Ken Nunn Collection)*

A North British Railway official view of the train at North Berwick, *c.* 1912. The engine is Reid 4–4–0 No. 359 *Dirk Hatteraick*, then almost new, which was to become an LNER class D29 and survive to become BR's No. 62412. Although six coaches are seen here, normally only three would be conveyed from North Berwick to the main-line junction at Drem, where the Dunbar portion would be attached. (The engine is named after a character in Sir Walter Scott's 1815 novel *Guy Mannering*.) *(NRM/SSPL)*

This time another D29 (named after Sir Walter Scott's 1817 novel of that name) rests on Glasgow's Eastfield shed displaying the 3rd style headboard, 9 July 1934. This is an LNER board fixed in the standard position, on the top lamp iron. *(J.T. Rutherford/Transport Treasury)*

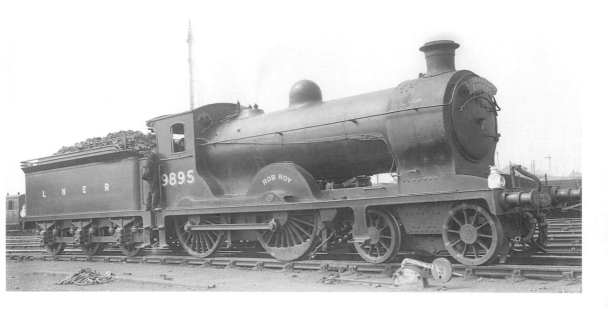

FIFE COAST EXPRESS

Glasgow (Queen Street)–Dundee via Crail and St Andrews
And Edinburgh (Waverley)–Crail via Thornton (from 1923)

Inaugural titled run	1 July 1912 (by NBR)
Title withdrawn	30 September 1914
Reintroduced	1 June 1920 (by NBR)
Title withdrawn	31 August 1939

(a) 1st style headboard	Introduced 1 July 1912(?) As for LOTHIAN COAST EXPRESS with FIFE replacing LOTHIAN.
(b) 2nd style headboard	Introduced 1 July 1912(?) As for LOTHIAN COAST EXPRESS.
(c) 3rd style headboard	Introduced c. 1932 Variation on 2nd style with all three words on top line and CRAIL centrally below. Refers to Edinburgh train only.

• These trains ran only during the months June–September.
• Between 1923 and 1939 the separate Edinburgh train was operated untitled in the timetable.
• The headboard wording did not match that printed in the timetable (for the Glasgow train), which was 'Fifeshire Coast Express'.
• The title was resurrected by British Railways in 1949. See the Eastern Section for details of the headboards carried.

Another NBR posed shot, again with No. 359 and again thought to date from 1912. Not only is the headboard lettering shaded, but so is the engine's name, painted on the splasher, below which the builder's plate reads 'Cowlairs Works 1911'. *(NRM/SSPL)*

D32 No. 9886 leaving the carriage sidings at Craigentinny (Edinburgh) with the stock of the FIFE COAST EXPRESS, *c.* 1926. *(T.G. Hepburn/Rail Archive Stephenson)*

Dundee shed's D32 No. 9885 with the 3rd-style headboard in Craigentinny carriage sidings, 8 August 1932. *(By permission of Hull University Archives)*

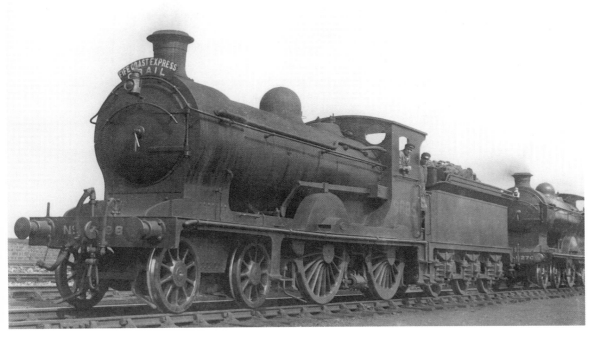

FLYING SCOTSMAN

King's Cross–Edinburgh (Waverley)/Aberdeen

Inaugural titled run	11 July 1927
Title withdrawn	(titled throughout the war years)

(a) 1st style headboard	Introduced 1 May 1928 (Haymarket version)
	15 May 1928 (King's Cross version)
	Painted-steel 'curved rectangle' with rounded corners. Black lettering on two lines with a white background. Central bracket on rear.
	NB: Being hand-painted, these two were distinguishable by virtue of differing letter styles and spacing.
(b) 2nd style headboard	Introduced 18 July 1932
	Visually identical to the 1st style, but 'mass produced' at Doncaster Works and incorporating a more substantial bracket on the rear, which also included a securing spring for tighter fixing of the board onto smokebox lamp irons. LNER standard pattern.
(c) 3rd style headboard	Used 20 May 1932 only(?). See below for details.

- Carriage roofboards describing the train as THE FLYING SCOTSMAN had been introduced from 1 October 1924, when new eleven-coach train sets were brought into service.
- During 1928–31 only the non-stop FLYING SCOTSMAN (which ran summer only) carried headboards into/out of King's Cross.
- 3rd style headboard. On this date an Imperial Airways 42-seat Heracles airliner paced the train between Newark and Doncaster at low altitude. This enabled train and plane passengers to speak to each other via wireless sets in the plane and in the Guard's compartment. Uniquely, engine No. 2744 carried a non-standard one-line curved rectangle headboard with THE FLYING SCOTSMAN in white letters on a dark background (not illustrated).
- These non-stop runs, covering some 393 miles and taking 8¼ hours of running time, plus time for engine preparation and disposal and movement between depots and stations, could not be accomplished by one set of foot-plate staff only. Hence, and concurrent with the introduction of the non-stop workings on 1 May 1928, the LNER also brought into use a unique innovation that enabled two sets of engine crews to change over, halfway between the two capitals, while travelling at speed. This invention was the corridor tender, whereby the relief crew (who had travelled in the front coach) could walk through a special vestibule connection between the first coach and the rear of the loco tender, through a narrow passageway within the tender (on the right-hand side) and emerge, fresh, onto the foot-plate. The crew being relieved then returned to the first coach the same way, and travelled 'on the cushions' for the second half of the journey, as their colleagues had for the first half. This feature was only ever used on the London–Edinburgh non-stop services. The corridor within the tender was 18ft long, 5ft high and only 18in wide, causing some staff no little difficulty in passing through.

King's Cross, 1 May 1928. A famous day, since this marked the commencement of non-stop running between London and Edinburgh, the first use of corridor tenders, and the first appearance of a titled train headboard in London. Standing beneath Haymarket shed's new headboard are fireman McKenzie (left) and driver Henderson, who were in charge for the first half of the southbound journey, while LNER Chairman William Whitelaw presents a souvenir of the occasion to driver Day, with his fireman Gray standing on the engine. A3 Pacific No. 2580 *Shotover* had arrived one minute early at 6.14 p.m. *(Getty Images)*

- The non-stop (summer only) service was accelerated over the years, as follows:

1928–31	8¼ hours	⎫
1932–5	7½ hours	⎬ Using A1 or A3 class Pacifics
1936	7¼ hours	⎭
1937–9	7 hours	Using A4 class Pacifics

From 1937 all twenty-one corridor tenders fitted to the A1 or A3 engines were transferred to A4 locos. The last to relinquish its corridor tender was Haymarket's A3 No. 2570 *Papyrus*, after working the non-stop on 6 and 7 August 1937. Non-stop working of the FLYING SCOTSMAN ceased during the war years, but was resumed in 1948 by British Railways.

The corridor tender attached to No. 4472 *Flying Scotsman* through which footplate crews changed over around 10 miles north of York. *(W.J. Reynolds/Rail Archive Stephenson)*

When the LNER decided to adopt the Gill Sans alphabet typeface throughout the company, this of course included titled train headboards. Eric Gill was himself commissioned to paint a FLYING SCOTSMAN headboard and is seen here standing on No. 4475 *Flying Fox*, having just fixed his own hand-painted headboard to the top lamp bracket. This engine went on to amass what is thought to be the highest lifetime mileage of any British steam engine of 2,642,860 miles over its forty-one years of service. The headboard, in contrast, seems to have disappeared immediately, as the author can find no further evidence of its use whatsoever. King's Cross, 21 November 1932. *(Monotype)*

King's Cross again, this time on the occasion when, on successive days, the four-cylinder high-pressure Compound engine No. 10000 worked its only two trips with the non-stop. After the southbound run on 31 July 1930 the four crew members stand on the buffer beam, and chief mechanical engineer H.N. (later Sir Nigel) Gresley stands on the platform. *(SSPL)*

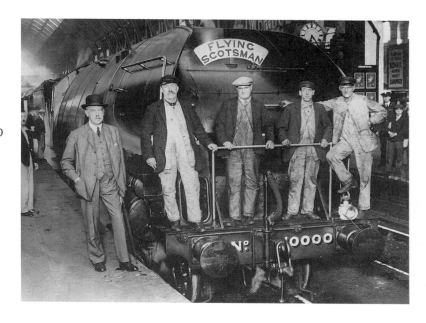

The following day, 1 August, No. 10000 departed north with the 10 a.m. return working. However, close inspection reveals that not only has the headboard-carrying position been changed, but the headboard itself has been modified. Two pairs of studs have now appeared (to the left of F, C and to the right of G, A), signifying the addition to the rear of the headboard of two extra brackets so that the headboard could be attached to the smokebox door handrail. Use of these brackets was specific to this loco only, and the 1932 Doncaster drawings included provision of these. In the event, this engine did not see further use on the non-stop, nor can evidence be found that it carried *any* titled headboard subsequently (pre-Second World War) before or after its rebuilding in 1937. *(Getty Images)*

- The non-stop service was the first to acquire a tailboard on the last coach, from the summer of 1932, saying THE FLYING SCOTSMAN. Inclusion of the definite article in the title was common (though not universal) practice in the public timetable, but was not adopted on LNER headboards until after the Second World War.
- Also in 1932, and as part of the LNER's adoption of the Gill Sans typeface, Eric Gill himself personally affixed the first headboard to use Gill Sans characters, appropriately that for FLYING SCOTSMAN, onto the engine at King's Cross. However, as the winter timetable included stops (and engine changes) at Grantham and Newcastle, four sheds became involved in the provision of the hand-painted headboards, namely King's Cross, Grantham, Gateshead and Haymarket. Hardly surprisingly, the signwriters at these depots did not do identical jobs in the painting of the wording, and at least sixty distinguishable versions have been identified. (This includes pre-1932 non-Gill Sans headboards, and such examples as were repainted for further use postwar.) In the photographs that follow, several differently painted headboards can be seen.

A3 No. 2795 *Call Boy* accelerates through Retford with the southbound non-stop in 1930. The racehorse *Call Boy* had won the Derby only three years earlier. The engine was new in April 1930 and spent almost all of its thirty-three years of working life allocated to Edinburgh's Haymarket depot. *(F.R. Hebron/Rail Archive Stephenson)*

Public exhibitions of rolling stock were a feature of the LNER's Publicity Department and this is Ilford in East London in June 1934. The 'double FLYING SCOTSMAN' combination is in evidence, while the loco on the left is one of Gresley's P2 2–8–2s, No. 2001 *Cock o' the North*, with its rotary-cam poppet valves being admired. *(NRM/SSPL)*

Accelerated timings were not the only aspect to be incorporated into the 1932 non-stop service; tailboards were also introduced. The first was to be found at the rear of the LNER's most prestigious express and is seen here passing through Newcastle, probably in its first summer of operation. *(By permission of Hull University Archives)*

The non-stop service had through coaches for Aberdeen, Glasgow and Perth, and the headboard was carried beyond Edinburgh on the Perth portion. That shed's D49 No. 250 *Perthshire* shows this to good effect at its home depot in about 1930 – which is as far north as the headboard got. *(T.G. Hepburn/Rail Archive Stephenson)*

Opposite, top: 1936 was the last year in which A1/A3 Pacifics were regularly diagrammed for the non-stop, the new A4s taking over for the summers of 1937–9. Here, No. 4489 *Dominion of Canada* hurries the twelve-coach, fully roofboarded northbound service through Finsbury Park in 1938/9. This A4 was unique in carrying a (steam-operated) bell presented by the Canadian Pacific Railway Company and fitted to the engine on 11 March 1938. Although rendered inoperative before the Second World War, it remained in position until December 1957, being removed only when the loco received a double chimney. *(NRM/SSPL)*

Opposite, bottom: The sleeping car train left King's Cross at about 7.30 p.m. and during the summer months it was therefore possible to photograph the express en route. Here, A4 No. 4465 *Guillemot* has at least fifteen vehicles in tow, all carrying roofboards, near Brookman's Park, probably in 1938. Note the lettering differences on the two headboards carried by Nos 2002 and 4465. *(Colling Turner/Rail Archive Stephenson)*

ABERDONIAN

King's Cross–Aberdeen/Elgin/Lossiemouth (Sleeping car train)

Inaugural titled run	11 July 1927
Title withdrawn	(titled throughout the war years)
Only headboard	Introduced 18 July 1932
	LNER standard pattern.

- Elgin and Lossiemouth were only served during the summer when the HIGHLAND-MAN was also running. At other times, portions for Inverness and Fort William took their place.

Aberdeen station on 6 August 1935 sees P2 2–8–2 *Earl Marischal* ready to depart southbound. This engine was the second of the powerful Mikado-type built in 1934 specifically to eliminate double-heading over the difficult road between Edinburgh and Aberdeen. It was, however, rebuilt as a Pacific type in 1944. *(By permission of Hull University Archives)*

NIGHT SCOTSMAN

King's Cross–Glasgow (Queen Street)/Perth/Dundee/Aberdeen (Sleeping car train)

Inaugural titled run	11 July 1927
Title withdrawn	(titled throughout the war years)
Only headboard	Introduced 18 July 1932
	LNER standard pattern.

- Strangely, the title related to the northbound service only. The corresponding southbound working was not named until after the war.

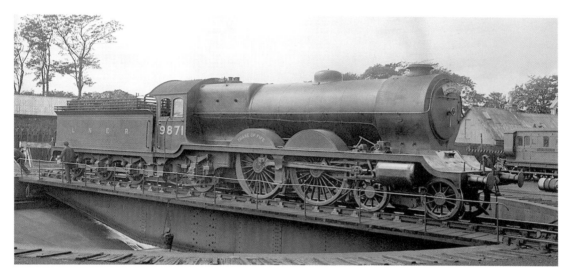

Above: Former NBR C11 *Thane of Fife* carries the headboard while being turned on the turntable at Aberdeen's Ferryhill shed in the early 1930s. All the class had been withdrawn by 1939. *(NRM/SSPL)*

A1 No. 2548 *Galtee More* stands at the King's Cross buffer stops in 1937. Although wearing the headboard, this is not the NIGHT SCOTSMAN (which was titled northbound-only at the time). However, No. 2548 will work this as its next duty. Interestingly, houses and bungalows in Edgware were being advertised as selling new for £755 freehold and £600 leasehold. *(E.E. Smith/Rail Archive Stephenson)*

HIGHLANDMAN

King's Cross–Fort William/Inverness/Nairn (Sleeping car train)

Inaugural titled run	11 July 1927
Last titled run	10 September 1939
Only headboard	Introduced 18 July 1932
	LNER standard pattern.

- This service operated in the summer timetable only, and was essentially a relief train to the ABERDONIAN. When this service was not running the ABERDONIAN included sleeping cars for the first two destinations above also.
- This title was not resumed after the Second World War.

A splendid shot of a rare headboard. Evening sun still shines on King's Cross as the sleeping car train that preceded the ABERDONIAN by about twenty-five minutes waits to leave behind (probably) A1 *Prince Palatine*. *(J.B. Hubback, courtesy John Hodge Collection)*

WEST RIDING PULLMAN

King's Cross—Leeds (Central)/Bradford (Exchange)/Halifax/Harrogate/Newcastle

Inaugural titled run	11 July 1927
Last titled run	28 September 1935
Only headboard	Introduced 18 July 1932
	LNER standard pattern.

- Several lettering variations are to be found in photographs of this headboard.
- The service was replaced by the YORKSHIRE PULLMAN on and from 30 September 1935. This train did not run north of Harrogate, but a portion served Hull instead.

The Ivatt large-boilered Atlantics enjoyed an Indian summer on the Leeds expresses, and some of their best work was done on the crack Pullman train. C1 4–4–2 No. 4444 is seen here with six cars for Leeds and beyond, and two (at the rear) for Bradford and Halifax. *(NRM/SSPL)*

SCARBOROUGH FLIER

King's Cross–Scarborough (Central)/Whitby (Town)

Inaugural titled run	11 July 1927
Title withdrawn	9 September 1939

(a) 1st style headboard	Introduced 18 July 1932
	LNER standard pattern.
(b) 2nd style headboard	Introduced 1935/6
	Shallow LNER pattern.

* This service operated in the summer timetable only.
* Use of the 2nd style headboard is thought to have been confined to the York–Scarborough Section.
* 'Flier' (on the headboard) was spelt 'Flyer' in the timetable.
* This title was reintroduced on 5 June 1950.

The first of the conversions from A1 to A3 class (in 1927), Pacific No. 4480 *Enterprise* heads the London-bound service over the water troughs at Langley, south of Stevenage, probably in 1932/3. Note the GNR somersault distant signal and the plethora of telegraph posts and wiring. *(Colling Turner/Rail Archive Stephenson)*

King's Cross again, this time at the buffer stops, where A4 No. 4903 *Peregrine* has recently arrived non-stop from York, where this loco was attached. No. 4903 was the last A4 to be built (in July 1938) and was one of only four of the class to receive a double chimney from new. It was renamed *Lord Faringdon* by British Railways in March 1948. The photo must date from the summer of 1938 or 1939, and several differences in lettering are evident from the earlier shot of No. 4480. *(The Stephenson Locomotive Society)*

The main-line engine was detached at York and the train taken forward by one of various smaller types. On this occasion D49 4–4–0 *The Percy* awaits the arrival of the train from London and carries the shallow-pattern headboard with Gill Sans lettering. The three different positions in which the headboards are being carried will be observed. The very high lamp iron on the D49 – above the boiler profile – was typical of engines allocated to former North Eastern Railway depots, and mitigated against the placing of any headboard here (especially the standard pattern) for fear of it being blown off. *(NRM/SSPL)*

QUEEN OF SCOTS

King's Cross–Glasgow (Queen Street) via Leeds and Harrogate (Pullman car train)

Inaugural titled run	1 May 1928
Title withdrawn	2 September 1939

(a) 1st style headboard	Introduced 18 July 1932
	LNER standard pattern.
(b) 2nd style headboard	Introduced *c.* 1936
	Shallow LNER pattern.

- This title was reintroduced on 5 July 1948.

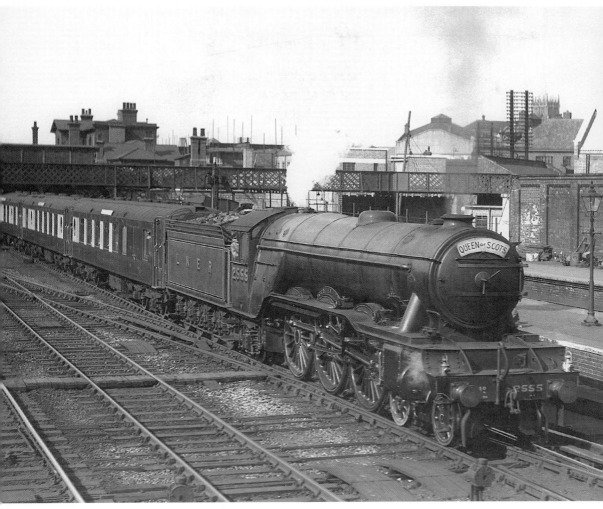

It was only after October 1936, when the bridge spanning the River Calder at Wakefield was strengthened, that Pacifics were allowed to work regularly over the Doncaster–Leeds sector. Copley Hill then immediately received two A1 class 4–6–2s and one of these, No. 2555 *Centenary*, is seen passing through Doncaster with the Up train on 12 August 1939. Note the 'mid-air' positioning, and small size, of OF. *(The Gresley Society/H.C. Doyle)*

Opposite, top: 'Director' class D11 4–4–0 No. 5510 *Princess Mary* was only allocated to Copley Hill shed (Leeds) between June 1931 and 8 February 1933. Since headboards were not provided until 18 July 1932, this shot was most likely taken in the summer of that year. *(NRM/SSPL)*

Opposite, bottom: Copley Hill A1 No. 2553 *Prince of Wales* has the southbound train near Askham Tunnel, with about 134 non-stop miles to go before reaching King's Cross from Leeds (Holbeck, High Level). The half-mile, two-minute run between Central and Holbeck was the shortest possible journey by Pullman train. *(R.S. Carpenter Photos)*

HARROGATE PULLMAN

King's Cross–Leeds (Central)/Bradford (Exchange)/Harrogate (Sunday only)

Inaugural titled run	6 May 1928
Title withdrawn	27 August 1939
Only headboard	Introduced 24 July 1932
	LNER standard pattern.

- In the timetable this service was designated 'The Harrogate Sunday Pullman' in full. This was the only titled train to run on one day of the week only, either before or after the Second World War.
- In 1927 the service had been introduced as the 'Weekend Pullman' (in the timetable), running northbound on Saturdays and southbound on Sundays, the first being 16/17 July.
- The title was reintroduced on 11 June 1950, this time with 'Sunday' included on the headboard, as well as 'The'.

NORSEMAN

King's Cross–Newcastle (Tyne Commission Quay) (Boat train service)

Inaugural titled run	13 June 1931
Title withdrawn	10 September 1939
Only headboard	Introduced 23 July 1932(?), very rarely carried
	LNER standard pattern.

- This service operated in conjunction with the B&N Line shipping route to Bergen, but (in 1939) was titled only on Saturdays (northbound) and on Thursdays and Sundays (southbound).
- The title was reintroduced on 7 June 1950.

A3 No. 2598 *Blenheim* was built new as an A3 and is seen here with the Down boat train on 23 July 1932, probably near Croft Spa. The Gateshead loco carries the distinguishable, but not pin-sharp, NORSEMAN headboard in the only known pre-war photograph of it. *(By permission of Hull University Archives)*

A1 No. 4472 *Flying Scotsman* again, this time at Doncaster, heading south. This was the only headboarded train to have a title operational on one day per week. Even then, only the timetable declared the day in question (pre-war). Ivatt C1 Atlantic No. 3273 stands, light engine, on the left. *(NRM/SSPL)*

YORKSHIRE PULLMAN

King's Cross–Leeds/Bradford/Halifax/Harrogate via Leeds/Hull

Inaugural titled run	30 September 1935
Title withdrawn	2 September 1939
Only headboard	Introduced 27 September 1937(?)
	Shallow LNER pattern.

- As this was effectively a renaming of the WEST RIDING PULLMAN (with Hull replacing Newcastle as a destination served), it is perhaps surprising that the redundant LNER standard-pattern headboards were not simply repainted to say YORKSHIRE PULLMAN. However, no evidence has been found that this occurred, and it appears that the express ran for some time without a headboard.
- The change of title was accompanied by a change in motive power, with A1/A3 Pacifics taking over from the ageing C1 Atlantics south of Doncaster.
- With the introduction of the WEST RIDING PULLMAN on 27 September 1937, the southbound train commenced at Harrogate and ran via York, the Hull portion again being attached/detached at Doncaster. The Halifax/Bradford/Leeds cars were worked empty to Wakefield, then by semi-fast to Doncaster, reuniting with the main train there. It is perhaps from this date that the service acquired its headboard, though no photograph has been found to support a date earlier than July 1938.
- This was the only service to have this type of headboard as its sole headboard.
- This title was reintroduced (by the LNER) on 4 November 1946.

Perhaps surprisingly, in pre-war days there is no evidence that the YORKSHIRE PULLMAN received the LNER standard-pattern headboard. A repainting of the withdrawn WEST RIDING PULLMAN headboards would have been an easy option, and yet the one-line, shallow board is the only one for which there is photographic proof. A1 No. 4481 *St Simon* (named after the winner of the 1884 Ascot Gold Cup) heads north on a summer evening in the late 1930s, first stop Doncaster, where the Hull portion will be detached. *(NRM/SSPL)*

With the introduction of the WEST RIDING LIMITED, the YORKSHIRE PULLMAN service southbound from Bradford and Leeds was superfluous, so the Harrogate cars were re-routed via York to Doncaster. Here they joined the Hull portion and the Halifax portion (which avoided reversal at Bradford by use of the Bowling curve), which itself had been united with the (empty stock) Leeds and Bradford cars at Wakefield. Back at York on 19 July 1938, Starbeck's No. 2020 has brought the Harrogate portion to a stand. Unusually for the NE Area, but common to this service, the headboard is being carried on the D20 4–4–0. *(J.P. Wilson/Rail Archive Stephenson)*

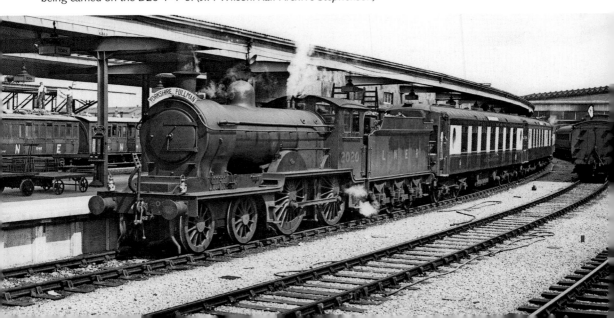

(THE) SILVER JUBILEE

King's Cross–Newcastle

Inaugural titled run	30 September 1935
Last titled run	31 August 1939

Experimental headboard	On wooden mock-up only.

- Interestingly, the proposed headboard included the definite article.
- The SILVER JUBILEE was the second service to receive a tailboard, again with 'THE' in the title, the lettering being dark blue on a silver-grey background (see page 153).
- An historic trial run (for the benefit of the press) was conducted on Friday 27 September 1935, when No. 2509 Silver Link touched 112mph, then a record speed.
- The schedule was four hours each way, inclusive of a stop at Darlington in each direction. This was maintained when the original seven-coach formation (one twin first-class, one twin third-class, and a restaurant/kitchen/restaurant triplet between them) was strengthened in February 1938 to eight coaches by the addition of an extra third-class, thus making a third-class triplet.
- Supplementary fares were payable. These were 5s (first class) and 3s (third class) for the single London–Newcastle journey.
- The stock of this streamlined train was stored during the Second World War, after which five coaches (one twin first-class, one triplet third-class, articulated sets) were reused in the formation of THE FIFE COAST EXPRESS upon the reintroduction of this title on 23 May 1949. The catering vehicles were used on a variety of other services.

Evidence that the LNER did at least consider providing a headboard for the service is shown here. Just how official or unofficial the rectangular-shaped headboard was we shall probably never know, but it certainly didn't appear in traffic. Note also the non-adopted livery and lining style. *(Doncaster Grammar School Railway Museum)*

CORONATION

King's Cross–Edinburgh (Waverley)

Inaugural titled run	5 July 1937
Last titled run	31 August 1939

No headboard provided

- Two beaver-tail observation cars were provided for this service, with CORONATION in stainless-steel letters below the rear windows. The title was similarly displayed on each coach's bodyside, at the same height. At each terminus, these cars required turning, this being accomplished at King's Cross by the use of a turntable, while in Scotland the car was turned by running round the Niddrie Triangle near to the Craigentinny carriage sidings.
- During the winter months when the observation car was not used (the runs being made largely in the dark), the last coach carried a tailboard declaring the title CORONATION, without the definite article.
- The two train sets were 'evacuated' during the Second World War to Ballater carriage sheds, Aberdeenshire, and did not return to Doncaster for restoration until April 1948.
- The schedule for the run was six hours, but was not non-stop, so crews did not need to use a corridor tender to change over. As a stop took place at Newcastle in both directions (and at York heading south only), foot-plate staff were changed at Newcastle.
- Supplementary fares were: 6s (first class) and 4s (third class) for the full London to Edinburgh journey.

In pre-service trials, the leading and trailing brake-composites bore large painted panels depicting a Scottish lion rampant on one, and the three lions of England on the other. The latter is seen here (on No. 1711) behind the tender of A4 No. 4489 on the Barkston triangle during the course of one of the pre-service runs. These panels were painted out before the train entered revenue-earning service. *(NRM/SSPL)*

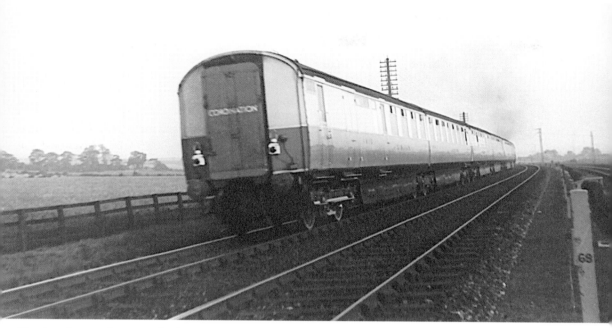

The two famous 'beaver-tail' observation cars were only used during the summer. At other times the last coach sported a single-word tailboard and two asymmetrically positioned tail lamps. *(By permission of Hull University Archives)*

The observation cars were numbered 1719 and 1729 (also in stainless steel). After wartime storage these did not see regular service again until E1729E (as it was then numbered by BR) was put into use between Fort William and Mallaig in the summer of 1956. The second car followed suit a year later between Stirling and Oban. Both cars still exist. *(NRM/SSPL)*

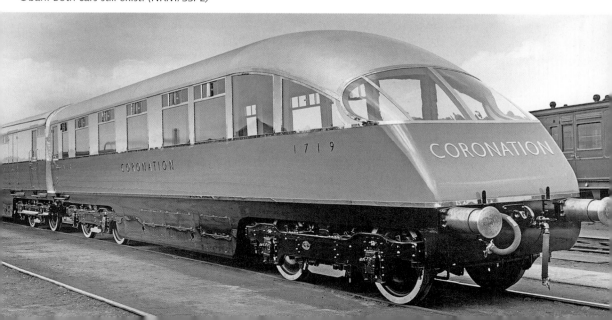

WEST RIDING LIMITED

King's Cross–Leeds (Central)/Bradford (Exchange)

Inaugural titled run	27 September 1937
Last titled run	31 August 1939

No headboard provided

- Like the CORONATION train sets, each coach displayed the title on the bodysides; this time, however, the wording was painted on.
- The service was also provided with a tailboard, which again included 'THE' in the title (not illustrated).
- Again the stock was stored for the duration of the Second World War, this time at Copley Hill carriage shed, Leeds. Six coaches were reused in the formation of THE WEST RIDING when this service was reintroduced on 23 May 1949.
- The entire train was worked to/from Bradford, not just a portion, with reversal at Leeds. The 185¾ miles from Leeds to King's Cross were to be run non-stop in 164 minutes.
- Although non-Pullman, all three of the streamlined services charged supplementary fares for both first- and third-class passengers. In this case, the rates were 4s (first class), 2s (third class) one way.

Twin-articulated set No. 45831/2 stands brand new at Doncaster in 1937. Only this service, and the CORONATION, had their titles displayed on each coach's bodyside. The stock dedicated to this service comprised four twin-sets per train, i.e. eight coaches, 290 tons gross (approx.). The schedule for the 185¾ miles from Leeds (Central) to King's Cross was 164 minutes, non-stop. *(NRM/SSPL)*

FLUSHING CONTINENTAL

Liverpool Street–Harwich (Parkeston Quay) (Boat train service)

Inaugural titled run	26 September 1927
Title withdrawn	10 September 1939
Only headboard	Introduced Summer 1932
	LNER standard pattern.

- The Flushing services had been transferred to Harwich from Folkestone with effect from 1 January 1927.
- After the Second World War the Dutch port of Flushing was renamed Vlissingen, and services were not resumed to this port but concentrated instead on Hoek van Holland. Consequently the service was retitled THE DAY CONTINENTAL.
- This was the only express, pre-war, to display the name of a European town or city on a headboard.
- These 69-mile non-stop runs were the shortest regularly timetabled, headboarded expresses.

B17 4–6–0 No. 2826 *Brancepeth Castle* stands, light engine, at Harwich Parkeston Quay, next to an electric lamp standard confirming the location, some time in 1937. *(W.H.C. Kelland Collection/Bournemouth Railway Club)*

HOOK CONTINENTAL

Liverpool Street–Harwich (Parkeston Quay) (Boat train service)

Inaugural titled run	26 September 1927
Title withdrawn	10 September 1939

No headboard provided

- The service had various titles in the LNER timetables, being first described (from 30 March 1925) as the 'Hook of Holland Continental Express'; and as the 'Hook and Antwerp Continental' between 18 July 1932 and 4 July 1937. It ran therefore under the title HOOK CONTINENTAL only between 26 September 1927 and 17 July 1932 and between 5 July 1937 and 10 September 1939.
- A tailboard was provided when a new set of ten pressure-ventilated coaches (a feature shared with the streamlined trains) was introduced from 10 October 1938. Two words only, white lettering on a black background.
- As this train ran non-stop and was for the sole conveyance of passengers making Continental ferry connections, the UK designation '3rd class' was altered to '2nd class' to conform with European practice.
- This title was reintroduced postwar by the LNER, though initially the new headboard read HOOK-OF-HOLLAND for a while before becoming HOOK CONTINENTAL.

The tailboard is seen here on the rear of brand-new coach No. 6487. Although the lettering of the tailboard and the carriage roofboard is in Gill Sans, that of 6487 is definitely not. This coach was a semi-open first (class), i.e. three compartments only, the rest open-plan with centre aisle, and only had twenty-four seats. *(NRM/SSPL)*

SCANDINAVIAN

Liverpool Street–Harwich (Parkeston Quay) (Boat train service)

Inaugural titled run	1 May 1931
Title withdrawn	10 September 1939
Only headboard	Introduced November 1932(?)
	LNER standard pattern.

- This service also went under different names in the LNER timetables, firstly as the 'Esbjerg Continental Express' (from 24 September 1928), then as the 'Scandinavian Continental Express' (from 22 September 1930), until adopting the shortest version, as above.
- This service operated in conjunction with sailings to Esbjerg (Denmark), and the title was reintroduced in 1945 by the LNER.

Another B17, this time No. 2836 *Harlaxton Manor*, carries the headboard at Stratford shed, as the driver prepares the engine for the run to Parkeston Quay. *(By permission of Hull University Archives)*

ADDITIONAL TITLES

EASTERN BELLE

Liverpool Street–various coastal destinations (Monday–Friday) (Pullman car train)
Liverpool Street–Clacton-on-Sea (Sunday only)

Inaugural titled run	3 June 1929
Last titled run	1 September 1939

Only headboard	Introduced Summer 1932
	LNER standard pattern.

- These trains operated in the summer timetable only, as half-day excursions on a Monday to Friday basis. In the first season, for instance, destinations were as follows: Felixstowe, Clacton, Frinton, Dovercourt, Thorpeness and Aldeburgh. Later resorts visited included Hunstanton, Lowestoft, Yarmouth, Cromer and – the furthest – Skegness. These weekday services were not advertised in the timetables.
- On Sundays the train ran regularly to Clacton and this was included in the LNER timetables, where it had previously been known as the 'Clacton Sunday Pullman' (no headboard of this title was ever carried, however). Although the headboard contained two words only, the full title printed in the timetable was 'The Eastern Belle Pullman Limited'.
- No such equivalent title ran postwar.

B12 4–6–0 No. 8509 has eight Pullmans behind the tender and an ultra-clear Gill Sans headboard to advertise the service. The ACFI feed-water heater mounted on top of the boiler does no favours for the engine's appearance. *(NRM/SSPL)*

NORTHERN BELLE

King's Cross–various destinations in north-east England and Scotland (Luxury touring train)

Inaugural titled run	16 June 1933
Last titled run	30 June 1939

Only headboard	Introduced 16 June 1933
	Shallow LNER pattern.

- During May 1933 a visual 'trial' of five alternatives to the LNER standard pattern headboard then in use took place inside Doncaster Works. The headboard selected to send the NORTHERN BELLE on its way was later to be used as a single-line alternative for three other timetabled services.
- The touring train left King's Cross on Friday evenings and returned there the following Friday morning. The stock comprised fourteen coaches, of which six were sleeping cars for the use of the sixty passengers, who paid £20 each for the week-long land cruise.
- The cruise only operated two, three or four times a year, in early summer, as follows:

1933	16, 23 June, 18 August	1937	4, 11, 18 June
1934	1, 8, 22, 29 June	1938	3, 17, 24 June
1935	31 May, 7, 21, 28 June	1939	9, 23 June
1936	29 May, 12, 19 June		

The doyen of the B17 class, No. 2800 *Sandringham*, is immaculately turned out and complete with the first (1932) non-Gill Sans headboard. This was, however, repainted for the following season's running. *(By permission of Hull University Archives)*

The Doncaster Works headboard 'trials' (May 1933) resulted in five designs being assessed (*NRM/SSPL*). Sequentially these were as follows:

On engine No. 4470 *Great Northern*

(a)   Very large two-line board of smaller radius that the standard 2ft 6in then in use, resulting in a large unused area. Gill Sans lettering.

(b)   The same as in (a) – it is thought – but with the 'spare space' cut away on the top line.

On engine No. 2574 *St Frusquin*

(c)   Enlarged version of LNER standard pattern (about 6in wider). Again in two lines containing the definite article, and much space on the upper line. Gill Sans lettering.

(d)   The same board as in (c) – probably – with the board now shaped to contain three words only, and no voids. (This strongly resembled the NBR boards).

(e)   The board as in (c), (d) but cut back further into a single line.

Notes: (i)   type (e) was accepted; the only version not to include THE in the title.

           (ii)   THE was again proposed for inclusion on the 'mock-up' SILVER JUBILEE headboard in 1935. It was adopted as policy, postwar.

           (iii)   type (d) was resurrected – more or less – for the last LNER headboard of all, THE MASTER CUTLER in 1947.

THAMES-FORTH EXPRESS (LMS/LNER)

St Pancras–Edinburgh (Waverley)

Inaugural titled run	26 September 1927
Last titled run	9 September 1939

Headboard	None provided, except that the LNER supplied destination boards between Edinburgh and Carlisle reading 'St Pancras' or 'Edinburgh' (See illustration).

- This service was reintroduced in 1957 under the title THE WAVERLEY, and can be found in the London Midland Section.

A3 Pacific No. 2749 *Flamingo* awaits departure from Edinburgh Waverley with the Up train in May 1937. The Carlisle (Canal) loco was rarely photographed, as was the 'St Pancras' destination board, as it applied to this train only. The board is a standard 'local' two-sided destination board (it will say 'Edinburgh' on the reverse) usually held in place by the two vertical pegs – beneath P and R – that slotted into holders specially fitted to the smokebox, above the door (see the North British titled trains also). This board has acquired a central bracket in addition, for fixing to the A3s lamp irons, as these engines did not work 'local' services. *(NRM/SSPL)*

Chapter Five

TITLED EXPRESSES OF THE POSTWAR LNER, BR (ER) AND BR (SCR EX-LNER LINES)

INTRODUCTION TO 'EASTERN' HEADBOARDS 1946–84

Part 1: Painted-steel headboards
1st Series: The black-on-white boards
2nd Series: The BR white-on-black/dark-blue boards
3rd Series: The Coronation boards
4th Series: The 'Deltic'-specific boards (including wood, fibreglass)
5th Series: Latter-day reintroductions
6th Series: Miscellaneous

1st Series

(a)   The latter days of the LNER
         Immediately before the outbreak of the Second World War the LNER was operating
         fourteen services that carried (or were supposed to carry) headboards. Between the
         resumption of this practice in 1946 and the end of the LNER's independent existence
         on 31 December 1947, nine expresses were again allocated headboards. Of these, only
         five titles had been headboarded pre-war, namely:

FLYING SCOTSMAN   YORKSHIRE PULLMAN
NIGHT SCOTSMAN   SCANDINAVIAN
ABERDONIAN

This new title was inaugurated by using the doyen of the class, No. 70000 *Britannia* itself, for both the Up and Down runs. Seen here close to the 5.27 p.m. departure time, the engine had received special attention for the occasion, and the circular steel headboard soon gave way to a plain Type 7 cast board. *(NRM/SSPL)*

Two titled trains that had not previously carried headboards gained them:

EAST ANGLIAN
HOOK-OF-HOLLAND (ex-HOOK CONTINENTAL)

One was headboarded again but was renamed:

THE DAY CONTINENTAL (formerly FLUSHING CONTINENTAL but now sailing to Hoek-van-Holland)

And one new title was introduced:

THE MASTER CUTLER (with a non-standard design).

The last title was a significant addition. Not only was it the last title conferred by the LNER, and the first titled train to run over the GC Section, but it was also the only service to have headboards provided privately. These were supplied by Firth-Vickers Stainless Steels of Sheffield and were additional to the painted-steel LNER boards. The Firth-Vickers version was a stainless-steel casting with polished letters on a black background. Four were presented, and remained in use until 1958.

(b)   LNER boards in early BR days
      Four further pre-war titles were reintroduced (and headboarded) by British Railways in the years immediately after nationalisation, all of which carried the LNER-style boards, at least for a while. These were:

QUEEN OF SCOTS   (the only shallow-pattern board to be re-used)
THE SCARBOROUGH FLYER (now spelt with a 'Y')
THE HOOK CONTINENTAL   (ex-HOOK-OF-HOLLAND, firstly without THE)
THE FIFE COAST EXPRESS   (non-standard version)

It is also worth noting that despite the general change-over to the inclusion of the definite article in the titles postwar:

(i)   QUEEN OF SCOTS never did (on a painted-steel board)
(ii)   EAST ANGLIAN never did (on a painted-steel board, but did receive, uniquely, a green background)
(iii) THE FLYING SCOTSMAN only became thus in late 1950 and is very rare
(iv)   THE NIGHT SCOTSMAN has not been found at all, with or without THE. (It is, however, believed to have existed.)

(c)   Transitional black-on-white boards
      Three of these appeared in the GE Section, probably in early BR days, but certainly in LNER colours. An entirely new 'elliptical top' design was applied to THE SCANDINAVIAN and THE DAY CONTINENTAL and this shape was confined to these services only. A further board, for THE DAY CONTINENTAL, was probably that which was intended for use on THE SOUTH YORKSHIREMAN (drawing W765) but was repainted, and was unique to this boat train.

2nd Series

In the early days after nationalisation there were some instances (again on the GE Section) in which BR simply repainted the LNER and transitional boards. Both the elliptical top boards were repainted, as was the EAST ANGLIAN, though as noted previously, this board also passed through a green-background phase, though only on some boards. On repainting, the LNER standard-pattern SCANDINAVIAN board also gained the definite article. However, BR soon supplied several of a new type to the same basic outline as three of their recently introduced cast-aluminium headboards. Drawings for these three, which date from March 1951, are illustrated. These were used particularly in this year – Festival of Britain year – when it is apparent that a big effort was made to ensure a sufficient number of headboards were available, as BR had introduced no fewer than eighteen Eastern Region titles in the years 1948–51 inclusive, on top of those it inherited from the LNER.

In all, ten expresses actually received these BR official steel boards (from photographic evidence), though it is possible that four others did as well (since these were 'designated' on the drawings), though there is no evidence for this. Additionally, a further four carried non-standard types, one pre-dating the official 1951 issues, the others several years later (see 6th Series for details). It must be emphasised here that the use of painted-steel headboards in the twelve or so years after nationalisation was a stop-gap measure, and that the standard-issue aluminium boards were to be deployed when available, as first choice. Once production of these had fulfilled requirements, steel boards were used to cover shortages only, and some depots were supplied with 'blanks' to be painted up as necessary.

3rd Series

In common with the WR and LMR, the ER selected four titled expresses to bear an extra commemorative headboard for the period 22 May to 14 June 1953. Three titles, namely THE FLYING SCOTSMAN, THE MASTER CUTLER and THE BROADSMAN, carried identical multicoloured headboards displaying the crown and cypher, but no name. The fourth was allocated to THE WEST RIDING and although the same shape, was specific to that train as it bore that title, and the arms (on two shields) and motto of the West Riding of Yorkshire.

These were the only ER headboards designed to be carried centrally on the buffer beam, a rare feature only replicated elsewhere by some earlier Southern boards.

4th Series

When the prototype 'Deltic' appeared in 1955 it was equipped with an upper lamp iron on each nose (just below the headlight), and could therefore display the aluminium headboards then common on BR. However, when the production models were introduced in 1961 no such high-level lamp iron was included, but two widely separated brackets low down on the nose were. Since a very wide headboard would be required to bridge this gap, it was decided instead to use the existing 1951 shape of large steel headboard (size A) and fix this within a wooden backing frame that would slot into the two holding brackets. Hence, before a production run of these, a further 'headboard trial' was held in Doncaster Works yard, on an English Electric 2,000hp diesel. A small batch of these (five only, Nos D345–9) had been built with the same extra 'low down' brackets, as had the 'Deltics' and D347 was the guinea pig for the trial. Two boards were successively displayed; first THE ELIZABETHAN with cream/yellow lettering on a black/dark blue background, then THE FLYING SCOTSMAN in the old LNER colours of black lettering on a white background. In both cases the backing frame was painted black. Given that in those days diesels were in overall green, without yellow warning panels, the black-on-white headboard stood out infinitely better against the dark-green nose, and this was duly adopted. No evidence has been seen that any of this batch carried such headboards ever again. When the 3,300hp 'Deltics' eventually received yellow nose panels, however, these black-on-white headboards then stood out rather less well. In addition, a high central lamp bracket was subsequently fitted to all 'Deltics'. This was used to carry a small number of cast-aluminium boards, and also some of the black-on-white painted steel boards, though these had to be shorn of their 'wing extensions' and provided with a central bracket on the rear in the conventional manner for this to happen.

These 'Deltic'-specific headboards were acquired by nine titles, though photographic evidence of this has only been seen for

THE FLYING SCOTSMAN	THE YORKSHIRE PULLMAN
THE TALISMAN	THE WEST RIDING

The headboards described above were not the only ones to be carried solely by this single class of diesel locomotive. Of the four others, three used only the top lamp iron, and the earliest two of these (1964) were distinctively unconventional. They were made in fibreglass resin, painted gold, bore no wording at all and were the product of the Design Panel, set up by BR to overhaul its public image. The first was for 'The Flying Scotsman' and was in the shape of a 'winged thistle'. The second design was similar in concept and featured a 'crown with three thistles'. This was intended for 'The Queen of Scots' service, but unhappily this was withdrawn (on 13 June 1964), almost as soon as the new headboard was available for it. Consequently, photographic evidence of it in service use has not been found.

The final headboard intended specifically to use the low-level brackets was that for THE SILVER JUBILEE in 1977. Any resemblance between this and others carried in this position should, however, be dismissed. Now, the board itself was multicoloured painted wood and the backing-plate was an open steel framework, the reverse of the materials used previously. The central disc contained the BR 'double arrow' symbol, and the years 1952 and 1977 were also displayed, both features being unique to this ER board. The legend itself was within a scroll and did not dominate the board, again a unique intention, and not least, the board was three-dimensional in that the timber was in two layers.

THE SILVER JUBILEE was so titled for one year only, and after a further gap of one year came the last of the 'Deltic' headboards, for by 1979 these machines were being replaced by HST sets. The headboard for THE HULL EXECUTIVE was produced (by Stratford depot) in recognition of the fact that the schedule between King's Cross and the first stop at Retford demanded the fastest-ever locomotive-hauled average speed of 91.3mph start-to-stop. The board itself was ultra conventional and was similar to the 1960s' black-on-white shape, except the lettering was silver grey and the background was red, the first and only time this colour was used on the ER. The board could of course have been carried on the top lamp iron of other diesel classes, but the service was diagrammed solely for class 55 haulage and evidence against this is totally lacking.

5th Series

A short series this, comprising two titles only, both reintroductions, and both on the GE Section. The earlier of the two was THE EAST ANGLIAN in 1980, THE FENMAN reappearing in 1984. To the same design, both were new Stratford creations, more rectangular than that for THE HULL EXECUTIVE, with white horizontal lettering on a blue background. Both boards also displayed two pairs of civic arms – a nice reminder of earlier times. The 1980 board repeated the two shields carried in its previous existence, while the arms of London and King's Lynn graced THE FENMAN for the first time.

6th Series

(i)   Freight Train headboards

    (a)   THE KING'S CROSS FREIGHTER. This ran between Tees yard and King's Cross freight terminal as a class C fully-fitted freight. The board itself had three lines of black letters on a white background with, apparently, the outline of a Type 7 aluminium board.

    (b)   The TEES–TYNE FREIGHTER. This was the northbound working of (a). However, this was a standard-issue (size A) board again in three lines but with white lettering on a dark blue background. Uniquely for the ER, the board mixed capitals and lower-case lettering, the definite article being painted 'The'.

(ii)   (a)   BUTLIN'S EXPRESS. These seasonal but non-timetabled holiday-camp trains were given size B BR boards, painted yellow with black lettering. The apostrophe S was only seen on this board, and (i) (a) above only.

    (b)   BUTLIN EXPRESS. Whereas the (a) trains departed from King's Cross, the (b) services departed from Liverpool Street and had a large circular headboard, again yellow but with the shorter title, the lettering being 'around the clock'.

(iii)   THE ESSEX COAST EXPRESS. This was inaugurated with a large circular headboard having white letters on a dark-blue background. ESSEX COAST was horizontal across the centre with THE above and EXPRESS below, clock-face fashion. It is possible that this was not new, but a repainting of a BUTLIN EXPRESS board.

(iv)   'Wool Wins.' A short-lived (March/April 1962) alternative to THE WHITE ROSE headboard. Again large and circular with a very prominent double white rose (smaller superimposed on a larger), this promoted a campaign by the Yorkshire Woollen Industry (not illustrated).

(v)   Whereas drawing W765 may have been worn by an alternative title, THE NORFOLKMAN – as per W773 – was carried, at least in the initial weeks of this service in 1948. W773 also shows a smaller board to have been destined for the EAST ANGLIAN, though there is no photographic evidence to support this. However, some years later (1959) THE TALISMAN did use a steel headboard that may have been this. Even later still (1960), THE TEES–THAMES carried a board strongly resembling W765 (see page 210 for engineering drawings of these).

(vi)   To mark the transition from diesel to electric traction, a special headboard was made for THE HOOK CONTINENTAL in 1985. Based on the size A board this was made at Stratford depot, and as previously, the Dutch and UK flags were included. Brief usage only.

(vii)   Headboards that never were. Intriguingly, drawings (DNE 1067, see page 210) were produced in April 1955 for steel headboards suitable to be carried both on EM1 and EM2 electric locos and steam engines. As far as is known, none of these was made. Whether or not a titled service from Manchester (London Road) via Woodhead to Sheffield and beyond was at some stage being planned is also unknown.

Part 2: Cast–aluminium headboards 1948–60

This medium was first seen at the end of May 1948, on the first new ER title to be introduced by British Railways, THE SOUTH YORKSHIREMAN. Pre-war there had been an LMS train, called simply 'The Yorkshireman', that provided Bradford (Exchange) with a direct service to St Pancras, and this postwar title was effectively a replacement for this, but running up the GC main line into Marylebone.

The headboard itself was what is described on the following pages as a 'Type 5', though this nomenclature is adopted for the purposes of this book only and was not a BR description. There were eight basic designs of BR cast-aluminium headboards, mostly differing in size rather than shape, and these were used nationally on all regions. Seven of these types were carried by ER titled expresses and no fewer than thirty-three services displayed these various headboards just on the ER. Sixteen of this total were each embellished with two extra discs, shields, etc. These mostly related to the civic arms of the destinations, but national flags were also represented, one title showed a depiction of 'the sun with rays' and another showed Viking longboats.

Doncaster Drawing Office produced the drawings for seven of the eight types, and the distribution of these types among the named expresses (nationally) was as follows, where (E) denotes 'embellished' and A, B, C, D and R denote the sizes thereof (see Notes).

Type 1: Drawings W764, W786
ER:	YORKSHIRE PULLMAN	THE LEA VALLEY ENTERPRISE (freight)
	TEES–TYNE PULLMAN	EAST ESSEX ENTERPRISE (freight)
	THE CAPITALS LIMITED (E)(C)	
	ANGLO-SCOTTISH CAR CARRIER	(similar but 45in wide overall)
ScR:	FIFE COAST EXPRESS	
WR:	CHELTENHAM SPA EXPRESS	
	CORNISH RIVIERA	(similar but only 33in wide overall)
	TORBAY EXPRESS	(similar but only 33in wide overall)

Type 2: Drawings W772, W786
ER:	EAST ANGLIAN (W772)	THE FENMAN
	THE FAIR MAID	THE TALISMAN
LMR:	THE COMET	THE MANXMAN
ScR:	THE IRISHMAN	

NB: Drawing W773 shows a steel-plate version of W772. See Part 1, 6th Series (v).

Type 3: Drawing W786
ER:	THE WEST RIDING	THE WHITE ROSE (E)(R)
	THE TEES–THAMES	BUTLINS EXPRESS
WR:	THE RED DRAGON	THE CORNISHMAN
	THE BRISTOLIAN	THE MAYFLOWER
	THE INTER-CITY	THE DEVONIAN

SR: PINES EXPRESS
LMR: THE MIDLANDER   THE RED ROSE
           THE IRISH MAIL   THE DEVONIAN
ScR: THE BON ACCORD   THE GRANITE CITY
           THE SAINT MUNGO
NB: THE DEVONIAN appears twice as they were not interchangeable, each region having
its own type of fixing bracket.

Type 4: Drawings W772, W790
ER: THE NORFOLKMAN (W772)   THE NORTH BRITON
           THE NORTHUMBRIAN (E)(C)
NB: Drawing W773 shows the steel-plate version of W772. This was carried. See Part 1,
6th Series (v).

Type 5: Drawings W766, W768
ER: THE SOUTH YORKSHIREMAN (W766)
           THE QUEEN OF SCOTS
NB: Drawing W765 shows a steel-plate version of W766, to be painted with
black letters on a white background. No evidence has been found that THE SOUTH
YORKSHIREMAN ever carried this. It is, however, suspected that it might have been
painted up as THE DAY CONTINENTAL instead. See also Part 1, 1st Series (c).
NB: Types 4 and 5 were confined to the ER only.

Type 6: Drawings W811, W859
ER: THE ABERDONIAN (E)(A)   THE SCANDINAVIAN (E)(D)
           THE TYNESIDER (E)(A)   THE FENMAN
           THE NORSEMAN (E)(A)   THE BROADSMAN (E)(A)
           THE ELIZABETHAN   THE EASTERLING (E)(A)
           THE MASTER CUTLER (E)(A)(C)   THE NORFOLKMAN
LMR: THE ROYAL SCOT   THE WAVERLEY
           THE MID-DAY SCOT   THE PALATINE
           THE ROYAL HIGHLANDER   THE ROBIN HOOD
           THE MANCUNIAN   THE DEVONIAN
           THE LANCASTRIAN   EMPRESS VOYAGER
           THE RED ROSE   CUNARD SPECIAL
           THE SHAMROCK   THE WELSH CHIEFTAIN
           THE WELSHMAN   CONDOR (freight)
           THE LAKES EXPRESS

Type 7: Drawing W811
ER: THE FLYING SCOTSMAN (E)(D)   THE HOOK CONTINENTAL (E)(D)
           THE NIGHT SCOTSMAN   THE DAY CONTINENTAL (E)(D)
           THE HARROGATE SUNDAY PULLMAN (E)(C)
           THE SCARBOROUGH FLYER (E)(B)   THE EAST ANGLIAN (E)(A)
           THE HEART OF MIDLOTHIAN   THE ESSEX COAST EXPRESS
WR: THE MERCHANT VENTURER   CAMBRIAN COAST EXPRESS
           THE WILLIAM SHAKESPEARE   PEMBROKE COAST EXPRESS
           THE SOUTH WALES PULLMAN   CAPITALS UNITED EXPRESS

LMR: THE NORTHERN IRISHMAN   THE EMERALD ISLE EXPRESS
          THE MERSEYSIDE EXPRESS   THE THAMES–CLYDE EXPRESS
          THE ULSTER EXPRESS   CAMBRIAN RADIO CRUISE (E★)

The types were distinguished by size, as in the following table.

Dimensions are in inches	Type 1	Type 2	Type 3	Type 4	Type 5	Type 6	Type 7	Type 8
Length of top arc	40	24	24	34	34	28	35	51
Distance between lowest points	31¼	28	31	35	35¾	28	31	51
Distance between top/bottom edges	9⅞	9⅞	9⅞	9⅞	9⅞	12½	14⅜	15
Drawing No.	W764 W786	W772 W786	W786	W772 W790	W766 W768	W811 W859	W811	N/A

NOTES

(i)   Type 8 was specific to the Southern Region (see Southern Section).
(ii)   Type 4 scalloping had 7in radius; Type 5 had 5in radius.
(iii)   Standard letter sizes were 3¾in or 3in, using the Gill Sans Medium letterface.
(iv)   E★ = LMR shield embellishments 6in wide, 7½in high.
(v)   The various ER embellishments were designed in-house at the region's headquarters offices at Liverpool Street and came in five sizes. With reference to the lists above, these were:
        A = large shields 6in wide, 7in high
        B = 'sunbursts' for THE SCARBOROUGH FLYER only; 8½in wide, 4½in high
        C = small shields 4½in wide, 6in high
        D = discs, 7in diameter
        R = disc, 3in diameter for THE WHITE ROSE only.

It will be noted from the drawings that only ER titles are quoted on these, whereas the designs were to be used nationally. The presumption is that Doncaster Works was, at least initially, responsible for casting headboards for all regions (except the Southern). It is, however, not possible to be definitive about this, and there is a possibility that in the early days after nationalisation, Gorton Works was partly responsible. Outside contractors may even have had a hand. The perceived wisdom is that Crewe (and probably Derby) were also involved at some stage and that Eastleigh cast the Type 8 boards. The only absolutes are that Swindon produced the WR's own individualised boards introduced in 1956, but did not cast the BR types listed above that were allocated to WR expresses pre-1956. It did, however, cast the PINES EXPRESS in 1962.

In common with all other regions, headboard usage on the ER declined in inverse proportion to the increase in dieselisation. After 1962, when 'Deltics' took over the most arduous ER workings, few other headboards were carried on a regular basis on the East

Coast Main Line. However, THE MASTER CUTLER was an exception to this, and it is likely that this was the last cast-aluminium headboard to be carried out of King's Cross in regular service, probably just before transferring to the Midland route in October 1968.

GENERAL NOTES ON ER HEADBOARDS

1. Where services had been headboarded pre-war, it is presumed that these boards were reused postwar (suitably repainted) rather than new ones being supplied.
2. The painted-steel headboards nearly all exhibit differences in letter form and spacing, according to which depot, and which signwriter, performed the task.
3. The cast-aluminium headboards all had either ER blue, or black backgrounds. Some for the Anglo-Scottish services also had ScR light blue as background, and this is noted where appropriate. All had polished edges and letters.
4. The task of designing and producing the various discs, shields, etc. that graced many of the headboards was performed at Eastern Region Headquarters at Liverpool Street. At the instigation, and under the supervision, of Mr Leslie P. Parker (Motive Power Superintendent of the ER), prospective young managers were assigned these jobs as and when they could fit them in. Under this direction, William Cattermole, Peter Smith and Peter Townend were, between them, and over a period of time from around 1950, responsible for all the designs illustrated in the following pages.

No. 60028 *Walter K. Whigham* was named after the last deputy chairman of the LNER (1946–8) in October 1947, the engine having been previously named *Sea Eagle*. Seen here in the purple/blue livery it received in June 1948, with 'British Railways' in full on the tender, the Down non-stop runs through York below gantries of semaphore signals soon to be replaced by colour lights. The rarely seen 4th version of the pre-war standard headboard identifies the service. 4 August 1950. *(W.S. Garth/Rail Archive Stephenson)*

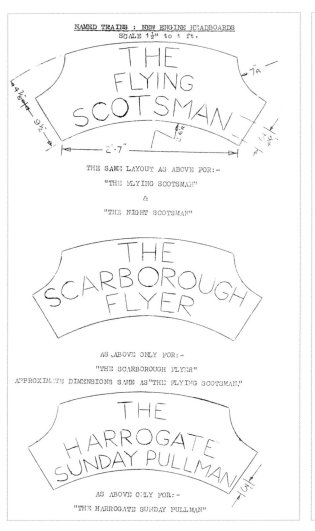

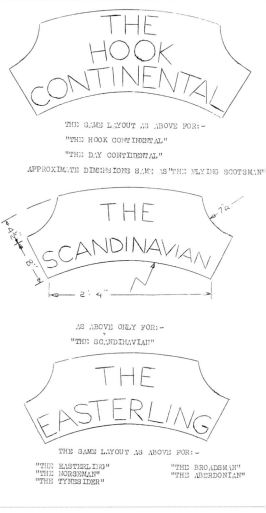

THE ABERDONIAN was diagrammed for 'Deltic' haulage for most of the 1960s at least as far as Edinburgh. No in-service photographic evidence has been found of this size A board with wooden backing. *(Courtesy Sheffield Railwayana Auctions)*

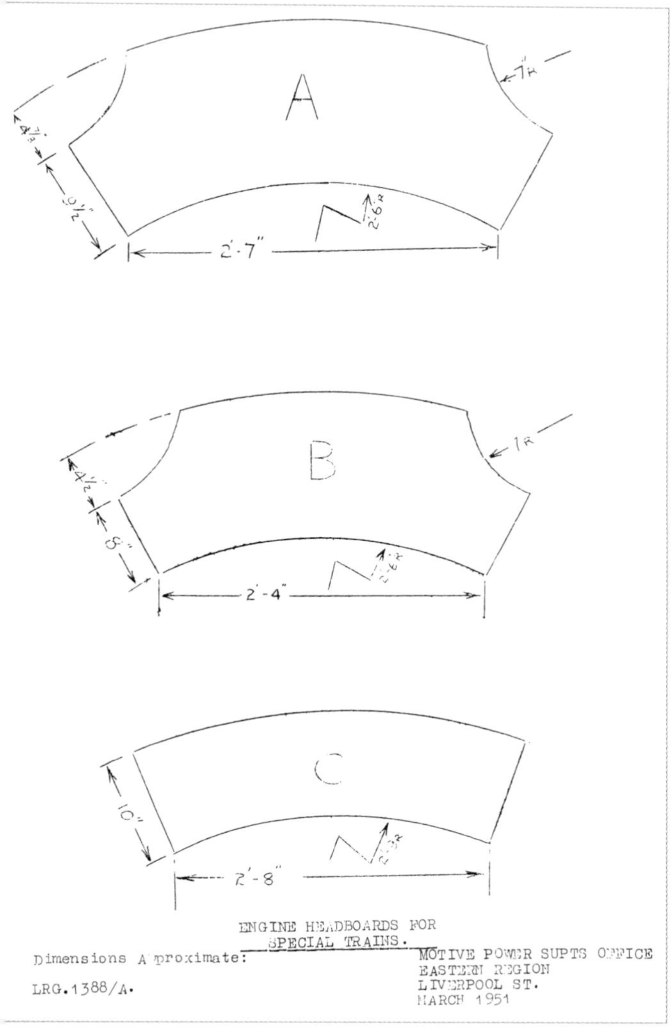
A
2'-7"
B
2'-4"
C
2'-8"
ENGINE HEADBOARDS FOR SPECIAL TRAINS.
Dimensions Approximate:
LRG.1388/A.
MOTIVE POWER SUPTS OFFICE
EASTERN REGION
LIVERPOOL ST.
MARCH 1951

Nine outline drawings for sizes A, B, C of steel blanks to be painted up either as indicated, or as necessary, see Part 1, 2nd Series. These correspond, more or less, to the cast Types 7, 6, 1 respectively. *(NRM/SSPL)*

Pages 210–12: In the Doncaster Works Drawings, W765/773 and DNE 1067 refer to steel-plate headboards, the other four to those in cast aluminium. W768/790 are for Types 5, 4 respectively. W786 covers Types 1, 2, 3 and W811 covers Types 6, 7. The table of embellishments on W811 (below) is of particular interest. *(NRM/SSPL)*

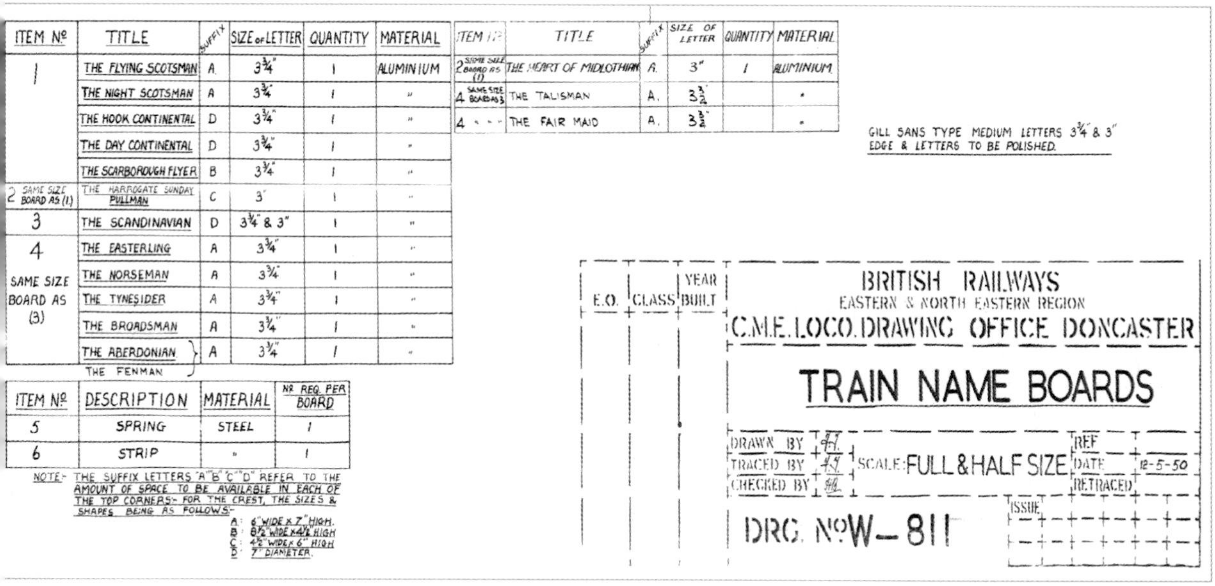

ITEM Nº	TITLE	SUFFIX	SIZE OF LETTER	QUANTITY	MATERIAL
1	THE FLYING SCOTSMAN	A	3¾"	1	ALUMINIUM
	THE NIGHT SCOTSMAN	A	3¾"	1	"
	THE HOOK CONTINENTAL	D	3¾"	1	"
	THE DAY CONTINENTAL	D	3¾"	1	"
	THE SCARBOROUGH FLYER	B	3¾"	1	"
2 SAME SIZE BOARD AS (1)	THE HARROGATE SUNDAY PULLMAN	C	3"	1	"
3	THE SCANDINAVIAN	D	3¾" & 3"	1	"
4 SAME SIZE BOARD AS (3)	THE EASTERLING	A	3¾"	1	"
	THE NORSEMAN	A	3¾"	1	"
	THE TYNESIDER	A	3¾"	1	"
	THE BROADSMAN	A	3¾"	1	"
	THE ABERDONIAN / THE FENMAN	A	3¾"	1	"

ITEM Nº	TITLE	SUFFIX	SIZE OF LETTER	QUANTITY	MATERIAL
2 SAME SIZE BOARD AS (1)	THE HEART OF MIDLOTHIAN	A.	3"	1	ALUMINIUM
4 SAME SIZE BOARD AS 3	THE TALISMAN	A.	3¾"		"
4 " " "	THE FAIR MAID	A.	3¾"		"

GILL SANS TYPE MEDIUM LETTERS 3¾" & 3"
EDGE & LETTERS TO BE POLISHED.

ITEM Nº	DESCRIPTION	MATERIAL	Nº REQ. PER BOARD
5	SPRING	STEEL	1
6	STRIP	"	1

NOTE:- THE SUFFIX LETTERS "A" "B" "C" "D" REFER TO THE AMOUNT OF SPACE TO BE AVAILABLE IN EACH OF THE TOP CORNERS:- FOR THE CREST, THE SIZES & SHAPES BEING AS FOLLOWS:-
A: 6" WIDE × 7" HIGH.
B: 8½" WIDE × 4½" HIGH
C: 4½" WIDE × 6" HIGH
D: 7" DIAMETER.

E.O.	CLASS	YEAR BUILT

BRITISH RAILWAYS
EASTERN & NORTH EASTERN REGION
C.M.E. LOCO. DRAWING OFFICE DONCASTER
TRAIN NAME BOARDS
DRAWN BY / TRACED BY / CHECKED BY — SCALE: FULL & HALF SIZE — REF / DATE 12-5-50 / RETRACED / ISSUE
DRG. Nº W-811

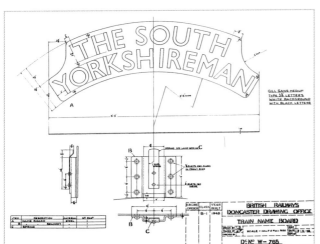

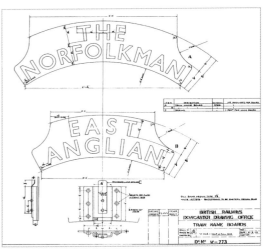

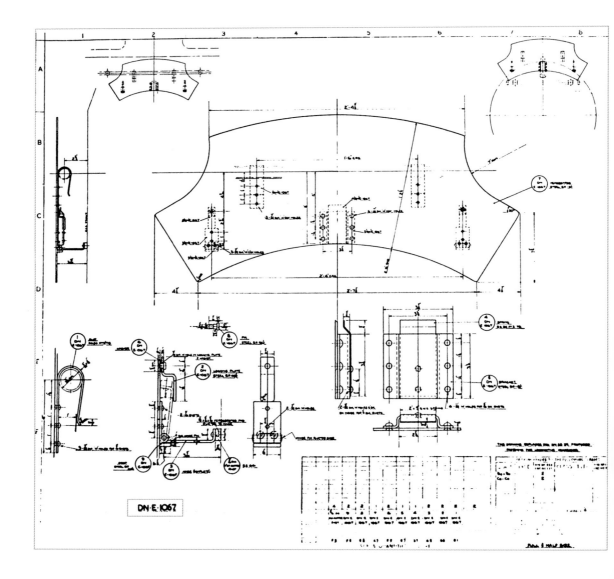

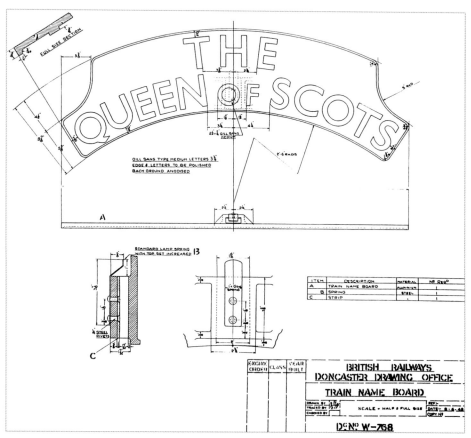

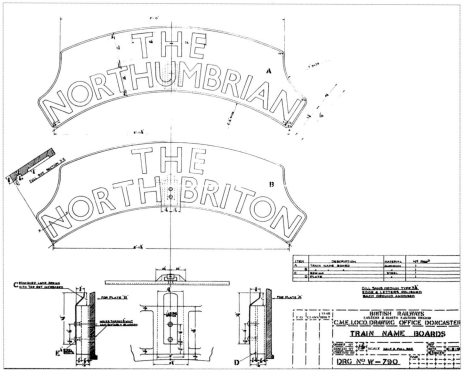

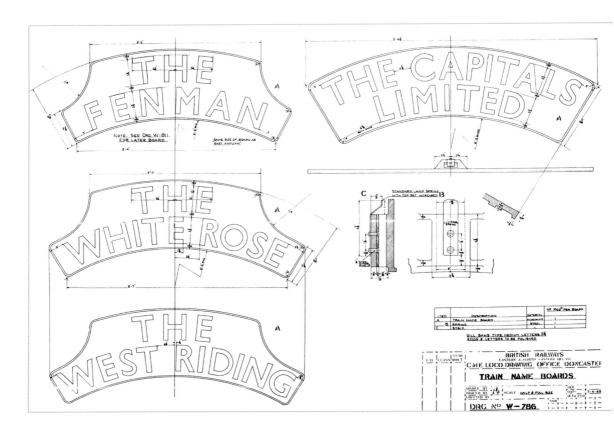

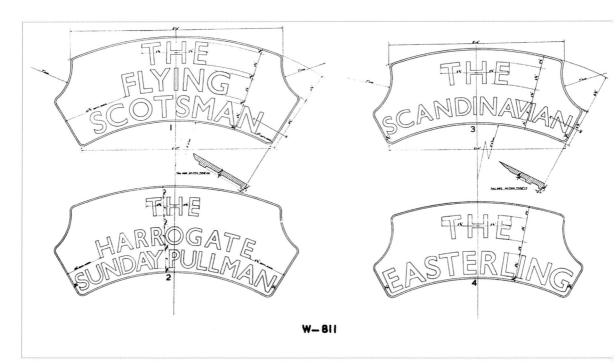

W—811

THE TITLED EXPRESSES

(a) Services using King's Cross

(THE) FLYING SCOTSMAN	(i) (v) (vi)	
THE ABERDONIAN		
(THE) QUEEN OF SCOTS	(v)	
THE NIGHT SCOTSMAN	(i)	
THE CAPITALS LIMITED		Anglo-Scottish services
THE HEART OF MIDLOTHIAN		
THE ELIZABETHAN	(v)	
THE TALISMAN	(v)	
THE FAIR MAID		
(THE) ANGLO-SCOTTISH CAR CARRIER	(i) (ii)	
THE SILVER JUBILEE		
TEES–TYNE PULLMAN	(v)	
THE NORTHUMBRIAN		Newcastle services
THE NORSEMAN		
THE TYNESIDER		
THE NORTH BRITON	(iii)	
(THE) YORKSHIRE PULLMAN	(i) (v)	
THE WEST RIDING	(vi)	Leeds services
THE WHITE ROSE		
THE HARROGATE SUNDAY PULLMAN		
THE SCARBOROUGH FLYER		
THE TEES–THAMES/THE TEES–THAMES LINK		Other services
THE HULL EXECUTIVE		

(b) Services using Marylebone

THE MASTER CUTLER	(iv) (vi)
THE SOUTH YORKSHIREMAN	

(c) Services using Liverpool Street

(THE) HOOK CONTINENTAL	(i)	
(THE) SCANDINAVIAN	(i)	
(THE) EAST ANGLIAN	(i) (v)	
THE DAY CONTINENTAL		
THE NORFOLKMAN		East Anglian services
THE FENMAN		
THE BROADSMAN	(vi)	
THE EASTERLING		
THE ESSEX COAST EXPRESS		

(d) Internal Scottish Service

(THE) FIFE COAST EXPRESS	(i)

NOTES

(i)   (THE) indicates that some styles of headboard included the definite article, others did not.
(ii)   This service commenced from Holloway loading terminal.
(iii)   This service was between Leeds (City) and Glasgow (Queen St.)
(iv)   This service was later transferred to King's Cross, and later still to St Pancras.
(v)   These services also carried tailboards.
(vi)   These services also carried a 1953 Coronation commemorative headboard.

ADDITIONAL TITLES

(e)   The BUTLIN EXPRESS holiday camp trains
(f)   HUMBER–LINCS EXECUTIVE
(g)   Headboarded freight trains

THE LEA VALLEY ENTERPRISE	THE KING'S CROSS FREIGHTER
EAST ESSEX ENTERPRISE	The TEES–TYNE FREIGHTER

Falcon, now renumbered as 60025 and in BR blue livery, bursts out of Copenhagen Tunnel on the exit from King's Cross on 3 March 1950. The LNER style (3rd version) headboard is still in use. The locomotive's allocated depot, Grantham, is not only stencilled below the headboard but also indicated by the oval shedplate above it, bearing the code 35B. *(J.C. Flemons/Millbrook House Collection)*

(THE) FLYING SCOTSMAN

King's Cross—Edinburgh (Waverley)/Aberdeen

Inaugural titled run	11 July 1927 and titled throughout the Second World War
Last titled run	(still running)

(a) 1st style headboard	**Reintroduced Summer 1946**
	LNER standard pattern. Versions possibly not sequential chronologically and may all have existed at the same time. Superseded by 2nd style.
(1st version)	3in letters on top line, 3¾in on bottom.
(2nd version)	3in letters top and bottom lines.
(3rd version)	3¾in letters top and bottom lines.
(4th version)	With THE in isolation on top line. Lettering 3¾in high but rather cramped on bottom line. Rarely seen.
(b) 2nd style headboard	**Introduced 6 June 1950**
	BR Type 7 also with ScR light blue background.
(1st version)	Without discs.
(2nd version)	As (1st version) but with twin 7in disc embellishments depicting the rose of England crossed with the thistle of Scotland in true colours on a white background.
	NB: Both versions concurrent. Not all headboards received the discs.
(c) 3rd style headboard	**Introduced Summer 1951**
	BR painted steel, size A. White lettering in three lines on dark-blue/black background.
(d) 4th style headboard	**Introduced Summer 1961 (1st version), (2nd version) closely following. Both existed simultaneously but were only used in 1961–6**
	'Deltic'-specific.
(1st version)	BR painted steel, size A. Black/dark blue lettering on a white background. This was fixed within a wooden backing frame whose ends slotted into vertical support brackets on the loco, below the headcode panel.
(2nd version)	As (1st version) but without backing frame and fitted with a central bracket for positioning on the upper lamp iron, above the headcode panel.
(e) 5th style headboard	**Introduced 9 March 1964**
	'Winged thistle.' Made in fibreglass resin, painted gold, with no wording. Carried on upper lamp iron only.
(f) 6th style headboard	'Sticker' types on HSTs.
(1st version)	8 May 1978 to celebrate the introduction of the Class 254 units on the service. Very short-lived. (Not illustrated)
(2nd version)	6 June 1981 to celebrate the service commencing its southbound journey from Aberdeen as a through train. Again, very short-lived.

- Non-stop running between London and Edinburgh was not resumed, postwar, until the 1948 summer timetable, commencing 31 May. However, the following year the non-stop 'baton' was passed to a new service THE CAPITALS LIMITED, which in turn passed it on to THE ELIZABETHAN in 1953.
- In 1953 the service was one of the four ER titled trains to carry the extra 'Coronation' headboard on the buffer beam. (see also Colour Section)
- Just as it had pre-war, the postwar express also carried a tailboard. Over the years at least three different versions were used.

The northbound service skirts the North Sea coast near Burnmouth behind No. 65 *Knight of Thistle*, recently converted from A1 to A3 (in March 1947). The train is composed of the then-new stock, with the exception of the triplet restaurant car set near the back. The date must be between March 1947 and July 1948, when No. 65 received its BR number 60065, and the 1st version of the LNER headboard is being carried. *(NRM/SSPL)*

31 May 1948 was a significant day in the postwar rehabilitation of the ECML, since on this date non-stop running was resumed over the 392¾ miles between King's Cross and Waverley, albeit on a 7 hour 50 minute schedule. Here, the first non-stop Down service is about to leave behind No. 60034 *Lord Faringdon*, one of only four A4s to be built (1938) with a double Kylchap chimney, the exhaust being clearly seen to rise in two columns. Until March 1948 the engine had been named *Peregrine*, before commemorating the LNER's deputy chairman from 1923 to 1934. LNER 3rd version headboard is on display, and LNER garter blue will remain on the engine until late October 1950, the last A4 to retain this livery. *(Author's Collection)*

Northbound again, but this time diverted away from the east coast route because of extensive flood damage. On 14 and 16 August 1948 the express was diverted via Selby to Leeds and over the Settle & Carlisle to Edinburgh via Carstairs. On one of these two occasions, A4 No. 25 *Falcon* is seen passing Marley Junction near Keighley, still in LNER guise, hauling 'teak' liveried stock and carrying the 2nd version of the LNER headboard. The ECML was not reopened for passenger traffic until 1 November, and during this diversionary period the non-stop service did, on several occasions, cover the 408½ miles, when running via Kelso and Galashiels, without a stop. This despite the longer, harder route and one less set of water troughs. *(NRM/SSPL)*

THE FLYING SCOTSMAN was the obvious choice to gain one of the extra Coronation headboards in 1953, and this is seen here at Grantham occupying the lower lamp iron while the steel plate (size A) version sits on the upper iron – a rare combination. The engine is No. 60006 *Sir Ralph Wedgwood*, previously named *Herring Gull*, the later name being transferred in January 1944 from the loco that was destroyed in the air raid on York on 29 April 1942, itself having been originally named *Gadwall*. Sir Ralph had been chief general manager of the LNER, 1923– 39. *(By permission of Hull University Archives)*

No. 60007 *Sir Nigel Gresley* was the only A4 originally to be named after a person, though no fewer than ten other A4s (out of a class of thirty-five) had their names changed to those of various personalities, nine of whom had been among the LNER's top management. Close to departure and blowing off steam, No. 60007 has the plain Type 7 headboard with Gill Sans lettering, though the number-plate does not have Gill Sans numerals. The shed-plate (34A) denotes 'Top Shed', as King's Cross was known, and the nameplate has a red background. BR Mk 1 stock in carmine and cream brightens the mid-1950s scene, and although the loco is immaculate in BR green livery, it would have to wait until December 1957 to receive a double chimney. Happily, after withdrawal in February 1966, No. 60007 was bought by the A4 Locomotive Society, in whose capable hands it lives on. Gresley himself was of course the engine's designer, and chief mechanical engineer of the LNER from 1923 until his death in 1941. *(NRM/SSPL)*

It is 18 June 1962 and the Eastern Region of British Railways is marking the centenary of the introduction of the ten o'clock Scotch Express. As remarked earlier, this train had to wait until 1927 before gaining official recognition, and the title is displayed here on the steam-age headboard retained, by this time, for special occasions only. English Electric 3,300hp 'Deltic' diesel No. D9020 *Nimbus* heads the northbound service and will leave King's Cross from Platform 8 only when the Lord Mayor of London, Sir Frederick Hoare, has given the 'right away'. The station itself was designed by the brothers Lewis and Joseph Cubitt, built on the site of the London Smallpox Hospital and opened in 1852 by the Great Northern Railway. As it was close to a crossroads where once had stood a monument to King George IV, the new station became known as King's Cross. *(Topfoto)*

Doncaster Works yard, 1961, and the brand-new 2,000hp diesel No. D347 displays, for inspection purposes, the new headboard designed to be carried in the future by the 3,300hp 'Deltics' (see the Introduction, Part 1, 4th Series for further details). D347 was built at the Vulcan Foundry, Newton-le-Willows, not only with the low headboard brackets, but also with a four-character train description panel, set here to describe the northbound service. *(NRM/SSPL)*

A late shot of the 'winged thistle' headboard, by now retained for special occasions only. Being 1 May 1978, the event being marked here is the Golden Jubilee of the very first non-stop working of the FLYING SCOTSMAN (and the first main-line usage of headboards, therefore). Haymarket's favourite 'Deltic', No. 55022 *Royal Scots Grey* (the erstwhile class leader D9000), pauses at Newcastle on its way to Edinburgh on what is believed to be the only time a blue liveried 'Deltic' carried this headboard in service. *(I.S. Carr)*

Even when the service had ceased to be formed of loco-hauled stock, there have been two notable 'firsts' when a headboard (of sorts) has graced the cab of an HST. The earlier of these, on 8 May 1978, was the first day on which the service became an HST working, and power car No. 254007 bore an adhesive 'advert' of an original design (not illustrated). The second occasion was on 1 June 1981, when the southbound train began running from Aberdeen as a through service. Here, an unknown power car leads the set beneath one of the Granite City's impressive signal gantries at the commencement of the 523½ mile journey. The 'headboard' itself strongly resembles the steam-age Type 7 (2nd version), though with LNER colours. *(C.J.M. Lofthus)*

The second version, seen here leaving Newcastle, has no emblem but does appear to have a light-blue background to the vestibule board. *(J.D. Gomersall Collection)*

The service had been the first to carry a tailboard pre-war, and this feature was repeated in the BR era, as seen here on 30 May 1953. At least two versions have been found (there were probably more), one of which carried the same 'rose and thistle' design (somewhat enlarged) that the Type 7 headboard received, the design being the work of Peter Townend, who later became shedmaster at King's Cross (34A). *(NRM/SSPL)*

THE ABERDONIAN

King's Cross—Aberdeen (Sleeping car train)

Inaugural titled run	11 July 1927 and titled throughout the Second World War
Last titled run	2 May 1971

(a) 1st style headboard	Reintroduced Summer 1946
	LNER standard pattern, with definite article.
(b) 2nd style headboard	Introduced 6 June 1950 (1st version)
	(2nd version) – by 16 May 1952. Precise date unknown.
	BR Type 6 also with ScR light blue background. Top line 3¾in letters; bottom line 3in letters.
(1st version)	Without shields.
(2nd version)	With two size A shields depicting the arms of the cities of London (left) and Aberdeen. (see Colour Section)
(c) 3rd style headboard	Introduced Summer 1962
	'Deltic'-specific. See THE FLYING SCOTSMAN, 4th style (1st version).

- It is not known whether all boards received the shields.
- THE ABERDONIAN was designated (on the outline drawings) to receive a BR painted–steel size B headboard. No evidence has been found for this.

The practice of identifying named trains by the use of loco headboards and carriage roofboards had been banned during the war, but was resumed in 1946. The new policy (not universally applied) was to include THE in the title, as seen in this shot of a V2 2–6–2 hurrying north at Brookman's Park on the outskirts of London on 5 July 1948. More than six months after nationalisation the engine still bears its LNER number 909. *(LCGB: Ken Nunn Collection)*

The southbound sleeping car train leaves Aberdeen behind A2 Pacific No. 60532 *Blue Peter* some time in the early 1950s. This engine was withdrawn from service at the end of 1966 but was then bought for preservation. Over the years since it has made many main-line appearances on excursion trains, but is currently inactive. *(Courtesy The Press Journal, Aberdeen)*

Peppercorn's A1 Pacific strongly resembled his A2 design, and No. 60128 *Bongrace* is seen here backing out of King's Cross having brought in the overnight service. The date is 16 May 1952 and it is likely that the shields have only recently been added. Note the higher position of the headboard, compared to the previous photograph, since on the A2 the number-plate is fixed to the smokebox door strap, allowing a lower position for the top lamp iron. *(H.C. Casserley, courtesy Richard Casserley)*

(THE) QUEEN OF SCOTS

King's Cross–Glasgow (Queen Street) via Leeds (Central) and Edinburgh (Waverley)
(Pullman car train)

Title reintroduced	5 July 1948
Last titled run	13 June 1964

(a) 1st style headboard	Reintroduced 5 July 1948
	LNER standard pattern, without THE.
(b) 2nd style headboard	Reintroduced 5 July 1948
	Shallow LNER pattern, without THE.
(c) 3rd style headboard	Introduced Summer 1949
	BR Type 5 also with ScR light blue background.
(d) 4th style headboard	Introduced 1964
	'Crown with three thistles.' Made in fibreglass resin, painted gold, with no wording. Designed to be carried on upper lamp iron, but no in-service use seen, (see Colour Section).

- The service reversed at Leeds (Central).
- The service carried a tailboard, supplied by the Pullman Car Co. (See page 294)

Setting off from King's Cross in the first year of British Railways, A3 No. 96 *Papyrus*, soon to become No. 60096, achieved a fully authenticated 108mph down Stoke Bank in 1935, the highest speed attained in this country by a non-streamlined engine. *(NRM/SSPL)*

No. 60119 was built in November 1948 by BR at Doncaster but was turned out in LNER green livery with 'British Railways' in full on the tender. Un-named until July 1950 (by which time it had been repainted in BR blue), No. 60119 became *Patrick Stirling*, after the second locomotive superintendent of the Great Northern Railway (1866–95). With its home depot (Copley Hill) just a train's length behind it, No. 60119 accelerates the Pullman service south from Leeds, probably in 1949. *(NRM/SSPL)*

Another of Doncaster's 1948-built A1 Pacifics, No. 60116 *Hal o' the Wynd*, waits to leave Leeds (Central) for points north. The deficiencies of the terminal's short platforms are all too obvious in this mid-1950s view, a dozen or so years before the station closed at the end of April 1967 and was immediately demolished. Nowadays even the site is difficult to locate. No. 60116 was not named until July 1950, gaining the name of a character from Sir Walter Scott's 1828 novel *The Fair Maid of Perth*. The engine spent fourteen of its seventeen years allocated to Heaton (52B) depot in Newcastle. *(NRM/SSPL)*

THE NIGHT SCOTSMAN

King's Cross–Edinburgh (Waverley) (Sleeping car train)

Inaugural titled run	11 July 1927 and titled throughout the Second World War
Last titled run	5 May 1968

(a) 1st style headboard	Reintroduced 1946(?)
	LNER standard pattern, with/without THE.
	NB: No photographic evidence of either of these has been found, though it is thought that at least one version existed.
(b) 2nd style headboard	Introduced 1950/1(?)
	BR Type 7 also with ScR light-blue background.
(c) 3rd style headboard	Introduced Summer 1962
	'Deltic'-specific. See THE FLYING SCOTSMAN, 4th style (1st version).

• THE NIGHT SCOTSMAN was designated (on the outline drawings) to receive a BR painted-steel size A headboard. No evidence has been found for this.

Although no photograph has been found of its in-service use, examples of the 'Deltic'–specific board still exist in private hands.
(Author, courtesy Fawley Museum Society)

A rare view of the Type 7 headboard in service, if not actually on the timetabled train itself, at Haymarket depot in October 1952. Haymarket (64B) shed's own A2/1 No. 60507 *Highland Chieftain* is looking immaculate, right down to the pristine buffer-beam lamps and the well-cleaned headboard. Originally nameless and equipped with a B1 six-wheeled tender, the name was applied about three years after building. The eight-wheeled tender seen here is, interestingly, that which was attached to A4 No. 4469 *Sir Ralph Wedgwood* when this engine was destroyed at York shed in an air raid in 1942. *(RAS Marketing)*

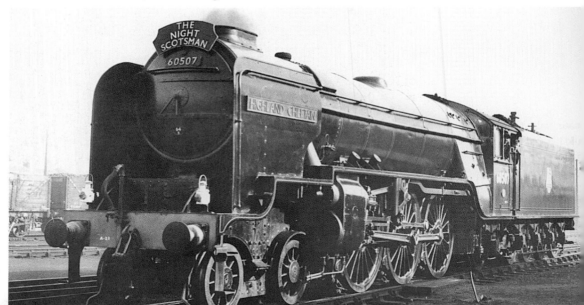

THE CAPITALS LIMITED

King's Cross–Edinburgh (Waverley)

Inaugural titled run	23 May 1949
Last titled run	13 September 1952
Only headboard	Introduced 23 May 1949 (1st version)
	(2nd version) – by 6 June 1950.
	Precise date unknown
	BR Type 1.
(1st version)	Without shields. Superseded by (2nd version).
(2nd version)	As (1st version) but with two size C shields depicting the arms of London (left) and Edinburgh, on bottom line.

- This prestige service ran summers only and took over the mantle of non-stop running from THE FLYING SCOTSMAN.
- Before departure of the inaugural train, the new headboard was unveiled ceremoniously at King's Cross by film star Anne Crawford.
- This was the only ER headboard to have embellishments on the bottom line.

Above, right: A close-up of the shield depicting a (stylised) Edinburgh Castle, to be carried on the right of the headboard. (See also rear cover). *(Author, with permission of NRM)*

Inauguration day, 23 May 1949, and it's 'hats off' to the newly named non-stop service as it leaves King's Cross for the first time. The engine is No. 60010 *Dominion of Canada*, still carrying the bell presented by the Canadian Pacific Railway in March 1938, which it did until receiving a double chimney in December 1957. *(Topfoto)*

THE HEART OF MIDLOTHIAN

King's Cross–Edinburgh (Waverley)

Inaugural titled run	3 May 1951
Last titled run	4 May 1968

(a) 1st style headboard	Introduced 3 May 1951 (1st version). (2nd version), date unknown
	BR Type 7 also with ScR light blue background.
(1st version)	With 3in lettering throughout.
(2nd version)	THE (only) in 3¾in lettering. Otherwise as (1st version).
(b) 2nd style headboard	Introduced Summer 1951
	BR painted steel, size A. White lettering in three lines on a dark–blue/black background.
(c) 3rd style headboard	Introduced Summer 1962
	'Deltic'-specific. See THE FLYING SCOTSMAN, 4th style (2nd version).

- The train was titled specifically for the Festival of Britain, when the 2 p.m. northbound and southbound departures from King's Cross and Waverley respectively were thus named and equipped with brand-new BR Mk 1 coaches in carmine and cream livery.
- The service was extended to Perth from 16 September 1957 for one year only.

Above, right: Although no in-service photo has been found, that which survives appears to be a 2nd version with non-Gill Sans lettering. *(Courtesy Sheffield Railwayana Auctions)*

No. 60043 *Brown Jack*, the final A3 to be built (in February 1935), emerges from the south end of Penmanshiel Tunnel (between Dunbar and Berwick) with the Up service on 17 September 1951. Only outshopped in BR green the month before, No. 60043 was always an Edinburgh-based engine. Note how the Type 7 headboard protrudes above the smokebox, obscuring (from this angle) the single chimney then carried. While the track level within the tunnel was being lowered in preparation for electrification in March 1979, a section of roof collapsed, killing two workers. So extensive was the collapse that it was not possible to recover the bodies, much less reopen the tunnel, which was then bypassed to the west on a new alignment. *(J. Robertson/Transport Treasury)*

Above: Stoke signal-box marked the highest point on the line between Peterborough and Grantham and was exactly 100 miles from King's Cross. Here, No. 60147 has had the task of hauling the thirteen-coach rake of new stock up Stoke Bank and will soon plunge into Stoke Tunnel and run downhill to Grantham. The size A steel headboard is displayed, but the engine's name, *North Eastern*, is not. This dates the photo between May 1951 and March 1952, when the name was eventually fixed, the loco having run almost three years nameless. *(NRM/SSPL)*

Right: Lord Faringdon again at King's Cross, but this time sporting the 2nd version of the Type 7 headboard, 20 July 1959. *(The late Michael Joyce)*

THE ELIZABETHAN

King's Cross–Edinburgh (Waverley)

Inaugural titled run	29 June 1953
Last titled run	7 September 1962

(a) 1st style headboard	**Introduced 29 June 1953**
	BR Type 6 also with ScR light blue background.
(b) 2nd style headboard	'Deltic'-specific type. Not used in traffic. Yellow/cream letters on dark-blue/black background. Doncaster Works viewing experiment only, 1961.
(c) 3rd style headboard	Painted steel. Unidentified, possibly drawing W773. White lettering (small) on dark background. Stop-gap measure.

- This service, a renaming of THE CAPITALS LIMITED to celebrate the Coronation of the new monarch, ran summers only and was non-stop.
- THE ELIZABETHAN brought to an end the era of non-stop running between London and Edinburgh. This ceased on 9 September 1961, since with one summer still to run before the title was withdrawn, the 'Deltics' took over the duty. Ironically, as these diesels had no 'corridor tender' facility for changing crews en route, a stop had to be made at Newcastle to do so.
- Tailboards were also fitted and over the years came in at least three varieties.

'Top Shed' coaling tower with No. 60028 *Walter K. Whigham* being coaled to the limit, supervised by the driver and fireman – who will have to shovel about 4 tons of it on his shift. Note the burnished buffers (and the cylinder cover) and that both the A4 and the V2 front number-plates have Gill Sans numerals. Just why 'electrification flashes' have appeared on No. 60028 is a mystery, as no work of this nature would commence on the ECML until the King's Cross suburban scheme was authorised in 1971. The date must be at least the summer of 1958, as No. 60028 did not receive a double chimney until November 1957. This loco inaugurated the service from King's Cross, 29 June 1953. *(NRM/SSPL)*

Above: No. 60032 *Gannet* at the Hadley Wood Tunnels, 12 July 1960, with an unidentified steel headboard being carried. Of the ten coaches, however, seven are of LNER design, now in the standard maroon livery, and only three are the later BR Mk 1s. *(NRM/SSPL)*

Right: No. D347 exhibiting the proposed headboard that was not adopted (see Introduction, page 201, Part 1, 4th Series), 2 June 1961. Why the headcode panel is incomplete is unknown. *(NRM/SSPL)*

Below: In its last summer of operation, THE ELIZABETHAN was diagrammed for 'Deltic' haulage on a six-hour timing and is seen here headed by No. D9021 awaiting departure from Waverley. Note the absence of electrification warning signs on the diesel, and no name either. The latter was not added until 29 November 1963, when *Argyll & Sutherland Highlander* plates were unveiled at Stirling. *(NRM/SSPL)*

In the early days of service the guard looks forward to establish why speed has fallen, and will soon see that the signal gantry ahead displays 'proceed with caution'. A blue tailboard was fitted at this time and the eleven coaches are of ex-LNER air-conditioned stock, now repainted in BR colours. This set was said at the time to be easily the best train running on the Eastern Region and probably the finest to be found on any ordinary service in the country. Photographed on 22 July 1954 between Brookman's Park and Hatfield, with No. 60032 *Gannet* letting off steam. *(NRM/SSPL)*

Again thought to be in the first year of operation, a different tailboard brings up the rear as the train climbs out of King's Cross. The well-controlled vegetation and the well-tended permanent way feature prominently. *(A.R. Carpenter)*

THE ELIZABETHAN was a Monday to Friday service only, and at weekends the stock could be used to cover shortages on summer Saturdays, or for excursions. One of these must be the case here, as the stock passing through Wellington (Somerset) in 1960 is a long way from the East Coast Main Line. *(I.E. Grinter)*

THE TALISMAN

King's Cross–Edinburgh (Waverley)

Inaugural titled run	17 September 1956
Last titled run	3 May 1968
(a) 1st style headboard	Introduced 17 September 1956
	BR Type 2 also with ScR light blue background.
(b) 2nd style headboard	Introduced 1957
	Painted steel, probably to drawing W773. White letters on dark background.
(c) 3rd style headboard	Introduced Summer 1962
	'Deltic'-specific. See THE FLYING SCOTSMAN, 4th style (1st version).

- This title was introduced as a new service, and was seen as a successor to the pre-war CORONATION, especially as the early eight-coach formations each included a first-class twin set from that train, and the old 4 p.m. departure time was also reinstated.
- On the commencement of the 1957 summer timetable, the service was doubled with the introduction of a 'Morning Talisman'. For either train the headboard still read simply THE TALISMAN. Now using roller-bearing stock, it became possible to use the same train sets for a double working in a day, thus covering 786 miles, the greatest daily mileage of any British coaching stock up to that date.
- For one year only the 'Morning Talisman' was extended to Perth, after which the 'double service' continued until the title's withdrawal (see THE FAIR MAID).
- Tailboards were also used on this service.

King's Cross again, but this time at the buffer-stop end, with No. 60021 *Wild Swan* having recently arrived with the morning departure from Edinburgh. The almost-new Type 2 board sits snugly behind the number-plate, and the immaculate A4 has a red-backed nameplate. The photo must pre-date April 1958, which is when No. 60021 lost its single chimney. *(Transport Treasury)*

No. 60039 was named *Sandwich* after the horse that won the 1931 St Leger, and the express itself after the famous novel of that name written by Sir Walter Scott in 1825. This is the afternoon service, 4 p.m. from King's Cross, on 8 October 1959. With two return workings now bearing the same name, the 'extra' headboard is a painted-steel version of that on No. 60021 in the previous photograph. On the right, A1 No. 60156 *Great Central*, the last of the class to be named (in July 1952), waits with the 4.05 p.m. departure for Leeds and York. *(The late Michael Joyce)*

Only a few months after entering service in May 1961, No. D9004 heads the Up 'Morning Talisman' under Holgate Bridge, just south of York station. No. D9004 was not named until 1964 and has neither yellow warning panel nor top lamp iron. The name *Queen's Own Highlander* was unveiled at a ceremony at Inverness on 23 May 1964. *(Cecil Ord/RAS Publishing)*

THE FAIR MAID

King's Cross–Perth

Inaugural titled run	16 September 1957
Last titled run	12 September 1958

(a) 1st style headboard	Introduced 16 September 1957
	BR Type 2 also with ScR light blue background.
(b) 2nd style headboard	Introduced 1957
	Painted steel, probably to drawing W773. White letters on dark background. (Not illustrated).

• This service was an experimental extension (and renaming) of the 'Morning Talisman'.

Right: The title may not have lasted long, but at least it was appropriate, and echoed that of Scott's novel *The Fair Maid of Perth*. At King's Cross shed before the inaugural run the pristine headboard is fixed to *Quicksilver*, itself newly fitted with the Kylchap double chimney. *(NRM/SSPL)*

Below: The eight-coach rake for THE TALISMAN is seen here approaching Scarborough on a special pre-service trial run on 11 September 1957. Although the tailboard features prominently here, the stock is an interesting choice, with four BR Mk 1s, two LNER vehicles of postwar design, and (the second and third coaches from the rear) a pre-war ex-CORONATION articulated twin, all in the latest maroon livery. *(Ken Hoole Study Centre)*

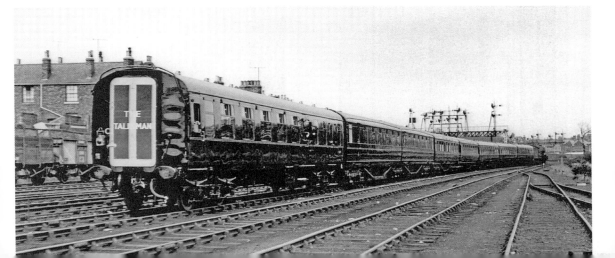

(THE) ANGLO-SCOTTISH CAR CARRIER

London (Holloway)–Newcastle/Edinburgh/Perth

Inaugural titled run	30 May 1960
Last titled run	24 September 1966
(a) 1st style headboard	**Introduced 30 May 1960**
	BR Type 1 (wider version). No definite article.
(b) 2nd style headboard	**Introduced *c.* 1962**
	'Deltic'-specific type, including THE. See THE FLYING SCOTSMAN, 4th style (2nd version).

- The 2nd style headboard has the distinction of having the greatest number of letters (26) on any headboard.
- (b) has only been seen on steam locos.
- The inaugural runs were from King's Cross goods yard, later transferring to Holloway.

30 May 1960, and another inaugural run, as No. 60032 *Gannet* backs down onto its train in King's Cross goods yard, again 'light engine'. Note the burnished buffers and the first-class appearance of the A4, its home depot being accessed through the right-hand archway. *(P.N. Townend)*

No. 60153 *Flamboyant* backs onto the southbound train at Newcastle. Whether or not the board seen here was made as a '2nd version' or is a conversion from a '1st version' is unknown. *(Campbell Lawson Kerr/Mitchell Library, Glasgow)*

THE SILVER JUBILEE

King's Cross–Edinburgh (Waverley)

Inaugural titled run	8 June 1977
Last titled run	5 May 1978

Only headboard	Introduced 8 June 1977
	Non-standard. Centrally, a crowned lion twixt the flag of St George and the Scottish Saltire surmounts a globe bearing the BR symbol and surrounded by laurels. The title, on a scroll, occupies a central lower position on the globe, this section being backed by a larger scroll bearing the years 1952 and 1977. Multicoloured and multilayered. (See also Colour section and title page)

- The title was conferred on the 7.45 a.m. from King's Cross and the 3 p.m. return service, and commenced running on a Wednesday, after the 'double Bank Holiday' following the Silver Jubilee celebrations.
- The service became an untitled HST diagram from 8 May 1978, on a 4 hour 40 minute schedule to Edinburgh.

14 September 1977, and class 55 No. 55 019 *Royal Highland Fusilier* departs York with the northbound service. This was the last 'Deltic' to be named, at Glasgow (Central) on 11 September 1965, and is now preserved. Note that 'corporate blue' livery is the order of the day by this time and that the headboard is backed by an open metal framework. *(Gavin Morrison)*

TEES–TYNE PULLMAN

King's Cross–Newcastle

Inaugural titled run	27 September 1948
Last titled run	30 April 1976
Only headboard	Introduced 27 September 1948
	BR Type 1. (See Colour Section for wooden pattern).

- The inaugural southbound run was hauled by brand-new Pacific No. 60115 of Gateshead shed. Before departing from Newcastle the headboard was unveiled by Miss Esther McCracken (author, playwright and broadcaster of the time).
- A tailboard supplied by the Pullman Car Co. was also carried (see Colour Section).
- After a lapse of over nine years, the title was reintroduced on 30 September 1985 as an HST service (no Pullman cars). This was preceded on 27 September by a special press run (southbound) on which a short-formation HST set completed the entire distance in a record 2 hours 20 minutes. This date was exactly fifty years after the press run that preceded the introduction of the SILVER JUBILEE in 1935 (itself setting records, though going northbound and only as far as the Barkston Triangle, south of Grantham), and exactly 160 years after the opening of the Stockton and Darlington Railway. The HST carried an adhesive headboard for a short while after the introduction of the service (see illustration).

Taken between September 1948 and August 1949, when it acquired BR blue, A3 No. 60072 *Sunstar* heads the eight-car, supplementary fare train south from York. It is seen passing Holgate excursion platforms, whence York racecourse (the Knavesmire) was served in those days. Private-owner four-wheel sheeted wagons and semaphore signals enhance the period scene. *(Cecil Ord/Rail Archive Stephenson)*

A rare sight indeed, as 'double headboarding' hardly ever happened. Often, when a spare headboard needed to be returned to its home depot it would be carried reversed, usually on any service going to the appropriate destination. Not here, however, with the world speed record holder for steam traction, *Mallard*, running south through Doncaster with the correct headboard in both the upper and lower positions on 26 August 1954. No. 60022 is preserved in the National Railway Museum. *(John Hodge)*

The service was reincarnated in 1985 as an HST working, and for a time the power cars carried 'sticker'-type headboards, as displayed on No. 43 038, seen here leading a 2+9 formation southbound near Stevenage on 11 October 1985. An elongated version of the Pullman crest appears above the title. *(David Percival)*

THE NORTHUMBRIAN

King's Cross–Newcastle

Inaugural titled run	26 September 1949
Last titled run	13 June 1964

Only headboard	Introduced 26 September 1949 (1st version); 5 June 1950 (2nd version)
	BR Type 4.
(1st version)	Without shields.
(2nd version)	With two size C shields depicting the arms of London (left) and the ancient Kingdom of Bernicia (the northern part of Northumbria).

- The triple articulated dining set from the pre-war SILVER JUBILEE was included in the formation of this train for some time.
- Northumberland County Council were not granted their own arms until 1951. These incorporated the (slightly modified) arms of Bernicia, and this county council shield is displayed alongside that for London on the headboard in the NRM. However, no evidence has been found for this shield being carried in service.

A1 No. 60157 *Great Eastern* heads south out of Grantham with the embellished headboard placed (unusually for this class) on the buffer-beam lamp iron. This engine was allocated to Grantham (35B) for five years from September 1951 which dates the scene at least roughly. The triplet dining set is fourth, fifth and sixth from the front. *(NRM/SSPL)*

A close-up of the headboard in the NRM which has the Northumberland County Council arms. *(Author, with permission of NRM)*

Below: Again photographed at York, Holgate and most probably in 1949, No. 60003 *Andrew K. McCosh* heads south in the early days of the service. The formation boasted the triple articulated dining set from the pre-war SILVER JUBILEE for a number of years, here forming the fifth, sixth and seventh vehicles, recently repainted in carmine and cream. No. 60003 had borne the name *Osprey* until October 1942, before being renamed after the chairman of the Locomotive Committee. In 1950 *Osprey* was used again, this time on the A1 No. 60131. *(Cecil Ord/Rail Archive Stephenson)*

THE NORSEMAN

King's Cross–Newcastle (Tyne Commission Quay) (Boat train service)

Title reintroduced	7 June 1950
Last titled run	3 September 1966

(a) 1st style headboard	Introduced 7 June 1950 (both versions, probably)
	BR Type 6
(1st version)	Without shields.
(2nd version)	With two size A shields, each depicting a Viking longboat on the open sea. On the left, the ship sails to the left, on the right it sails to the right. (See also Colour Section).
(b) 2nd style headboard	Introduced 1951
	BR painted steel, size B.

- The service ran two or three days a week, summer only, to connect with Bergen Line sailings to Norway.
- Having opened on 16 June 1928, the Tyne Commission Quay closed on 4 May 1970 (last train 2 May). Until 24 November 1968 through trains were loco–hauled from Newcastle (in steam days usually by a V1 or V3 2–6–2 tank engine). After that date, a DMU connecting service was instituted until closure of the rail facility. Buses then substituted.
- No evidence has been found that the headboard on display in the NRM ran thus embellished in service.

A3 No. 60040 *Cameronian* attacks Holloway Bank with some vigour at the start of the northbound journey, probably in 1951. A Gateshead (52A) engine at the time, No. 60040 would be in BR blue livery until May 1952, and here carries the 2nd style headboard. *(F.R. Hebron/Rail Archive Stephenson)*

Gateshead engines were not renowned for their cleanliness, and grubby A4 No. 60016 *Silver King* bears this out. The loco was another of the original four built in 1935 for the SILVER JUBILEE service, and the last of these to be withdrawn, in March 1965, being scrapped at Motherwell two months later. *(Milepost 92½/ A.W.V. Mace)*

The climb out of King's Cross again, this time at Belle Isle (with the North London line flying over), with two A4s in echelon, *c.* 1954. On the right, No. 60033 *Seagull* (one of only four A4s to be built with a double chimney) waits to slip down the shed exit road onto the main line, and will later head THE ELIZABETHAN. Meanwhile, No. 60026 *Miles Beevor* is the main subject of the photograph, nicely under way with the boat train, which it will haul through to Newcastle before handing over to a tank engine for the trip down to the Quay. Miles Beevor was another of those obscure personalities hidden away at the top of the LNER management tree, being the acting chief general manager at the time of nationalisation.No. 60026 (as 26) gained his name at Marylebone in November 1947 as a replacement for *Kestrel*, which was reused on A1 No. 60130 in 1950. *(NRM/SSPL)*

THE TYNESIDER

King's Cross–Newcastle (Sleeping car train)

Inaugural titled run	5 June 1950
Last titled run	4 May 1968

(a) 1st style headboard	Introduced 5 June 1950 (both versions, it is believed)
	BR Type 6.
(1st version)	Without shields.
(2nd version)	With two size A shields depicting the arms of London (left) and Newcastle.
(b) 2nd style headboard	Introduced 1962
	'Deltic'-specific. See THE FLYING SCOTSMAN, 4th style (1st version).

- THE TYNESIDER was designated (on the outline drawings) to receive a BR painted-steel size B headboard. No evidence has been found for this.
- As the train operated almost wholly within the hours of darkness, no in-service photograph has been found of any style of headboard.

The 'Deltic'-specific board, with backing frame (not shown). Seen from the rear, the wood is cut to match the profile of the steel plate, with sideways extensions, as one piece (see also page 208, THE ABERDONIAN). *(Courtesy Sheffield Railwayana Auctions)*

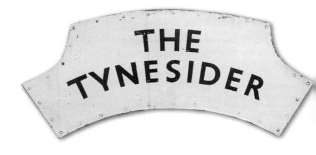

One of the huts at Grantham shed has five titles displayed on the rack outside, including three of the sleeping car train's rarely seen headboards, in both versions, 9 August 1955. Grantham (105 miles from London) was traditionally an engine change-over point and always had a good stock of headboards. *(Gavin Morrison)*

THE NORTH BRITON

Leeds (City)–Glasgow (Queen Street) via York.

Inaugural titled run	26 September 1949
Last titled run	4 May 1968
Only headboard	Introduced 26 September 1949
	BR Type 4.

- The title was conferred on the 8.48 a.m. from Leeds and the 4 p.m. return working from Glasgow. When introduced it was scheduled to cover the 44.1 miles from Darlington to York in 44 minutes, the first 60mph timing since before the war.
- This was the only ER titled train to use the City station in Leeds.
- The title lapsed for four years but was resurrected in 1972 and applied to a Leeds–Dundee service until May 1975. No headboard was carried during this time.

25 March 1961, and the 9.15 a.m. to Glasgow prepares to leave the east end of City station behind the Neville Hill (55H) A3 *Gainsborough*. This station has since undergone not one but two total rebuilds and is now electrified, though not for eastbound departures, as the 20 miles (or so) between Neville Hill Traincare Depot (as it now is) and Colton South Junction on the outskirts of York are currently wire-less. Having taken this picture, the photographer then travelled (officially) on the foot-plate to Newcastle. *(Gavin Morrison)*

(THE) YORKSHIRE PULLMAN

King's Cross–Leeds (Central)/Bradford (Exchange)/Harrogate/Hull

Title reintroduced	4 November 1946 (by LNER)
Last titled run	5 May 1978

(a) 1st style headboard	Reintroduced 4 November 1946
	LNER standard pattern with definite article.
(b) 2nd style headboard	Introduced 31 May 1948(?)
	BR Type 1.
(c) 3rd style headboard	Introduced Summer 1962
	'Deltic'-specific. See THE FLYING SCOTSMAN, 4th style (1st version). (See also Colour Section).

- Because of the fuel shortage this train was withdrawn (along with many others) for a large part of 1947. Operation resumed on 6 October.
- This service also carried a tailboard. Perhaps surprisingly there is no evidence that a 'standard' Pullman Car Co. type was used.
- Friday 5 May 1978 closed the era of Pullman car trains on the East Coast Main Line. The Hull Pullman (not headboarded) was withdrawn at the same time, having been introduced as a separate service in March 1967. The brand name 'Pullman' lived on, but not the rolling stock.

No. 60047 *Donovan* received its BR number in May 1948, and as the cast headboard would shortly appear on the scene the photo is likely to have been taken not long after this. The location is Beeston Junction, just south of Leeds, and the Up service carries the postwar LNER headboard. The engine itself was repainted into LNER green in January 1948 – the BR era – and was one of three A3s to receive this treatment that year. *(NRM/SSPL)*

No. 60051 was named *Blink Bonny* after the horse that won both the Derby and the Oaks way back in 1857, the earliest year from which race winners were commemorated on the Pacifics. Again heading south out of Leeds, probably in 1953 or 1954, but with the rear of the train still passing Copley Hill shed (37B), No. 60051 has one of the first cast headboards to appear, though without the definite article in comparison with the previous shot. *(NRM/SSPL)*

A murky day at King's Cross, and with the front of the train already inside Gasworks Tunnel the rear advertises the service again for those watching the departure from the platform end. *(Kenneth Oldham)*

THE WEST RIDING

King's Cross–Leeds (Central)/Bradford (Exchange)

Inaugural titled run	23 May 1949
Last titled run	4 March 1967

(a) 1st style headboard	Introduced 23 May 1949
	BR Type 3.
(b) 2nd style headboard	Used only for a fortnight or so either side of the Queen's
	Coronation, 2 June 1953
	Painted-steel 3rd Series, Coronation board, the only one specific to a particular title. The arms are those of the West Riding of Yorkshire and the motto translates as 'Heed Counsel' (see also Colour Section).
(c) 3rd style headboard	Introduced 1962
	'Deltic'-specific. See THE FLYING SCOTSMAN, 4th style (1st version).

- For several years the formation included six of the coaches from the pre-war WEST RIDING LIMITED streamlined train, these having been in storage at Copley Hill carriage sidings (Leeds) during the war.
- Headboard embellishments were designed for this service, but were never produced.

With a Copley Hill A1 in charge of the service, No. 60123 *H.A. Ivatt* is seen between Stevenage and Hitchin with the Down train on 6 June 1953. The engine carries the Coronation commemorative headboard, and the name of the Great Northern Railway's locomotive superintendent between 1896 and 1911 (Gresley's predecessor). *(The Gresley Society/G.W. Goslin)*

No. 60006 *Sir Ralph Wedgwood* climbs past Ganwick (just south of Potter's Bar) with what is thought to be the inaugural northbound run, though the King's Cross A4 is somewhat shabby for such an occasion. The first six coaches behind the (non-corridor) tender are three articulated twins from the pre-war streamlined train, newly repainted in carmine and cream. *(NRM/SSPL)*

Probably taken between Doncaster and Leeds in 1961-2, the express has now shrunk from fourteen coaches to eight BR Mk 1s in maroon, and gained 'Deltic' power in the form of No. D9007 *Pinza*. This engine was the first of the class to receive its name (on 22 June 1961, the day it entered service), and was named after the winner of the 1953 Derby. *(NRM/SSPL)*

THE WHITE ROSE

King's Cross–Leeds (Central) / Bradford (Exchange)

Inaugural titled run	23 May 1949
Last titled run	13 June 1964

(a) 1st style headboard	Introduced 23 May 1949 (1st version) March 1950 (2nd version)
	BR Type 3.
(1st version)	Without discs.
(2nd version)	With twin size R discs depicting the White Rose of York.
(b) 2nd style headboard	Introduced 1951
	BR painted-steel size C. Also size B (see THE TYNESIDER for this illustration).
(c) 3rd style headboard	Used between 26 March and 14 April 1962 only
	Painted steel, 6th Series (iv). Large circular board promoting the 'Wool Wins' campaign of that time (not illustrated).

- After 13 June 1964 the service continued to run, untitled. However, with the simultaneous discontinuation of THE QUEEN OF SCOTS, two sets of Pullman cars became spare, one of which was used to form a new 'White Rose Pullman' which operated from 15 June 1964 until this was in turn withdrawn on 4 March 1967. This train was not headboarded.

Wakefield was the county town of the old West Riding of Yorkshire, and the distinctive clock tower at the Westgate station was a familiar landmark. With this feature as a backdrop, No. 60046 *Diamond Jubilee* will shortly depart for London, having had the Bradford portion, worked via Morley (Top), attached at the rear. *(NRM/SSPL)*

Another of Copley Hill's A1 Pacifics, No. 60114 *W.P. Allen* is about to depart from the cramped terminal at Leeds (Central), probably in 1950. Unusually, the 2nd style headboard is being carried. No. 60114 was the first engine of the new A1 class to be built, and the only one to be accorded an official naming ceremony. This took place at King's Cross on 28 October 1948, when Sir Eustace Missenden, chairman of the Railway Executive, named the engine after the trade union member of the Executive. It was to be eighteen months before any other class member was named. *(NRM/SSPL)*

A rather battered example of the embellished headboard sits astride the chevrons on the nose of the prototype 'Deltic', seen here at King's Cross on 7 July 1959. Initially allocated to Hornsey depot, then on its completion to the new diesel depot at Finsbury Park, the 'Blue Deltic' (as it was always known) worked almost exclusively between London and Leeds until its retirement back to the Vulcan Foundry in March 1961. Not for scrap, however, as the loco has been preserved ever since, firstly at the Science Museum, latterly at the National Railway Museum. The 'Blue Deltic' is flanked at King's Cross by 'Baby Deltic' No. D5906. As a class, these were singularly unsuccessful, in total contrast to their larger cousins. (See also Colour Section). *(NRM/SSPL)*

THE HARROGATE SUNDAY PULLMAN

King's Cross–Leeds (Central)/Bradford (Exchange)/Harrogate.

Title reintroduced	11 June 1950
Last titled run	5 March 1967

(a) 1st style headboard	Introduced 11 June 1950 (1st version). Others later, dates unknown BR Type 7.
(1st version)	Without shields.
(2nd version)	With two size C shields depicting the arms of London (left) and Harrogate. Shields aligned normally.
(3rd version)	As (2nd version) but with shields angled across the top corners.
(b) 2nd style headboard	Introduced 1951 BR painted-steel size A.

- Only this headboard displayed two different shield alignments. It is not known why.
- This board has the second-largest number of letters (25).
- The Harrogate portion reversed at Leeds (Central).

A close-up of the Type 7 2nd version headboard showing the normal alignment of the London and Harrogate shields. *(Courtesy Sheffield Railwayana Auctions)*

Copley Hill depot with No. 60123 fully coaled and standing in the shed yard with the 1st version of the Type 7 headboard prominent. *(NRM/SSPL)*

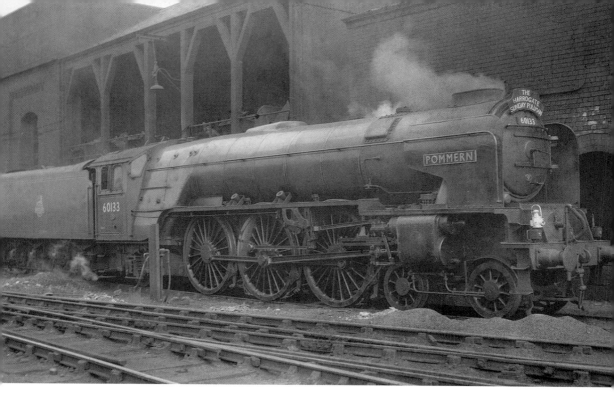

One of Copley Hill's own A1s being coaled at its home depot, c. 1951-2. The large-size painted-steel board sits in front of the unlipped double chimney. In 1915 the racehorse *Pommern* won the Derby, the 2000 Guineas and the St Leger. This loco was the second of the class to be named, in April 1950. *(RAS Marketing)*

No. 60118 *Archibald Sturrock* (the first locomotive superintendent of the GNR, 1850–66) simmers in the sun at Leeds (Central), sporting the 3rd version headboard with the angled shields uniquely 'lying' on the 3in lettering. *(The Stephenson Locomotive Society)*

THE SCARBOROUGH FLYER

King's Cross–Scarborough (Central)/Whitby (Town)

Title reintroduced	5 June 1950
Last titled run	8 September 1963
(a) 1st style headboard	Introduced 5 June 1950
	LNER standard pattern, with definite article.
(b) 2nd style headboard	Introduced 5 June 1950
	BR Type 7.
(1st version)	Without 'sunbursts' (see THE TYNESIDER for this illustration).
(2nd version)	With twin size B 'sunbursts' (in brass).
(c) 3rd style headboard	Introduced 1951
	BR painted-steel size A.

- The exact chronology of (b) is uncertain. The inaugural southbound run carried (a) but both versions of (b) appear to have been available at much the same time also.
- This service operated summer only.

One of York's own V2s, No. 60979, heads south past the racecourse platforms on the exit from York with a substantial thirteen-coach train of varied stock, probably in 1951. *(By permission of Hull University Archives)*

The BR painted headboard sits uncomfortably high on B16/3 No. 61434 as it leaves York for Scarborough in the early 1950s. Former NER designs such as this had the top lamp iron on the smokebox itself (rather than the door) and staff were always reluctant to use this position. *(Author's collection)*

An extremely rare view of the unique W1 4–6–4 No. 60700 carrying a headboard. Here it's the Type 7 board complete with 'sunbursts' and is seen passing Escrick, about halfway between Selby and York (where engines will be changed). As the engine is still allocated to King's Cross, the photo cannot be later than the summer of 1953, since it was transferred to Doncaster in October of that year. Always known as 'the un-named streak', two sets of nameplates were in fact made for it, *British Enterprise* (by Darlington) and *Pegasus* (by Doncaster), but neither was ever fitted. (See also Colour Section). *(Cecil Ord/Rail Archive Stephenson)*

THE TEES–THAMES

King's Cross–Middlesbrough / Saltburn

Inaugural titled run	2 November 1959
Last titled run	9 September 1961

(a) 1st style headboard	Introduced 2 November 1959
	BR Type 3.
(b) 2nd style headboard	Introduced 2 November 1959
	Painted steel. Possibly to diagram W765. Unusually, all three words were on one line.

- Both styles were available from the start. Probably the 2nd style was only used north of York where engines were changed and the 1st style to the south of York.
- The start of the winter timetable 1959/60 was delayed from 13 September owing to a printing dispute. This was a new, additional service.

THE TEES–THAMES LINK

Middlesbrough–Doncaster (southbound only) (DMU Service)

Inaugural titled run	27 October 1958
Last titled run	30 October 1959

Only headboard	Introduced 27 October 1958(?)
	Non-standard type for DMU (see Colour Section).

- In an attempt to give Teesside a better service to London this connecting service was provided, using a then brand-new DMU set complete with headboard. The venture was successful enough for BR to provide a steam-hauled through express from the beginning of the winter timetable (see above).
- This was the only DMU service to carry a headboard (the LMR 'Trans-Pennine' was a brand name for an entire service, rather than an individual title).

The 2nd style headboard was rarely seen, but here it is carried by Thornaby (51L) shed's V2 No. 60846, probably in 1960, on the Up service. *(By permission of Hull University Archives)*

No. 60103 *Flying Scotsman* is ready to leave Peterborough after making the northbound stop, and the relatively small headboard (with a black background) shows up none too well against the engine's smokebox, especially as the scene is back-lit. This famous locomotive was the first A1 to be completed under the auspices of the LNER, the preceding two Pacifics having been built entirely in GNR days. Converted to an A3 (i.e. receiving a 220psi boiler instead of the 180psi original) in January 1947 and withdrawn sixteen years later, the engine covered more than two million miles during its forty years of service. It has, however, now been in preservation for even longer. In this era it has not only been very active on BR metals but has also undertaken extensive tours of the USA and Canada (1969–73, disastrously) and Australia (1988–9, successfully). Now out of private hands, the engine is at last part of the national collection and is based at the NRM at York. *(NRM/SSPL)*

Right: Introduced too late for inclusion in the winter 1958/9 timetable, the only timetable in which THE TEES–THAMES LINK ever appeared was for summer 1959, operational between 15 June and 1 November. *(BRB (Residuary) Ltd)*

Table 2—*continued*

NEWCASTLE, DURHAM, FERRYHILL, DARLINGTON,

MONDAYS to FRIDAYS

D—Diesel Train.
A—Commences 16th June.
B—On Suns. departs Aberdeen 5.40, and Dundee 7.44 pm.
C—Runs 20th July to 28th August inclusive.
E—Calls to set down only.
F—Liverpool (Exchange). Change at Harrogate and Leeds (Central).
G—2 minutes earlier on 15th June.
H—Applies Sunday to Thursday nights.
J—Commences 15th June.
K—Connection at Eaglescliffe.
L—Applies Sunday to Thursday nights and only conveys Sleeping Car passengers.
M or MO—Mondays only.
MX—Mondays excepted.

N—Mondays only. Runs 13th July to 24th August inclusive.
P—Change at Peterborough.
R—Via Ripon (Table 39).
RC—Restaurant Car.
T—One minute earlier on 15th June.
V—Mondays only. Also runs Tuesdays and Thursdays commencing 21st July.
Y—Tuesdays and Thursdays only. Commences 21st July.
d—Sunday night.
f—Via Church Fenton and Selby (Table 13). On Mondays arrives Hull 4.56 am.
g—Mondays 20th July to 24th August only.
h—Connection at Stockton.

k—Via Doncaster. Applies Tuesdays and Thursdays commencing 21st July.
n—From 20th July to 4th September inclusive arrives Scarborough 9.44 am.
q—Applies 20th July to 21st August inclusive.
s—Via Selby (Table 13).
t—Except Sunday nights.
u—Change at Doncaster.
w—On Sundays departs Glasgow 9.0 pm.
y—Only conveys Sleeping Car passengers. On Sundays departs Glasgow 9.0 pm.

THE HULL EXECUTIVE

King's Cross–Hull (Paragon)

Inaugural titled run	8 May 1978
Last titled run	2 January 1981
Only headboard	Introduced 14 May 1979
	BR painted steel, 4th Series, resembling the earlier 'Deltic'-specific type but may have been a slight variation of this. Red background silver/grey lettering.

- Faster scheduling from 14 May 1979 resulted in a record average speed (for a loco-hauled train) of 91.3mph being maintained between King's Cross and Retford. The express was headboarded in consequence of this.
- Class 55 diesels ('Deltics') were diagrammed for this service until HST sets took over on 5 January 1981.

Taken at Stratford depot on 14 July 1979, Finsbury Park 'Deltic' No. 55 015 *Tulyar* carries the last newly introduced traditional headboard to be used regularly out of King's Cross. The racehorse of this name won the Derby and the St Leger in 1952 and was owned by the Aga Khan. No. 55015 lives on as one of the six preserved examples of this class. *(Geoff Cann)*

THE MASTER CUTLER

Marylebone–Sheffield (Victoria) 6 October 1947 to 13 September 1958
King's Cross–Sheffield (Victoria) 15 September 1958 to 1 October 1965 (Pullman car train)
King's Cross–Sheffield (Midland) 4 October 1965 to 4 October 1968 (Pullman car train)

Inaugural titled run	6 October 1947 (by LNER)
Last titled run	4 October 1968 (on ER lines)
(a) 1st style headboard	**Introduced 6 October 1947 (Down service). Soon superseded by (b), (c)** LNER non-standard type. 1st Series (a), with THE (in small letters) on upper line, but with board 'stepped down' on either side of this. Unique to this service. Painted steel.
(b) 2nd style headboard	**Introduced 6 October 1947 (Up service)** BR Type 1 shape, but wider (46in) privately supplied and made in stainless steel (see 1st Series (a)). Polished edges and lettering on a black background, one line only. Unique to this service.
(c) 3rd style headboard	**Introduced c. 1950 (1st version); c. 1954 (2nd version); c. 1958/9 (3rd version); 21 April 1959 (4th version); c. 1960s (5th version)** BR Type 6. THE with 3¾in letters; others 3in.
(1st version)	Without shields.
(2nd version)	With two size A shields depicting the arms of the Company of Cutlers in Hallamshire (left) and the City of Sheffield.
(3rd version)	As (2nd version) but with two size C shields.
(4th version)	As (3rd version) but with letters and shields in stainless steel, privately supplied, each individually attached to the board. Shields unpainted, size C (see Colour Section).
(5th version)	As (3rd version) but in fibreglass resin. Shields unpainted.

In the early days of the service motive power was provided by the B1 4–6–0s, and here Leicester's No. 1187 is seen with the Down train at Wembley Hill on 27 April 1948. The last new LNER headboard is carried and a long neat rake of teak-liveried stock trails behind the tender. *(LCGB: Ken Nunn Collection)*

As loadings became consistently heavier, A3s were drafted onto the GC main line. No. 60102 *Sir Frederick Banbury* was reallocated to Leicester (from Grantham) in May 1949. This engine was the second (and last) Pacific to be completed by the GNR (in July 1922, as No. 1471) and was appropriately named after the last chairman of that railway before amalgamation in 1923. Here at Marylebone in the mid-1950s No. 60102 has just come in and the fireman is already busy in the tender. The large size A shields decorate the Type 6 headboard. Note the water column and the engine run-round pointwork. *(E.M. Johnson)*

- This was the last title to be conferred by the LNER. Indeed, it was the only new title to be introduced by that company postwar that had no previous pre-war connections.
- This was the first named train to run down the GC main line into Marylebone. In 1947 the name was applied to the 7.40 a.m. from Sheffield and the 6.15 p.m. return working.
- Firth-Vickers Stainless Steels (of Sheffield) made (b) and the lettering and shields for (c) (4th version), the only private firm to supply headboards to either the LNER or BR. When the service became a Pullman car train, the original 1947 stainless-steel headboards were taken out of use and one of these was presented back to the then Master Cutler (Mr J. Hugh Neill) for permanent display in the Cutler's Hall in Sheffield. Mr G.F. Fiennes, Line Traffic Manager ER (Great Northern lines), made the presentation on behalf of British Railways, and in return received a new headboard (described above as (c) (4th version)) from Firth-Vickers' chairman Mr W.D. Pugh and the Master Cutler. This official ceremony took place at Staybrite Works, Sheffield on 21 April 1959, some seven months after the train had been re-routed.
- In 1953 the service was one of the four ER titled trains to carry the extra 'Coronation' headboard on the buffer beam.
- After 4 October 1968 the service was transferred to St Pancras and the Midland main line, lost its Pullman cars, and initially lost its title also. See the London Midland Section for further details, post-1968.

The man elected Master Cutler in 1979, Mr B.E. Cotton CBE, has one of the 1947 stainless steel headboards in front of him and a very appropriate background behind him in the Cutler's Hall, Sheffield. *(Courtesy Sheffield Newspapers Ltd)*

Even before its re-routing to King's Cross as a service, the annual 'special' from London to Sheffield for the Cutler's Feast ran from King's Cross, and here No. 60021 *Wild Swan* has the 1957 train, on 5 April. The 'Feast' has a long history. First held as an annual dinner in 1625 – even before the original Cutler's Hall was built in 1638 – and called a Feast from 1680, it has been held every year, with only eight exceptions, ever since. The special train ceased in about 1970, however. The headboard for this is of particular interest, being of size A painted steel complete with size A shields, the wrong way round. (Note, being a privately chartered train, this headboard is unlisted.) *(NRM/SSPL)*

Nottingham (Victoria), south end, on Saturday 13 September 1958, the very last day of operation of this train over this route. From the following Monday, the title would apply to a diesel-hauled Pullman train running via Retford and up the ECML into King's Cross. So, for the final time the crew look expectantly for the 'right away' before easing their V2 on its way to Marylebone. Without the shields on the headboard, the difference in letter size seems even more noticeable. *(T.G. Hepburn/Rail Archive Stephenson)*

And so to King's Cross as a timetabled train, where No. D206 is seen emerging from Gasworks Tunnel soon after the commencement of the Pullman service, 7 October 1958. Surprisingly, the size A shields are again the wrong way round, with the Sheffield shield on the left (compare with No. 60102 at Marylebone). Note the suburban tank engine with 'Finsbury Park' displayed on the bunker. *(NRM/SSPL)*

The next diesel in number sequence, No. D207, poses for a publicity shot in which it will be seen that four of the six Pullmans are now of the latest stock and that the headboard with stainless-steel letters and small size C shields is deployed. (Note that the Sheffield shield is on the right.) Taken on 25 September 1960, the new formation entered service on the 28th. *(NRM/SSPL)*

THE SOUTH YORKSHIREMAN

Marylebone–Bradford (Exchange) via Huddersfield and Halifax

Inaugural titled run	31 May 1948
Last titled run	2 January 1960
Only headboard	Introduced 31 May 1948 BR Type 5.

- This was the first title to be conferred by BR, and the first therefore to be provided with a cast-aluminium headboard.
- This was the second (of two) titled services to utilise the GC main line into Marylebone.
- Pre-war, there had been an LMS express named 'The Yorkshireman' running between Bradford (Exchange) and St Pancras, for which this was effectively a replacement service.
- THE SOUTH YORKSHIREMAN was allocated a painted-steel headboard to drawing W765, but no evidence has been seen for this.
- Exchange station saw its last trains on 13 January 1973. Services were then transferred to the new Interchange station a short distance up the line from the previous terminal.

In the early postwar years a newly titled train was an event that was well reported locally and was seen as a sign of recovery, a restoration of normality. BR's first brand-new title was duly unveiled at the unprepossessing terminus of Bradford (Exchange) by a large gathering of local dignitaries on 31 May 1948. Here the Lord Mayor of Bradford (Alderman F.J. Cowie) performs the ceremony and later gave the 'right away', being then presented with the whistle and green flag as souvenirs. The Mayor and Mayoress of Huddersfield (Mr and Mrs O. Smith) were also present and travelled in the train to Huddersfield where he too whistled the train off, again retaining the whistle as a memento. Note the short-lived letter prefix M in front of the old LMS engine number, all of which later had 40000 added to them. At the time the shed-plate 25A denoted allocation to Wakefield depot. *(NRM/SSPL)*

Opposite, bottom: Before the advent of the 'Britannia' Pacifics in 1951, B1 4–6–0s were the staple motive power for GE line expresses, with many of the 410 locos built being brand new in the early BR period. Passing Stratford on 12 June 1949, No. 61226 is looking neat and tidy and carrying the 2nd version LNER headboard. A Gresley wooden-bodied full brake and a Thompson steel-sided coach are the first two vehicles, in BR carmine and cream. *(W. Hermiston/Transport Treasury)*

HOOK-OF-HOLLAND/(THE) HOOK CONTINENTAL

Liverpool Street–Harwich (Parkeston Quay) (Boat train service)

Title reintroduced	14 November 1945 (by LNER)
Last titled run	10 May 1987
(a) 1st style headboard	Introduced Summer 1946(?) (1st version); 1947–9 (2nd and 3rd versions)
	LNER standard pattern.
(1st version)	HOOK-OF-HOLLAND.
(2nd version)	HOOK CONTINENTAL. Also repainted by BR (not illustrated).
(3rd version)	THE HOOK CONTINENTAL.
(b) 2nd style headboard	Introduced 5 June 1950
	BR painted steel, size A, in three lines. Dutch flag (left) and Union Jack on either side of THE on top line.
(c) 3rd style headboard	Introduced Summer 1951 *et seq*, order unknown. All three versions probably coexisted
	BR Type 7.
(1st version)	With two size D enamelled discs in the top corners, depicting the same flags as in (b).
(2nd version)	As (1st version) but with the flags now painted onto discs that were cast integral with the headboard.
(3rd version)	Without embellishments. Rarely seen.
(d) 4th style headboard	Introduced 1985
	Painted steel 6th Series (vi). Blue background with antique silver letters and edging. Flags 4½in by 2¼in. Letter size 3in.

- This was the first titled train to be reintroduced after the war, the inaugural run leaving Liverpool Street behind apple green B1 class 4–6–0 No. 8304 *Gazelle*.
- This service operated in conjunction with British Railways' Royal Mail route sailings overnight to and from the Hook of Holland.
- No evidence can be found that this service carried a tailboard postwar, in contrast to its pre-war counterpart.

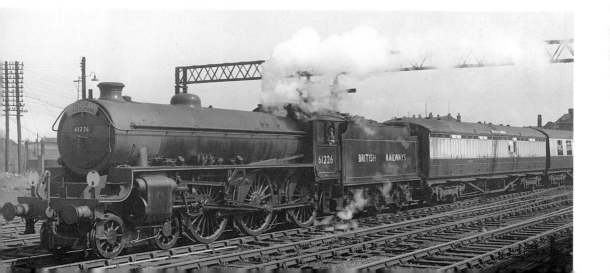

Parkeston Quay 1947, still in LNER days, and B1 No. 1149 displays the pristine twin white discs favoured by the GE lines to distinguish their express services. The 'L5' on the buffer beam denoted 'Load Classification 5' when hauling freight trains, and was applied only to LNER freight or mixed-traffic engines and by no means universally. The double-hyphenated headboard is unique. *(NRM/SSPL)*

Below: No. 61264 was a Parkeston (30F) engine for many years and a regular performer on the various boat trains to Harwich. Seen here at Liverpool Street, probably in 1950, the cheerful crew have no qualms about tackling Bethnal Green and Brentwood banks with a 'class 5' locomotive and a trailing load approaching 500 tons. Fortunately No. 61264 still exists. It now resides at the Great Central Railway at Loughborough and is currently in working order. The photographer was not only the Parkeston shedmaster at the time, but he also designed the embellishment on the painted-steel headboard. *(W. Cattermole)*

Type 7 headboard, without discs, seen [nea]ring Liverpool Street on No. 70007 *Coeur-[de-L]ion, c.* 1957. On the left, No. 70010 *Owen [Glen]dower* prepares to leave with the 9.30 a.m. [to N]orwich. The arrival of the 'Britannias' enabled [tot]al recasting of the East Anglian services in [195?]. *(Lance King)*

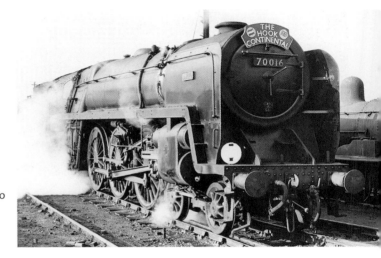

[Str]atford shed yard on 25 January 1953 sees [No.] 70016 *Ariel* bearing the 'twin discs' [he]adboard. This engine was normally allocated to [th]e WR and was a short-term transfer to the [GE] lines to ease a motive power shortage. *[(]K.B. Green Collection/ Initial Photographics)*

[Man]chester, 12 May 1986 with a class 86 electric [lo]w in charge. Photos of any 25kV ac electric [loco] in a titled train headboard are extremely rare. *[(Ma]lcolm Root)*

A close-up of a rare survivor, the 3rd version headboard (or blade as it was known locally). *(Harwich Railway & Shipping Museum/ Bob Clow Collection)*

(THE) SCANDINAVIAN

Liverpool Street–Harwich (Parkeston Quay) (Boat train service)

Title reintroduced	7 December 1945 (by LNER)
Last titled run	4 May 1975

(a) 1st style headboard	Introduced 6 May 1946(?) (1st version); 1948/9 (2nd version)
	LNER standard pattern.
(1st version)	In LNER colours, no definite article.
(2nd version)	Repainted by BR. White lettering on dark blue background, with THE on top line.
(b) 2nd style headboard	Introduced 1948/50 respectively
	Transitional 'elliptical top' design.
(1st version)	In LNER colours.
(2nd version)	Repainted by BR. Now with white lettering on a dark background.
(c) 3rd style headboard	Introduced 5 June 1950
	BR painted steel, size B. Danish flag (left) and Union Jack on either side of THE.
(d) 4th style headboard	Introduced Summer 1951
	BR Type 6 with two size D enamelled discs in the top corners depicting the same flags as in (c). THE in 3¾in letters, others 3in.

- The service operated in conjunction with the United Steamship Co. Ltd of Copenhagen. Sailings were overnight to and from Esbjerg, with onward rail connections to principal towns in Scandinavia.

Occasionally, if a 4–6
was not available,
a 4–4–0 would be
substituted. Here it's
D16/3 No. 2532 doin
the honours on the
service train, of which
nine roofboarded
coaches are visible, at
Parkeston Quay on 1
July 1947. *(NRM/SSP*

On 3 June 1946 a new motor vessel, *Kron Prinz Frederik*, was introduced on the Harwich–Esbjerg route. In connection with this the Crown Prince of Denmark made an unofficial visit to this country on board the eponymous vessel on 28 May – its maiden voyage. A special train from Parkeston Quay to Liverpool Street was placed at the disposal of the Crown Prince and his party, and is seen here at Harwich. The engine reserved for Royal duties, B2 No. 1671 *Royal Sovereign*, had been recently rebuilt and renamed, and was drafted in from its depot at Cambridge for the event. In addition, a large circular board with the Union Jack and Danish flags superimposed and attached to it was fixed over the smokebox door. The pre-war headboard, suitably repainted, enhances the scene, although this was not the service train. This title was almost certainly the first to be re-headboarded postwar. *(London News Agency Photos Ltd)*

Harwich again, this time with Stratford (30A) B17/1 No. 61612 *Houghton Hall* departing for London, 1 July 1950. The LNER headboard has been repainted by BR. *(LCGB: Ken Nunn Collection)*

Still at Harwich, the now-preserved B1 No. 61264 reverses the empty stock out of the carriage sidings and into the platform on 16 August 1950. The headboard has now undergone 'colour reversal'. *(NRM/SSPL)*

Somewhat earlier, on 10 September 1949, B17/4 No. 61648 *Arsenal* (another Stratford engine) wears the 'elliptical top' headboard in LNER colours. Note the extremely grimy state of the engine. *(LCGB: Ken Nunn Collection)*

B17/1 No. 61606 *Audley End* at Liverpool Street with the brand-new painted-steel headboard in place, June 1950. *(NRM/SSPL)*

B1 No. 61226 tops Bethnal Green Bank with the Down train in 1951 carrying the cast-aluminium headboard. The electrification is for the Shenfield services, which had been authorised in 1936, delayed by the war and energised in 1949 at 1,500V dc. This was the first postwar electrification scheme to be completed, and was very well received. *(NRM/SSPL)*

(THE) EAST ANGLIAN

Liverpool Street–Norwich (Thorpe)

Title reintroduced	7 October 1946 (by LNER)
Title withdrawn	16 June 1962 until
Reintroduced	12 May 1980
Last titled run	Ran until privatisation

(a) 1st style headboard	Introduced 7 October 1946 (1st version); 1948/9 (2nd and 3rd versions)
	LNER standard pattern, without definite article.
(1st version)	In LNER colours.
(2nd version)	Repainted by BR, white letters, green background.
(3rd version)	Repainted by BR, white letters, dark-blue/black background.
(b) 2nd style headboard	Introduced 1949
	BR Type 2 without definite article.
(c) 3rd style headboard	Introduced June 1951 (1st version); July 1951 (2nd version)
	BR Type 7, with definite article.
(1st version)	Without shields.
(2nd version)	With two size A shields depicting the arms of London (left) and the Kingdom of East Anglia. (See also Colour Section).
(d) 4th style headboard	Introduced 12 May 1980
	Painted steel, 5th Series. White lettering, horizontal, on blue background. Two shields, depicting the same arms.

- This service had been introduced on 27 September 1937 as a fast 'streamlined' service, similar to the three GN lines expresses (though no surcharge was made), and lasted until 31 August 1939. Like these other three, no headboard was carried in that period.
- Postwar the six dedicated coaches were refurbished and then reused, at least initially, on the reinstated service. The two class B17 4–6–0s that had been streamlined (A4 fashion) specially for this service pre-war, again operated the diagrams, but were no longer reserved solely for these runs, and were both de-streamlined in 1951.
- In BR days the service carried a tailboard, at least two varieties being noted. These were the only examples to be seen on GE lines.
- Drawing W773 shows a steel-plate version of (b) above, but no evidence has been seen for this.
- The reintroduced service (1980) ran through to Yarmouth (Vauxhall), but only until 1984, when Norwich became the final destination.

other of Norwich's B1s taking water before working
e Up service. The engine has received its BR number
ough neither its smokebox number-plate nor shed-
te) but retains LNER on the tender at this time. The
d version headboard is now in use. *(R.K. Blencowe
llection)*

till in LNER days, Norwich's B1 No. 1052 leaves
verpool Street on 10 May 1947 to begin the
15-mile run back to its home base.
CGB: Ken Nunn Collection)

he 2nd version was very much an intermediate
ep, and was taken so that those (few) B1s that had
ceived LNER apple green livery could be paired
ith them. Here the Up train has the matching colour
heme near Chelmsford on 2 October 1948, though
e new number and tender lettering now denote BR
wnership. *(LCGB: Ken Nunn Collection)*

e recently introduced Type 7 board sits on B1
. 61270 a few minutes before departure time from
verpool Street on 11 June 1951. *(LCGB: Ken Nunn
llection)*

This title received its first cast-aluminium headboard in 1949 and B17/5 *East Anglian* displays this at the Liverpool Street engine-servicing area in August of that year. From this angle the 4–6–0 is giving a very passable imitation of an A4, though the latter never worked the GE lines. The combination of engine name and train title being identical was only possible in very few instances, and to find them photographed together was rarer still. In 1937 two B17s had received this form of streamlining (the other became No. 61670 *City of London* in BR days) and were dedicated to the working of this service. *(C.I.K. Field)*

Yet another B1, this time Stratford's No. 61399 (the last of the class to be delivered), stands at Norwich with the Up train in 1957. This is likely to have been a replacement engine, since the 'Britannia' Pacifics had been in charge of this service for a number of years by this time. Two typical young spotters of the era engage the crew's attention, and a Metro-Cammell DMU lurks on a local, thus completing the period scene. *(T. Scarsbrook/Initial Photographics)*

The last of the headboards designed for this service appeared when the train was accelerated again in 1980, the 16.20 ex-Liverpool Street then taking 110 minutes inclusive of the stop at Ipswich. Which is where No. 47170 *County of Norfolk* stands on 15 May 1980 bearing the new board (which has shaded lettering). The very large BR logo catches the eye. *(John D. Mann)*

The earlier version of the two tailboards is seen at the back of the Up train climbing Belstead Bank, south of Ipswich, on 25 July 1953. The two shields on the headboards are repeated, overlapping and contained in two concentric circles on this tailboard, which is yellow and of a one-piece non-folding type. The stock nearest the camera appears to be the reused 1937 stock. (G.R. Mortimer)

Five years or so later the 11.45 a.m. to Liverpool Street leaves Norwich with the 2nd-style tailboard bringing up the rear on 18 August 1958. This style clearly folds and is devoid of shields, though the LNER vehicle carrying it may well be the same as before. The depot coaling plant, large mechanical signal-box and prominent semaphores belong to the steam age, though the train was powered by No. D200 itself, not long 'out of the box' and more likely to have been a 'cop' for those witnessing the departure than the familiar 'Britannias'. (G.R. Mortimer)

THE DAY CONTINENTAL

Liverpool Street–Harwich (Parkeston Quay West) (Boat train service)

Inaugural titled run	8 June 1947 (by LNER)
Last titled run	10 May 1987

(a) 1st style headboard	Introduced 8 June 1947
	LNER standard pattern with definite article.
(b) 2nd style headboard	Introduced 1948/50 (2nd version presumed, not seen)
	Transitional 'elliptical top' design.
(1st version)	In LNER colours.
(2nd version)	Repainted by BR. White lettering on dark background.
(c) 3rd style headboard	Introduced 1949
	Transitional type. Possibly drawing W765 repainted.
(d) 4th style headboard	Introduced 5 June 1950
	BR painted steel, size A, in three lines. Dutch flag (left) and Union Jack on either side of THE in the top corners.
(e) 5th style headboard	Introduced June 1951
	BR Type 7 with two size D enamelled discs, depicting the same flags as in (d). (See also Colour Section).

- This service ran before the war as the FLUSHING CONTINENTAL, but was re-routed in 1947 to Hoek van Holland, and renamed.
- This service was operated in conjunction with the Zeeland Steamship Company's Royal Mail route daytime sailings.
- Parkeston Quay was opened in 1883 by the Great Eastern Railway and named after its then chairman, Charles Henry Parkes.

Having already seen the SCANDINAVIAN headboard used 'incorrectly' on a special working, here's another instance of headboard 'misuse', though in total contrast to that seen previously. Here, Parkeston's J69 shunter has the shed's breakdown tool van in tow and carries the LNER headboard. *(William Cattermole)*

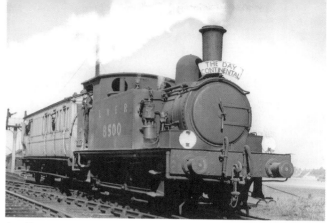

Right: More usual power in the early days of the service was B17/4 No. 61666 *Nottingham Forest*, seen charging west through Mark's Tey with the Up service *c.* 1949. The unusual 'elliptical top' headboard identifies the boat train. No photograph has, however, been found of BR's repainting of this. *(P.M. Alexander/Millbrook House Collection)*

Below: Witham, eastbound, 16 April 1949, with No. 61236 carrying the painted-steel board thought to conform to drawing W765. An F5 2–4–2T waits with the Braintree branch train, behind a ubiquitous platform trolley. *(Rex Conway Collection)*

Opposite, left: The new-looking 4th style headboard rises nearly to chimney height in this view at Liverpool Street on 5 June 1950. Note, however, the high position of the number-plate and the close spacing of the smokebox door straps in comparison with previous photographs of B1s. *(NRM/SSPL)*

Opposite, right: When the recently arrived 'Britannias' had teething problems and had to be temporarily withdrawn for modifications, the only engine type of similar power that was within the GE line axle-loading restriction was the Bulleid Light Pacific. Several were ultimately drafted to the Eastern Region as replacements, and No. 34039 *Boscastle* stands at the London terminus with the Type 7 headboard in the low position. *(William Cattermole)*

THE NORFOLKMAN

Liverpool Street–Norwich (Thorpe)

Inaugural titled run	27 September 1948
Last titled run	16 June 1962

(a) 1st style headboard	**Introduced 27 September 1948 but superseded by (b)** Painted steel, 6th Series (v) to drawing W773. White letters on a dark blue background.
(b) 2nd style headboard	**Introduced 1949** BR Type 4.
(c) 3rd style headboard	**Introduced 3 May 1951** BR Type 6. Top line 3¾in letters; bottom line 3in.

- In summer only, the service was extended to Cromer, and in the early years to Sheringham also.
- In 1951, to mark the Festival of Britain, this train was equipped with brand-new Mk 1 stock in carmine and cream, from 3 May of that year.
- There is no evidence that the embellished headboard on display in the NRM actually ran thus.

B1 No. 1236 again, but this time in purely LNER guise, standing in Liverpool Street prior to the inaugural run, 27 September 1948. This departed at 10 a.m. and was given the 'right away' by the Mayor of Ipswich Alderman J.B. Cullingham, and on arrival at Norwich the train was met by the Lord Mayor of Norwich Mr W.G. Cutbush, himself a railwayman. On the left, class leader B17/1 No. 61600 *Sandringham* (named only after Royal permission had been granted) awaits further duties. *(Getty Images)*

Stranger in the camp. Southern Region Light Pacific No. 34059 *Sir Archibald Sinclair* stands in the shed yard at Norwich after working the Down train. This May 1949 trial was of short duration, but transfers were repeated in 1951 on a more extensive basis, when the new 'Britannias' developed mechanical problems (see THE DAY CONTINENTAL on pages 276–7). *(NRM/SSPL)*

English Electric 2,000hp diesels (later to become class 40) began taking over some of the GE services in 1958. In May of that year, the first of the class is seen here between Manningtree and Ipswich with the 3rd style headboard fixed centrally among the clutter on the nose. These heavy (133 tons) units had a low power/weight ratio compared with later designs, but nevertheless the timetables were accelerated when sufficient units became available. *(Harwich Railway & Shipping Museum/Bob Clow Collection)*

THE FENMAN

Liverpool Street–King's Lynn via Cambridge and Ely

Inaugural titled run	23 May 1949
Title withdrawn	4 May 1968
Reintroduced	1 October 1984
Last titled run	13 May 1990

(a) 1st style headboard	Introduced 23 May 1949(?)
	BR Type 2.
(b) 2nd style headboard	Introduced 1951
	BR Type 6.
(c) 3rd style headboard	Introduced 1 October 1984
	Painted steel, 5th Series. White lettering, horizontal on blue background. Now with two shields, depicting the arms of London (left) and King's Lynn.

- In its early years the service ran through to Hunstanton, with reversal at King's Lynn. After May 1961 this service became a DMU connecting service, though only until the line to Hunstanton closed on 5 May 1969, by which time the service had lost its title anyway.

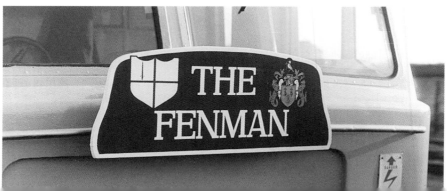

Although the use of 2–6–0s was uncommon, smaller 4–4–0s were regular power north of Ely. This was mainly because the turntable at King's Lynn could not accommodate the B1/B2/B17 4–6–0s that worked the service from London to Ely, and so engines were changed at that point. Hence D16 No. 62580 – a King's Lynn (31C) engine – leaves its home town for the south on 21 May 1957, this time equipped with the larger headboard. *(K.L. Cook/ Rail Archive Stephenson)*

Opposite, top: K3 class 2–6–0s were rarely turned out for titled express workings, but on 25 May 1953 the Down train was about to depart Liverpool Street behind Stratford's No. 61830, complete with the Type 2 headboard. *(Stanley Creer)*

Opposite, bottom: A close-up of the painted-steel board used when the title was reintroduced in 1984, photographed at Cambridge on the inaugural southbound run. No. 47582 provides the power. *(Pat Sumner)*

THE BROADSMAN

Liverpool Street–Cromer and Sheringham

Inaugural titled run	5 June 1950
Last titled run	16 June 1962

Only headboard	Introduced 5 June 1950 (1st version); November 1950 (2nd version)
	BR Type 6.
(1st version)	Without shields.
(2nd version)	With two size A shields depicting a 'Cruiser' or 'Bermudan' type yacht sailing left (on the left), and a Norfolk wherry sailing right. Both shields include a windmill on flat land beyond the bow of each craft.

- THE BROADSMAN was designated (on the outline drawings) to receive a BR painted-steel size B headboard. No evidence has been found for this.
- The service became distinguished in September 1952 when the Down train was allocated the first-ever mile-a-minute timing in East Anglia, with only 45 minutes allowed for the 46¼ miles between Ipswich and Norwich.
- In 1953 the service was one of the four ER titled trains to carry the extra 'Coronation' headboard on the buffer beam.

Norwich B1 No. 61042 arriving at Liverpool Street on 26 August 1950 with the plain headboard. *(LCGB: Ken Nunn Collection)*

The official photo of the
headboard itself. THE NORSEMAN
headboard also depicted two
sailing vessels. *(NRM/SSPL)*

Of the various GE line titled expresses, THE BROADSMAN was the one chosen by the authorities to carry
the Coronation decorative headboard. Seen leaving Ipswich on 28 May 1953, 'Britannia' Pacific No. 70007
Coeur-de-Lion carries both boards. *(H.N. James/Ipswich Transport Museum)*

THE EASTERLING

Liverpool Street–Yarmouth (South Town) and Lowestoft (Central)

Inaugural titled run	5 June 1950
Last titled run	6 September 1958

(a) 1st style headboard	Introduced 5 June 1950(?)
	BR painted steel size B.
(b) 2nd style headboard	Introduced Summer 1950 (1st version); Summer 1951 (2nd version) (?)
	BR Type 6.
(1st version)	Without shields.
(2nd version)	With two size A shields depicting the arms of Great Yarmouth (left) and Lowestoft. (See also Colour Section).

- This service operated summer only.
- The train divided into two portions at Beccles, and was rejoined at the same place on the southbound run.

The painted-steel board seems to have been available at much the same time as the Type 6 headboards, and smartly turned out B1 No. 61205 stands (temporarily light engine) wearing this at Liverpool Street. *(NRM/SSPL)*

The summer-only train about to leave Liverpool Street with the plain Type 6 headboard, 15 July 1950. Note the white oil lamps sitting on top of the electric lights. *(LCGB: Ken Nunn Collection)*

Another well-presented engine, B17/4 *Bradford City*, heads north through Ipswich with an entire rake of Gresley stock in carmine and cream, carrying the embellished headboard. This was the only train not to call at Ipswich, running non-stop between London and Beccles. *(H.N. James/Ipswich Transport Museum)*

THE ESSEX COAST EXPRESS

Liverpool Street–Clacton

Inaugural titled run	9 June 1958
Last titled run	3 May 1968

(a) 1st style headboard	Introduced 9 June 1958, soon superseded by (b)
	Painted steel, 6th series (iii). (See page 199)
(b) 2nd style headboard	Introduced June 1958; probably both (a), (b) were available at the commencement of the service
	BR Type 7 with 3in lettering throughout.

- The name was bestowed on the 7.51 a.m. from Clacton and the 5.27 p.m. return working from Liverpool Street, both accelerated and provided with 'Britannia' Pacifics recently displaced from the Norwich main line by diesels.
- When the Clacton line was electrified in 1963 new multiple units took over the (again accelerated) service. Surprisingly, the title remained in the timetable for a further five years, though no headboard was carried on the multiple units.

One last look at Liverpool Street, with an extremely rare view of a 'Clan' Pacific bearing a titled train headboard. For a couple of months in 1958, late August to late October, this engine was temporarily moved to Stratford from Carlisle (Kingmoor) – the 12A shed-plate is still in place – for evaluation. Management had in mind switching round five 'Clans', 'Britannias' and 'Royal Scots' between Stratford, Holbeck (Leeds) and Kingmoor, but Stratford regarded the move as a retrograde step and the triple transfers did not go ahead. No. 72009 *Clan Stewart* stands, blowing off, in the engine bay on 17 September, while on the right 'Britannia' No. 70001 *Lord Hurcombe* does the same. *(R.F. Smith/Transport Treasury)*

(THE) FIFE COAST EXPRESS

Glasgow (Queen Street)–St Andrews

Title reintroduced	23 May 1949
Last titled run	5 September 1959

(a) 1st style headboard	Introduced 23 May 1949(?) (1st version), (2nd version) soon after
(1st version)	Non-standard. Painted steel in LNER colours, including the definite article. Two lines, with only EXPRESS on the lower. A repainting of an LNER/NBR-style destination board carried on two fixing pegs on the smokebox, rather than on the upper lamp iron.
(2nd version)	As (1st version) but now provided with a standard central bracket for attaching to the upper lamp iron.
(b) 2nd style headboard	Introduced Summer 1951(?)
	BR Type 1 without THE.

- This service operated summer only from 1952–9 inclusive, and out of Buchanan Street for its last three years.
- For a number of years the twin first-class and triple third-class articulated sets from the pre-war SILVER JUBILEE were used on this service. After wartime storage these were painted in BR carmine and cream, but at least initially retained their stainless-steel lining in place of the standard yellow and black.

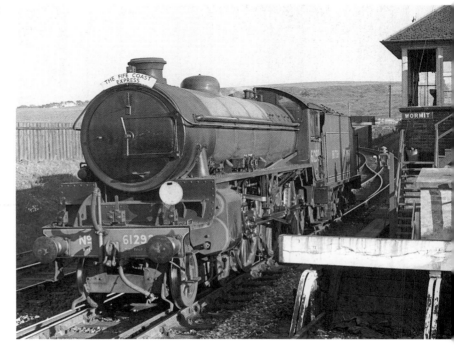

B1s worked widely throughout former LNER territory (and beyond), and No. 61292, still in apple green, has the 1st version headboard at Wormit, on the south side of the Tay Bridge, working light engine from its home shed (Dundee) to St Andrews. Note the tablet-exchange apparatus on the cabside for single-line working. Many (but not all) B1s were fitted with electric lighting, four lamps being seen on the buffer beam and a fifth behind the headboard. The generator can be seen at the front of the running board, on the left. *(NRM/SSPL)*

Sister engine No. 61263, again at Wormit with a J38 for company, now has the 2nd version headboard fixed comfortably on the top iron. Note that the two versions have slightly different letter spacing. *(NRM/SSPL)*

Glasgow's Eastfield shed hosts No. 61293 bearing the Type 1 headboard, 16 September 1955. While the B1 takes water, Haymarket A3 No. 60099 *Call Boy* (the 1927 Derby winner) rests on the adjacent track with the Leeds (City) service's headboard. *(Philip J. Kelley)*

ADDITIONAL TITLES

THE BUTLIN HOLIDAY CAMP TRAINS
Duration: 1950s and early 1960s.

(a) 1st style headboard	BR painted-steel size B, reading BUTLIN'S EXPRESS. Black letters on yellow background. Used on the King's Cross–Skegness trains.
(b) 2nd style headboard	Painted steel, 6th Series (ii) (b), circular and reading BUTLIN EXPRESS. Black clock-face lettering on a yellow background. Used on the Liverpool Street–Clacton trains.
(c) 3rd style headboard	BR Type 3 reading BUTLINS EXPRESS on a yellow background. Used on GE line trains after dieselisation (see Colour Section for illustration).

•   These were by no means the only 'holiday camp' specials, but they were the only ones specific to a particular company that were headboarded.

The GN line version of the headboard is displayed on B1 No. 61139 as it leaves King's Cross for Skegness in June 1958. Note that this smartly turned-out loco doesn't have electric lighting. The BR Mk 1 stock is, however, roofboarded in the manner of a prestige titled express. *(By permission of Hull University Archives)*

Yet another B1, No. 61230 has the GE line's large circular headboard covering the entire smokebox door. (K.L. Cook/Rail Archive Stephenson)

HUMBER–LINCS EXECUTIVE

King's Cross–Cleethorpes

A short-lived HST title with a 'sticker' headboard. This showed two interlocking shields (of Cleethorpes and Lincoln) on a plain black background, with the legend in yellow beneath these.

HST set No. 253 024, with power car No. 43048 leading, heads south out of Doncaster station, 31 July 1983. (Andrew Thompson)

HEADBOARDED FREIGHT TRAINS

THE LEA VALLEY ENTERPRISE

NE London–Whitemoor (March), north of England and Scotland

Inaugural titled run	2 November 1959
Only headboard	Introduced on commencement of service BR Type 1.

EAST ESSEX ENTERPRISE

Chelmsford–Colchester–Ipswich–March, Midlands and Scotland

Inaugural titled run	13 June 1960
Only headboard	Introduced on commencement of service BR Type 1.

THE KING'S CROSS FREIGHTER (SOUTHBOUND)
The TEES–TYNE FREIGHTER (NORTHBOUND)

King's Cross Goods–Newcastle (Forth Goods), and vice versa

Inaugural titled run	13 June 1960
	Introduced on commencement of service
southbound headboard	BR Type 7 in reverse colours, i.e. black letters on a white background.
northbound headboard	BR painted-steel size A. Uniquely, the definite article is painted 'The'.

King's Cross yard with A1 Pacific No. 60140 *Balmoral* waiting to go north on 1 July 1960. The archways leading to 'Top Shed' are on the right. *(By permission of Hull University Archives)*

Above: On the Friday before its official introduction on Monday 2 November 1959 a 'dry run' was conducted, and hence Brush A1A-A1A diesel No. D5531 carries the new headboard and a class C (express freight) designation on the four-character train description panel. *(NRM/SSPL)*

The similar headboard for the service that was introduced seven months later. *(Courtesy Sheffield Railwayana Auctions)*

The southbound service with No. D283 and a string of short-wheelbase four-wheel wagons forming the trailing load. *(NRM/SSPL)*

INDEX OF TITLED EXPRESSES

Tailpiece; third-class car No. 67 brings up the rear of THE QUEEN OF SCOTS, leaving King's Cross behind A3 No. 96 in 1948. (See page 224). Complete with tailboard, the title is thus advertised at both ends of the train. (*NRM/SSPL*)

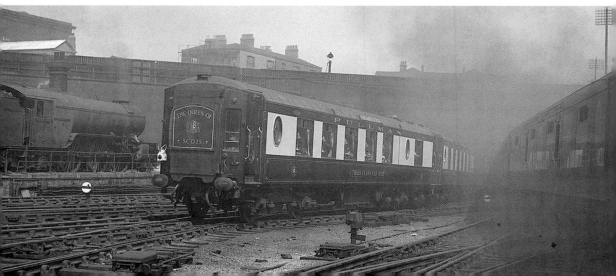